This is Volume One of the series, *Covenants of the Almighty, According to the New Testament and Other Considerations*. The purpose of this series is to make covenant theology accessible to students and leaders who speak English as a second language, and to anyone else interested. Collegiate language is minimal, colloquial idiosyncracies are avoided, and illustrations aim at being universally understood. Difficult points are explained as simply as possible, sometimes from several approaches to assist readers who may not quickly grasp non-concrete theological concepts.

This series views the divine covenants through the lens of the New Testament, especially the writings of the apostle Paul. The apostle's comments are taken as divinely inspired commentary explaining the true meaning of the text.

The first part of the book is a "Synopsis of Covenant Theology" for readers who want an overview of the covenants or need to understand how to bring together the details described in later chapters of the series.

The second part of this first volume explains the history, meaning and application of the Covenant of Works, and its importance for a correct understanding of Biblical concepts such as the covenant, the fall of man into sin, the final judgment, redemption, Christ's role as Mediator and Last Adam, and Edenic themes in the promises of the new covenant in Christ Jesus.

*"The earth lies defiled under its inhabitants; for they have transgressed the laws, violated the statutes, **broken the everlasting covenant**. Therefore, a curse devours the earth, and its inhabitants suffer for their guilt..."* Isa. 24:5

*" "...**my covenant that they they broke**, though I was their husband," declares the Lord."* Jer. 31:32

*"As I live, surely it is my oath that he despised, and **my covenant that he broke...**"* Ezekiel 17:19; ESV

*"**You have broken my covenant**, in addition to all your abominations."* Ezekiel 44:7, ESV

Broken Covenant, Fallen World

Broken Covenant Fallen World

Covenants of the Almighty
According to the New Testament
and other Considerations

Steven T. Poelman

First of five volumes in the series,
Covenants of the Almighty According to the New Testament

Volume One: **Broken Covenant, Fallen World**
Volume Two: **Camp of the Saints**
Volume Three: **The Lighthouse Kingdom**
Volume Four: **Dawn of Heaven's Light**
Volume Five: **Heaven's Lamps in the Valley of Sorrows**

Available at www.narrowpathway.com

NarrowPathway Books

Print Version ISBN: 978-1-937754-01-3
Kindle Version ISBN: 978-1-937754-00-6
iBooks Version ISBN: 978-1-937754-03-7

Book layout and cover design by author.
Cover drawing by Sandhya R. Poelman, © 2011.

Published for NarrowPathway Books.

Printed in the United States of America

Contents

Pg. No.

i.   Description

iv.   Title Page

v.   Copyrights

viii.   Acknowledgments

x.   Foreword

1.   PREFACE: Modern Challenges

13.   INTRODUCTION

PART ONE: AN OVERVIEW OF THE COVENANTS

29.   Chap. 1: Garden Paradise

51.   Chap. 2: Noah, the Second Adam

59.   Chap. 3: Heaven in Abraham's Heart

73.   Chap. 4: The Foreshadow Kingdom

87.   Chap. 5: David and the Coming Messiah

93.   Chap. 6: Climax: The Covenant of Heaven

PART TWO: THE COVENANT OF WORKS

111.   Chap. 7: Old Theology, New Questions

119.   Chap. 8: The Covenant of Works Doesn't Belong Here Anymore?

147.   Chap. 9: Why These Features in Sinai?

169.   Chap. 10: Obedience Came First

183.   Chap. 11: The "Eternal Purpose" of God

211.   Chap. 12: The End is the Beginning

215.   BIBLIOGRAPHY

Affectionately

Heartfelt thanks to dear friends Elbert Shackleford for countless hours of proofreading for grammar and spelling mistakes, and Sandy Jackson's readings for easy comprehension, to Pastor James Admiraal for reviewing doctrinal content, to Dr. Gerald Bilkes for reviewing most of the entire series and offering helpful advice and encouragement, and to Dr. Mohan Chacko, for his kind words in the foreward.

Gratitude also must go to elder Glenn Hop and Dr. Jeff Doll for encouraging me to begin writing. You were God's instruments to push me to do what I never would have tried.

And unceasing thanks to my wife, Nalini, and our three children still at home, for permitting me to take so much time to write the four volumes of this series. I could not do it without you. I dearly love you.

FOREWORD

I consider it a privilege to offer this "Foreword" to *Broken Covenant; Fallen World*, written by my colleague, Rev. Steven Poelman.

It is no secret that Reformed theology is essentially covenant theology. The covenantal scheme is not something imposed on the Bible, but derived from it. In form and content, the Bible is covenantal. Reformed theologians insist that one cannot truly understand the central message of the Scriptures without grasping its covenantal framework. The glory of the gospel of Christ shines the brightest when its revelation is traced through the pages of the Bible as one unfolding story.

Yet it is sadly true that there have been those who refused to see this marvelous unity in biblical revelation. Their approaches have resulted in serious misunderstandings of the gospel, rendering large chunks of biblical revelation moral lessons at best and irrelevant at worst.

Even within the Reformed camp there has not always been unanimity in thinking about the covenant. Concepts such as "Covenant of Works" and "Covenant of Redemption" have been disputed even by distinguished Reformed theologians.

Questions related to the covenant have taken on a new urgency in the current theological discussions of the church. Scholars of the New Perspective school of thought have re-ignited a controversy on justification by faith – the most crucial doctrine of the Reformation, and one that was considered settled long ago. Questions regarding grace and works in relation to the covenant have become even more complicated and relevant.

In such a context, a biblical-theological discussion on Covenant, as presented by the author here, is most welcome and useful. Along with exegetical insights, he draws on various theologians of the past to argue his case. In the first part of this work, the author presents a survey of the covenants in biblical history. The second part is devoted to an elaborate examination of the Covenant of Works.

The present volume is the first in a four-part series on the covenant. It is evident from the pages of this book that the author is familiar with classical as well as contemporary literature on the subject, and is well-equipped to illuminate the reader on this complex topic.

It is my sincere prayer that the present volume will cause many to think on this central theme of Scripture, and gain a greater understanding of the glory of the gospel of Christ.

Mohan Chacko, Principal
Presbyterian Theological Seminary
Dehradun, India

Preface:
Modern Challenges

Old is always Bad, New is always Good

No one would expect the twentieth century to leave any field of knowledge undisturbed by its revolutionary changes, stamped by remarkable advances in every field—astronomy, archeology, nuclear physics, computer science, medicine, and electrical engineering, to name a few. And so Christianity, after a 19th century slumber dominated by theological liberalism[1] and rejection of the supernatural, shook off its drowsiness in the 20th century to spawn new expressions of faith: fundamentalism,[2] evangelicalism, dispensationalism,[3] neo-evangelicalism,[4] Pentecostalism (and other forms of charismatic expression), neo-dispensationalism,[5] the marketing mega-church movement,[6] and finally, the "emerging church." The winds of change swept through the halls of theological seminaries, sirens wailing for something new, for fresh approaches, new insights, and change from the old and tired patterns of doctrinal ruts that seemed, to some critics, worn far too deep into frequented pathways. It wasn't surprising that in such a century of transformation, some began to search out entirely new ways of thinking about very ancient texts of Scripture, sometimes, for no other reason than to try something new.

This book, however, is not an analysis of modern culture, but of the ancient Bible's theology. It will not make any attempt to explore the underlying causes of changes in the church and changes in how we do

1

theology. Let it simply be noted that most of the evangelical world has been swept into the threshing machine of change, and Reformed theology has not escaped unscathed.[7]

Throughout the twentieth century this need for change was impressed upon evangelicals. As quickly as change was introduced, however, new voices rose on the horizon to further change what had recently been changed. This pattern continued because the necessity of always doing something new had become a function not only of Western politics and culture, but of the church, as well.

Covenant theology, however, was one discipline that seemed to grow stronger the more it was tested. It has withstood challenges both within and without, subject to only minor adjustments, but certainly not prone to any radical changes that would uproot its basic foundations or transform its overall structure. The century of change saw it stand firm against its main contenders, sometimes even causing them to adjust their own stance.

It was inevitable, however, that some would declare the need for radical transformation in this arena of covenant theology, also. So it is not surprising that some should arise, toward the end of the 20th century, declaring that nearly all expositors since the time of Augustine have misunderstood the Word of God, and that both the gospel, and justification, and Reformed covenant theology and nearly all that has been taught of the writings of Paul for 1500 years, needs to be understood from *"a new perspective"*.

The Covenant of Works is among those doctrines that have come into the spotlight of the change machinery in recent years. This was an idea popular in Reformed theology for more than 400 years, that God made a covenant of law with the first man, Adam. "Reformed theology" is so named because it came from the great Reformation of the Christian faith in the 16th century. In the Reformation, God raised up spiritual men in many nations to "reform" the church by rejecting traditions introduced by man to return to the Holy Scriptures as the only spiritual knowledge truly inspired by God. For centuries Reformed theologians have insisted that the Biblical plan of redemption, revealed throughout the Scriptures, cannot be rightly understood without a correct knowledge of the Covenant of Works. This is the view that mankind's relationship with God, in the beginning, was established through a covenant God made with Adam, the father of the human race. Because Adam rebelled and broke the terms of the covenant, all descendants of Adam are separated from the true God and need redemption.

2

The concept of the Covenant of Works held an important place for a very long time, passing under the lens of many generations of able exegetes (Bible teachers who explain). But these are times of change. Since the term, Covenant of Works, only became popular toward the end of the 16th century, it was thought that the concept itself was only an invention of theologians, rather than *a truth finally understood rightly.* The title, "Covenant of Works," was declared inappropriate. Some were for doing away with an Adamic covenant altogether, while others charged that there was no distinction between the graciousness of God in establishing the Adamic covenant, and the grace God provided to redeem those who broke it.[8]

Such changes in thinking affect theological perceptions throughout the entire Bible, not only understanding of the Old Testament, but even more, the New, including the letters of Paul. This is important to the subject matter of this book, since Paul's commentaries on the older covenants are one of our most fruitful sources of understanding the true spiritual dimensions of the ancient pacts God established with man in Old Testament times.

Those who do advocate the *Covenant of Works* propose a simple structure of Scripture, in which the first three chapters of the Bible describe how Adam broke God's first covenant with man, to then introduce the plan of redemption revealed throughout the rest of the sacred Scriptures. From the perspective of those who hold to this view, it is easy to see that this first covenant was a simple test of obedience, a test of Adam's love for God, so basic and foundational to consequent major doctrines such as the awfulness of sin against God, man's hopelessly fallen nature, the moral law of God, the coming day of judgment, the need for salvation, the incarnation of Christ as the only acceptable sacrifice, the sinless obedience of Christ and His atoning death, cursed on a tree to restore mankind from disobedience at a tree.

Besides the rejection of the covenant of works, there is another modern challenge. Today, some insist that the central doctrine of the Protestant Reformation, justification by faith alone, as a free gift from God received only by God's grace and through Christ alone, was not right after all, because the Reformers, you see, could not understand the gospel. This view has been advanced by proponents of the New Perspective on Paul (NPP). It is called the "new perspective" because it rejects the established New Testament understanding of past centuries. For example, the New Perspective insists that Luther was mistaken on justification and he parted ways from the church for the wrong reasons. Staunch Protestants point out that the New Perspective looks too much like old arguments repackaged with a new twist, because NPP arguments, when all is said and done, easily lead toward a conclusion that the Roman Catholics had been right all along, with their view of a gospel that includes a final justification based on doing good works. N.T. Wright, a leading proponent of New Perspective ideas, has stated that our final justification is on the basis of "the complete life lived."[9]

These things are mentioned here, at the beginning of a study of covenant theology, only to show that the doctrine of God's covenant is facing some important challenges today. Students of the Bible need to be well-grounded in a sound understanding of the covenants, or they may be easily swept along by those proposing these new views.

No doubt some will misunderstand and read these words as an attack against all who embrace NPP ideas. Look more closely and you will discover that I'm not launching missiles at all who disagree with covenant theology, but merely describing several ways that covenant understanding has been in the line of fire from others.

Another angle looking to dismantle not only covenant theology, but nearly all theology, comes from the "emerging church." *Emerging church* is a misnomer because it is not a church but a movement (which is called a *conversation* to be novel), characterized by a *way-of-thinking* affecting and changing the church today, thus the name, "emerging". Today's generation has passed through university classrooms shaped by postmodern philosophy, which insists there are *no absolutes in any field of knowledge or education*. The children of postmodernism, now leaders themselves, raising their followers out of the religious landscape of the West, are the "emerging church." Don Carson, analyzing the movement, explains the necessity to communicate to the postmodern generation, "Those who fail to do so are blind to the cultural accretions that hide the gospel behind forms of thought and modes of expression that no longer communicate with the new generation, the emerging generation."[10] It's true that emergents are as important to the gospel cause as anyone else, but even among emergent leaders there is disagreement as to how far the church should step over the postmodern threshold. Ed Stetzer, a missiologist, points out that all Emergents are not the same, but that the movement has developed into at least three categories: *"relevants"* retain the same gospel known in historic Christianity and try to explain it in ways that are relevant to emerging culture, *"reconstructionists"* hold to the historic gospel but want to redesign the church, and *"revisionists"* would do away with all old creedal expressions and change not only the church but the gospel itself.

4

It is this third kind of emergent that has become most vocal against all forms of doctrinal precision, rejecting historical creeds and theological arguments. Reacting to them, John MacArthur warns, "...in the Emerging Church movement, *truth* (to whatever degree such a concept is even recognized) is assumed to be inherently hazy, indistinct, and uncertain—perhaps even ultimately unknowable."[11] For example, Brian McLaren, a well-known symbol of "revisionist" emergents, strangely feels that even the simple gospel has never been understood by anyone after the Bible has been studied for two thousand years. McLaren states, "I don't think we've got the gospel right yet." He rejects *systematic theology*[12] as an effort to "have final orthodoxy nailed down, freeze-dried, and shrink-wrapped forever." The very idea of holding to a doctrinal interpretation of Genesis 2 and 3, such as the concept of the Covenant of Works, is a useless effort to "nail down" orthodoxy. This kind of thinking is fashionable, in step with changing times, but leaves the church in a vacuum without solid objective truth or any clearly marked path to follow.

Paul's extensive letters are crucial for understanding both justification and the true meaning of the ancient covenants. Consequently, anyone who has the superior intellect to give a clever twist to Paul wields the power to manipulate long-standing doctrines, or send the church racing on a track bordered with fascinating billboards but leading to nowhere. Therefore, getting Paul right is extremely important. The past thirty years has seen many attempts at viewing Paul from new angles—sometimes with the result that a reinvented wheel has left us with a very bumpy ride. But that hasn't stopped an increasing number of people from buying a ticket to ride the train of change, even when the price is set far too high for Protestants—especially those of Reformed persuasion. Some advertising the benefits of the change train, rising in Protestant camps, appear prepared to derail the entire Protestant Reformation, aligning themselves not only against Luther & Calvin, but against the time-tested doctrines of Protestant churches and believers everywhere.

This book explores Paul's understanding of the covenants of the Bible, written with a desire to keep the wheels on the tracks, and make the ride as smooth as possible for ordinary Christians who have no formal theological education. With some modern critics insisting that Protestant theologians have been wrong about justification for the past 500 years (or 1600 years, as N.T. Wright suggests, or 2,000 years according to MacLaren), and that the real truth can be found only in their own books, new books must also continue to be written explaining and defending both justification and covenant theology. If the doctrine of justification by grace through faith in Christ is correct, every believer should gather around this banner, "Contend earnestly for the faith once delivered to the saints." Therefore, this book is pulled along by certain convictions: that some important things that should never be forgotten are in danger of being lost in the new wave, other things that should be simple have been made unnecessarily complicated, and some things "hard to understand" have been handled too simplistically.

Because of the genre of the writings of the apostle Paul—doctrinal letters to the churches—he may be the most significant author of the New Testament.[13] This will not seem an overstatement when we consider that the major part of doctrinal understanding that has guided the church for the past two millennia is based on the letters from the pen of this brilliant apostle. Unlike narrative literature, the letters are densely packed, like suitcases crammed full of everything necessary for a long journey. It is the job of the exegete to unpack the suitcases, without wrinkling the carefully placed contents.

Yet Paul did not present us with a systematic theology, an overview of the main points of his entire doctrine, or a lengthy creed. He may be the foremost theologian of the Holy Scriptures, but we run into problems when we attempt to organize Paul's theology. This is because his letters are not a complete systematic theology on any of the common loci (*section* or *category* of theology) studied in theological seminaries, but take the form of theological comments on specific issues and doctrinal controversies faced by the churches. For example, Paul never attempted to compose a comprehensive treatise on the divine covenants.

R.P. Martin, in the *Dictionary of Paul and His Letters*, comments on the wide variety of views about Paul's theology: "The endeavor to ascertain whether there is a central organizing principle in Paul's theology has been pursued actively in recent studies. All students agree that Paul's thinking is not so much systematic as "occasional." But there the agreement stops. When we ask about a "Pauline center," or the underlying principle of coherence in Paul's theology, we are faced by a bewildering variety of answers."[14]

Because Paul's remarks are "occasional," it is necessary to study Paul within the overall context of New Testament theology, instead of in isolation. But when we decide to do this in today's theological environment, we run aground in the mucky stuff of another field of difficulties, especially

6

with new covenant theology. There are so many studies on Paul today, each a "fresh reading" with "completely new insights". Shall we take pathways well-marked by trusted theologians of past centuries, many of whom were brilliant, or the post-modernist trailblazing of casting aside every path followed in the past in pursuit of an entirely new and fresh approach? Can we trust the labors of earlier theologians and the great creeds they developed that brought stability to churches for centuries, or follow the chorus of divergent theologians calling for change, those promoting Emerging Church ideas, or the latest breed of Neo-orthodoxy, or the New Perspective on Paul (NPP), or the Federal Vision adherents, or the new breed of aggressive and dynamic Roman Catholic apologists?

Recent years have seen a plethora of new books on justification: both those redefining its meaning, "correcting" views of the past, reinterpreting Paul's comments from various angles, and those defending what is called "the traditional meaning." Living in a time in which the very word, "traditional," implies old dinosaur bones, some dismiss the guard and throw open the gates to any troop marching under the banner of "something new and fresh". But should the hingepin of the Reformation now be laid aside (the Protestant doctrine of justification by grace alone through faith alone) just because certain men want to replace it with postmodern ideas free of any definition?

It is easy for those who have become masters of rhetoric to cast behind their backs as nothing an entire age of the scholarly studies of spiritual men—while themselves claiming to stand in the Calvinistic, orthodox and Protestant heritage. But those who have feasted on the banquet of Reformed theology with open hearts, to discover that its spiritual promises are fulfilled in their very own lives, having tasted of the fruit of so satisfying a supper of Reformed preaching—I mean of course to be convicted of one's sin, and the righteousness of God set forth in His law and in the day of judgment, by the good Spirit who leads us first to Sinai and the futility of our own works, only so that He may employ the Law as our tutor to lead us to Christ, so that we may be saved from sin and justified by faith alone, sharers in Christ Himself, being grafted into Him to share in His death, resurrection, life, righteousness, ascension and glorification, and in His eternal inheritance—those well fed in sound doctrine will not soon be scavenging off the wayside for a morsel of "new" bread.

I've mentioned only a few of the modern challenges to covenant theology and the gospel of the Reformers (Luther, Calvin, and others) to demonstrate that these are hard times for the Covenant of Works.

The purpose of this book, however, is not to debate those who challenge Reformed covenantal theology. Such arguments will soon be outdated, replaced by something else that is "new and fresh."

In this day when so many voices are calling for us to, "Reject the doctrines of the past!" volume one of this series simply hopes to show that some of the most sound doctrine has already been served by a countless cloud of witnesses who have gone before us, and that today we're being coaxed to exchange golden treasures for cheap baubles and glass beads. Alas, the beloved apostle wrote that the time will come when they will not endure sound doctrine, but having itching ears will heap up teachers according to their own desires—and those who read the signs of times are no longer waiting for this day to arrive. No doubt, some have been riding the change train so long that it will be unbearable to consider any doctrine bearing the label "older," or explore Paul's understanding of the covenants without unique novelties. But, there is very little antagonistic polemic[15] in the chapters that follow. This book is not written to be a point-by-point refutation of anyone's views. Why this preface then, if there is no battleground herein? Simply to emphasize that the need is greater now than ever before for church elders and ordinary believers to understand what the Reformers saw in Scripture and defended to the death. In several arenas, the tide is rising against Reformed covenant theology. But much that is written against Reformed views fails to rightly understand what it is so determined to tear down.

Many excellent books have already been written to answer the challenges mentioned in this preface. The interested reader will seek and find them.

This book takes another path. In a dark storm of striking thunderbolts and flooding rain, it is hard to see clearly. Brilliant lightning flashes appear, only to be chased by threatening thunderclaps that drive one to run for shelter or stand and defend house.

But when the stormy contest has subsided and all is at rest, the air is fresh and everything looks better and more appealing. One of my favorite Puritan authors once wrote, "We stand at better advantage to find truth, and keep it also, when devoutly praying for it, than fiercely wrangling and contending about it. Disputes roil the soul, and raise the dust of passion; prayer sweetly composes the mind, and lays the passions which disputes draw forth; for I am sure a man may see further in a still clear day, than in a windy and cloudy."16

To paraphrase a favorite passage on God's sovereignty in Ecclesiates, "There is a time for clashing swords, and there is a time for peace." The time for clashing swords comes without seeking, but our aim is peace.

While teaching seminary classes in Asia over the years, I began to realize that one of the greatest needs for students of English as a second language are theology books written in simple English, presenting deep and difficult doctrines but without impressive collegiate language. The covenant is a fascinating subject, one in which many parts of inspired Scripture fit together in a marvelous harmony. Like almost all other loci of theology, many of our Asian students fail to comprehend almost all the books available on the subject of the covenants. My prayer is that this one will be different. Some terms are defined in footnotes. Theological concepts are explained as simply as possible and sometimes at greater length for clarity. Illustrations are designed to be universal, and will hopefully fit any culture of any age. Except in one chapter detailing the history of the Covenant of Works, the reader is not overwhelmed by numerous quotes from unknown authors. Seminaries in the West may also find this series useful as alternative reading material for their foreign students. Since the aim is comprehensible, easy-read theology, ordinary Christians and lay leaders may find this book helpful.

Preface Notes

1. *Theological Liberalism* is denial of the supernatural and rejection of miracles by modern "theologians" who reject divine inspiration and historical accuracy of the Bible. Universities in Europe had been overtaken by atheists who influenced appointments of professors in seminaries under control of the universities.

2. *Fundamentalism* originated early in the 20th century as a reaction against theological liberalism. A series of about one hundred articles defending five or six essential evangelical doctrines were printed in magazines and journals, then published in several volumes in 1918. It was felt that these were the essential doctrines that must be preserved

from theological liberalism's attacks on the authority of Scripture. Thoughout the first half of the twentieth century, this resulted in a resurgence of believing churches in North America. Most of these churches held to a creed or doctrinal statement that was very brief, generally including little more than the essential points of fundamentalism.

3. *Dispensationalism* is an approach to understanding Scripture that divides Biblical history into distinct periods known as "dispensations." Each dispensation is marked by a different administration designed by God. The administration of each age ends where the next age begins. Doctrinal statements by dispensationalists are typically brief, composed by denominations or individual churches. Premillennialism is promoted as confessional truth and included in every doctrinal statement.

4. *Neo-evangelicalism* rejected fundamentalism's separation from theological liberalism, encouraging Christians to remain in the same church with liberals and continue in fellowship with them in the hope of winning them to a more fundamental Biblical faith. It was promoted by Fuller Seminary, the Billy Graham Association and Christianity Today magazine. Fuller Seminary took the lead in world missions and neo-evangelical ideas rapidly spread around the world. By 1970, neo-evangelicals became known as simply, evangelicals.

5. *Neo-dispensationalism* is a new form of dispensationalism that began in the mid-1980's. The movement adopted a handful of significant positions against views of classic dispensationalism. Earlier dispensationalism believed Christ's kingdom could not begin until God resumes His plan for Israel at the Second Coming of Christ. New dispensationalism agrees to some extent with the view of covenant theology, that Christ's kingdom began through the incarnation, anointing, death, resurrection and ascension of Christ into glory.

6. *The Marketing Mega-Church* movement began in the 1980's and continued into the 21st century. Marked by glossy professionalism and repackaging of the gospel, the movement has minimized the importance of many Christian doctrines in favor of broader acceptance of the church's message and increasing the number of converts.

7. For a cutting-edge analysis that describes what has happened to the Christian mind, and why we are endlessly changing today, David F. Wells book is a must read. David F. Wells, *The Courage to Be Protestant: Truth*

Lovers, Marketers and Emergents in the Postmodern World (Grand Rapids: Wm. B. Eerdmans, 2008.) Over the past thirty years, Wells composed a comprehensive series of four stellar books that probed into every nook and corner of the progress (or deconstruction) of Western culture and the American church scene, beginning with *No Place for Truth or Whatever Happened to Evangelical Theology,* in 1982. Those books catered more to the intellectual mindset, especially for theology professors, pastors and seminary students; so Wells wrote The Courage to Be Protestant for the ordinary Christian.

8. Among the Reformed churches today this idea is primarily promoted by certain adherents of what has become known as the "Federal Vision."

9. N.T. Wright, *Paul in Fresh Perspective,* 148.

10. D.A. Carson. "The Emerging Church," *Modern Reformed Magazine 14*, no. 4 (2005), http://www.modernreformation.org/default.php?page=articledisplay&var1=ArtRead&var2=128&var3=issuedisplay&var4=IssRead&var5=12, 06-15-2011.

11. John MacArthur, *The Truth War: Fighting for Certainty in an Age of Deception.* (Nashville, Thomas Nelson (2007), x.

12. Systematic theology arranges all the revelations, truths and doctrinal teachings of Scripture into a meaningful order, a logical system. For example, to explain the doctrine of the Trinity, systematic theology takes whatever is revealed about the Trinity from all parts of the Holy Scriptures, and summarizes the complete doctrine in one detailed statement. Systematic theology attempts to present all that God has revealed for every important doctrine found in Scripture.

13. Paul's letters and his place in Acts may have produced more books, doctrinal studies, and sermons, than any other author. Obviously, Jesus Christ is the most significant person, but He is not an author.

14. R.P. Martin, *Dictionary of Paul and His Letters* (Downers Grove, Ill.: InterVarsity Press, 1993): 92.

15. Polemic is "an aggressive attack on or refutation of the opinions or principles of another."—*Merriam Webster's Collegiate Dictionary,* 10th Ed.

16. William Gurnall

Introduction

S ince we are surrounded by so great a cloud of witnesses, let us run the race marked out for us..." These words of Hebrews 12:1 direct the stagelights of history on the faithful saints of the Old Testament in one dramatic sweep through thousands of years. Their testimony is recorded in the many historical books of the Old Testament, tracing a line of history from creation to the coming of the Promised One, *the Messiah*, known in Greek as, *the Christ*. This "great cloud of witnesses" were believers who stood all along that line, whose life and faith testified that the true God keeps His promises, until the greatest of all promises was fulfilled by the appearance of Jesus Christ.

Paul once wrote that the Lord's promises were only for those who had "membership" in the "covenants of promise" (Ephesians 2:12). He knew that all of God's promises belonged to one covenant or another. The *cloud of witnesses* were not only members of these covenants, but each had learned to trust God, and by faith and perseverance finally received the things promised to them in those covenants.

With the great cloud of OT witnesses on the sidelines the New Testament thrusts many new witnesses into the spotlight. These new witnesses stood firm upon new promises with a greater testimony than those of the Old, just as Christ is the "Mediator of a better covenant, founded on better promises" (Hebrews 7:22; 8:6), where all the promises are "yes and yes in Him" (2 Corinthians 1:18-20).

The New Testament witnesses hiked over treacherous mountains and through perilous valleys, climbed through chasms, swam rivers, hacked out trails in dense jungles, and sailed the seven seas—to testify that the Christ had finally come (just as the Old Testament prophets kept predicting for centuries). They announced that in his short life on earth He did everything God had promised: He went about doing good; He healed every sick and deformed person who came to him; He released those in bondage to Satan, raised the dead to life and preached the kingdom of heaven to the poor. Having proved Himself to be the Son of God with power, He stamped the final seal upon His brief earthly ministry by shedding His own blood for the sins of all who would trust in Him, and rising again to prove that He is the Lord and giver of life. Thus He provides salvation for people from all nations. The message of His cross, promising forgiveness of sins for all who believe in Jesus Christ as their only Lord and Savior is the gospel. Gospel means good news. It is "good news" to those whose families have been enslaved to Satan and to deceiving spirits for centuries, good news to people bound up by countless superstitions inspired by demons, good news to every person who begins to fear the eternal misery that is coming for sins committed in hard service to the god of this present evil age—the misery of facing the final great day of judgment without a Savior.

The rejection of Christ by the Jewish leaders, and His violent death—"lifted up" to hang over the city of Jerusalem on a bloody tree, so passionate, sorrowful, and destructive, throwing its dark shadow over the citizens and their temple—loomed over the ancient city with finality, as if it were the very sign of God's rejection of the Israelite nation and the end of the older covenant.

The same bloody cross that was the crudest symbol of death and condemnation has emerged as the sign of victory for a new covenant that rushed like wind from the tomb, ascended triumphantly into heaven with authority over heaven and earth,[1] and rushed down again from heaven in the poured-out Spirit of Pentecost. The Messiah's resurrection is the greatest victory of history. The stone that sealed His death, now cast aside, stands as an Ebenezer[2] of the New Testament, declaring, "This far the Lord has brought us!" The light blazing from that empty tomb turned the whole world upside-down with the life-changing power of the new covenant promises.

Such was the power of the new covenant.

But we should not think that the older covenants had no power or purpose in God's grand eternal plan. In fact, these covenants also were perfect, spiritual and very important.

The *older* "covenants of promise," as Paul names them in his letter

14

to the Ephesians,[3] were two. These two covenants were the terms for a very special relationship God established with Abraham and his descendants. The first covenant of promise (Genesis 15 &17) taught them that the death of animals and forgiveness of sin, regeneration, faith and justification, are closely related. The second covenant (Exodus 24, renewed with additional words in Deut. 29) established them as a nation, separating them from all other nations to be God's very own possession, His own people.

The *new covenant*, like those older covenants, brought people near to God in a special relationship with Him. Unlike the old covenants, this new relationship put Jews and Gentiles on equal footing. All who would trust in Christ from every tribe, language and people of the earth were now accepted as equal. The promises of the new covenant establish this new and greater people of God as the citizens of the kingdom of heaven, just as the older covenant of Mt. Sinai made the people citizens of an earthly nation.

This dramatic change, from old covenant to new, is the end of the older covenant ages and the beginning of a new age. This change is Eschatology, the doctrine of last things. *Eschatology* is the study of things future. For those living in the Old Testament, eschatology was concerned with the promise of the future coming of the Messiah, the worldwide kingdom He would establish, the New Covenant that would be introduced at that time, and the salvation the Messiah would provide through the New Covenant. For those living during and after the New Testament, Eschatology includes events preceding, surrounding and following the glorious second coming of Jesus Christ.

Eschatology and the New Covenant in Christ Jesus are as closely related as ice and water; they are the same thing, but in different forms. One cannot have a complete understanding of Eschatology without becoming well-acquainted with covenant theology, because covenant theology provides one of the Biblical road maps that gets us through the maze of prophetic signs and symbols without getting lost. What I mean by this is that prophecy is like a tree that develops as history progresses. The trunk of the tree is the main path. There are many important facts and details scattered throughout the sixty-six books of the Bible, but many of these seem to stand alone without any visible connection to events or times described in passages that precede or follow. Surveying dozens of these passages is like looking at a green full tree from the outside and you see only hundreds of little leaves everywhere. But on closer examination of the tree, you see there is a main trunk, and every branch is connected to that main trunk somewhere, and every leaf is connected to a branch, and prophecy is very much like that. Just like leaves standing side by side can be connected to different limbs that tie into the main trunk at different places, future events described within one chapter of the Bible may actually occur hundreds or thousands of years apart.

There is an important difference between a tree and prophecy, however—a tree has only a single main trunk, where Biblical prophesy has at least two. One of these is the trunk of world history, in particular the history of the great empires of the Middle East that would surround and oppose God's people. Like nearly all things in Scripture, that trunk has its roots in the first chapters of Genesis.

The succession of God's major covenants with His people, throughout the course of their history, is the other main trunk of Eschatology. The revelation of Jesus Christ is the true vine that grows with this main trunk and appears here and there throughout its branches and leaves. Bible students who fail to understand the covenantal nature of Biblical prophecy can go astray like blind men trying to see with a pair of glasses. The most brilliant Bible teacher, lacking knowledge of the covenant connections, may fail to see many important connections in Scripture. Most people look at the end times from a different angle than from the covenants, or by misconstruing the covenants. This approach can result in taking many passages out of their proper context and aligning them incorrectly. Since new covenant theology is almost synonymous with end times theology, Eschatology only finally makes complete sense when viewed through covenant lenses. This roadmap, like the other one described above, originates in Genesis, leading along quite a different route throughout history, but converging at certain main intersections, and finally finishing at the same destination. This is mentioned here to trace an important connection between covenant theology and eschatology, but it will have to be fleshed out more fully in a study of eschatology, including Paul's eschatology, to be published as a companion text to this series.

But now we return to the shift between the older covenants and the new covenant.

If the books of the Bible were divided, not by the birth of Christ, but according to new covenant and old covenants, the four Gospels might be included in the Old Testament, since they conclude the old covenant period, and clearly declare it's end (e.g., Matthew 21:40-45).[5] Without the Gospels, the new covenant is left with only one historical book, *The Acts of the Apostles*.[6] Following, as it does, on the heels of the old covenant of Law, the

16

Book of Acts is the only Bible story that traces the progress of the new covenant nation as it proclaimed the kingdom of heaven first in Jerusalem, then in widening circles all the way to Rome, the capitol city of the empire.

The book of Acts is the bridge of the New Testament, connecting the end of Christ's earthly ministry to the beginning of the labors of the apostles, that first small cloud of witnesses of the new covenant. *"Acts"* links the twelve apostles in Jerusalem, to the last great apostolic witness of Christ's resurrection, Paul, sent forth from Antioch to carry the brilliant torch of the gospel into a Roman empire languishing in blackest darkness. Introducing Peter as the apostle to the Jews, the book of Acts concludes with Paul, the apostle to the Gentiles. Thus, it is the vital bond between Christ's training of the apostles in the Gospels and the inspired letters of Paul that would train the church in all nations to ride tightly upon the tracks of apostolic doctrine through all future ages.

The change from old to new covenant is the hinge of history. A long series of covenants leading to Christ, in the history of the Bible, has come to an end. The life of Christ, His death for our sins, and His resurrection for our justification, give birth to a people who belong not to the world nor the past as much as they belong to the future. For all who are in Christ belong to the new heavens and the new earth that will be revealed in the second coming of Jesus Christ. Indeed, the kingdom of heaven that is coming is already present within their hearts.

For many, it would be confusing to examine Paul's teaching on various portions of covenant theology without seeing how these segments fit into the overall doctrine of the divine covenants. Therefore, before considering what the New Testament apostles have written, the reader should have a basic introduction to covenant theology, as it has stood for the past 500 years—focusing especially on those parts addressed by Paul. When we have a sense of where covenant theology is going, we have the best vantage point to analyze Paul's comments and His interpretation of the divine covenants within their greater theological context. Does the Reformed position[7] really fit Paul's theology? This section is designed to give readers enough understanding of the covenants to judge for themselves. I personally believe the grid of covenant theology, as it has been known since the Reformation of the 16th century, properly flows from and snugly fits the writings of Paul. The emphasis is *Reformed* theology because it is the only corner of Christendom that has consistently plumbed the depths of the covenant doctrine. A comment from an issue of the Dispensational journal,

Bibliotheca Sacra, illustrates this:

> *"This subject (Covenant Theology) is one peculiar to Reformed circles as a brief survey will demonstrate. Leading Catholic writers ignore it entirely. Liberal authors, such as Burrows and Case, also pass over it without comment. Reformed writers, on the other hand, give a large place to the covenants of works, grace, and redemption."*[8]

Coming from the Reformed camp, S.M. Baugh emphatically agrees, "Let me make a bold assertion about Covenant theology: It is not incidental to Reformed theology—it is Reformed theology."[9]

Many today, who call for a completely fresh understanding, a new perspective on Paul, insist that the Reformers misunderstood both the covenant and justification. On the other hand, a common complaint of Reformed authors and teachers is that those who hold such views generally fail to explain the Reformed position correctly. Then, as if they have successfully demonstrated Reformed covenant theology to be in error, they set out dismantling the straw man they've fabricated—when all the while they have been blasting away at a misconstrued blunder they've wrongly named, "Reformed theology," or "covenant theology." In a humble attempt to clarify misconceptions about covenant theology right from the starting gate, Part One of this book sketches a Reformed view on the divine covenants as simply as possible. In Part One, special attention will be paid to Calvin's writings,[10] keeping an eye to succinct detail, but bringing in Paul where appropriate, with the other eye observing where the same tradition of covenant theology is today. The aim throughout will be to make difficult concepts easier and meaningful to the ordinary Christian reader.

If you prefer reading smaller books, this synopsis, or summary, of covenant theology (Part One of this book) actually stands alone and complete in itself, as a summary of some of the important features found in all four volumes in this series. While breezing through it, if you want to dig deeper into one or more sections, you can find related chapters in the Table of Contents and read only those chapters. Part Two is a study of the Covenant of Works. The remaining three volumes follow the pattern laid out in Part One, expanding some things summarized in this synopsis, exploring certain other concepts more deeply, or introducing additional points not found in this initial sketch.

In Part One we will jog along the pathway blazed by the major covenants, to arrange a panoramic of the covenants like a snapshot of the earth from a satellite, to serve as the background map for our study of specific segments later—to better understand how various parts of New Testament commentary, especially Paul's letters, fit into the overall puzzle of covenant interpretation. Insights gained studying and preparing numerous lectures and seminars on the divine covenants over the past ten years will also compose this mural. The reader should understand that the many diverse Reformed and Presbyterian churches in the world do not agree on every minute detail of covenant theology. There may be those who differ and wish to debate certain points expressed in this text. However, most if not all readers should find this brief presentation treads familiar ground.

This bird's eye view of the covenants in history may be sprinkled with some freshness, but it will not be a flight to worlds unknown, nor sensational, nor controversial. It will simply take into account the main streams and thoughts emphasized by the prophets themselves, and especially those footprints that the Holy Spirit, directing each prophet, steps upon again and again, guiding all who have ears to hear to "stand in the ways and see, ask where the good way is, and walk in it; there you will find rest for your souls." (Jer. 6:16) Those pathways that can be traced back to Adam are of greatest importance, because they are the basement of origin and doctrinal foundation—the paramount themes that are grounded in the garden, and are afterward discovered in every covenant God made with mankind—such things as:

- the promise of life, represented by the tree of life;

- death as the wages of sin, threatened at a tree where Adam would learn a hard lesson of the difference between real good and real evil—a threat that is multiplied a hundred times over much later in the laws and curses of the covenant of Sinai—so that man might by this means get the point of the single command that once set life and death, blessing and cursing, always before Adam's eyes, always in the very center of the garden;

- the justice of God against sin, portrayed in banishing Adam from the tree of life (with its promise of life) with no hope of returning on his own, for the flaming sword which guarded the way back "turned every way;"

- the theme of election that the prophets, and Jesus and the apostles are ever reminding the people of—"before the foundation of the

19

world"—which must then be unfolding from the very dawn of human history;

- the presentation of the world to Adam, only to be later presented in covenant first to Noah, then to Abraham (as a token of the whole), then to the kingdom of Israel, then to David, and at last to Christ, of whom the ancient prophet spoke when he wrote, "I will tell of His decree, "He said to me, 'You are my Son, today I have begotten you. Ask of Me and I will give you the nations as your inheritance, the ends of the earth as your possession" (Psalm 2:7-8);

- that most obvious strand that begins in the garden as a few words until more strands and more are braided into it, that is, the developing written Word of God, which grew by Christ's time to be a thick rope with thousands of strands—like those great ropes used to secure a huge ship to dock in a fierce storm—each strand with a lesson of its own, woven together and closely interacting with all the others, and all moving forward toward the Creator's central and objective purpose—the revelation of Jesus Christ—so focused in Him alone that in His coming He is revealed to be both the giver of the Word, the subject of the Word, and the Word itself;

- finally, though many other points might be noted, the love of God weaving itself in and out of the fabric of the Word, appearing time and again, as the great promise held forth for all who trust God, all who love God, all who listen to His Word, all who walk sincerely in His ways, all who repent of their sins, and especially all who find their hope in Christ alone. God's unfailing and absolute love, expressed as a promise of the covenants only for those who believe, is so frequently established, so consistently promised, as the treasured reward for all who keep the covenant by faith down through all the ages. It is not surprising to see that from ancient times God has commanded His people to show the same love for Him and for each other, as their first and second greatest commandments to obey in His covenant.

- And how can we pass over the types and signs and symbols and foreshadows of Christ that are at the front and center of every covenant? We cannot, if there will be a complete picture of the covenantal background of Paul's writings. One of the most common foreshadows was the animal sacrifice. When Adam broke covenant with God, the Lord put the hope of Christ before him in the Garden, both by promise and by illustration. He promised the "Seed of the woman" would be born, then illustrated how this man would strike the serpent's head in a wonderful picture of Christ, where God shed the blood of animals then covered Adam and Eve with their skins. This is the first picture of the Lamb slain and the sin of God's people covered by His righteousness, the spotlessly pure garment. Every soul dressed in this robe is accepted by God. This is the first act of God gathering his people, scattered by sin and judgment, back under His wings by clothing them with Christ. It is the first illustration demonstrating exactly how this shall be done, stated plainly in His own words, in Psalm 50:5, "Gather my consecrated ones unto me, those who made a COVENANT with me by SACRIFICE, and the heavens proclaim His RIGHTEOUSNESS for God Himself is JUDGE." This one verse is a synopsis of the whole scheme of redemptive covenant theology.

When God made a new covenant with Noah, it was over the slaughtered body of a sign of Christ crucified. The same was true of Abraham, who cut animals in half and God swore the words of His covenant over their sprinkled blood and dead bodies; and of Israel, whom Moses gathered at the mountain to enter into covenant with the Lord their God. After reading the whole book of the covenant to them, to seal the Lord's promise of grace to those who believe, Moses sprinkled all the people with the blood of the sacrifices. Until finally Christ Himself was slain as the only acceptable sacrifice of the final and greatest covenant. Surely the real sacrifice of Psalm 50:5 (quoted above) is Christ, who would be slain for the sins of His people to satisfy the demands of the righteous judge. God has appointed death as the wages for all sin, demonstrating that there is no possibility of a covenant with God, after the dreadful fall of Adam, unless sin is covered through the shed blood of a sacrifice.

All of these points are important facets of the covenant. But describing them all heaped upon each other like this is not fitting. Greek teachers emphasize, "Context determines meaning!" And the same holds true here. All the features mentioned above, characteristics of God's covenant, are like sparkling jewels stored in a dark, dim box. They are not yet seen rightly until they are brought out into bright light, arranged in their proper place, and set into their bases—only then can we see all their natural beauty. In this first part of the book, then, we will unfold the covenant with a view to its natural development, the progressive revelation from Adam to Christ. Beginning with the covenant God made with Adam in the Garden of Eden, we will proceed to the Noahic Covenant, the Abrahamic Covenant, the Davidic Covenant, and finally, the New Covenant in Christ Jesus. However, it should be understood that Reformed interpretation does not view all of these as distinct and separate covenants (as Dispensationalism does), but follows, rather, a "two covenant" structure. The two covenants are named, the Covenant of Works and the Covenant of Grace.[11] The Covenant of Works was established with Adam, the first head of the human race. When he rebelled against God a new covenant was needed, the Covenant of Grace, to redeem fallen people and reconcile them to God. The covenants established after Adam's fall are regarded as successive revelations of the Covenant of Grace, because each covenant finds its ultimate fulfillment only through Jesus Christ in His incarnation.

S.M. Baugh writes, "Integral to all Covenant theology is the two-covenant schema of the Covenant of Works and the Covenant of Grace. These two overarching covenants are classically expressed in the Westminster Larger Catechism of 1648 (WLC), which is still used today as an expression of faith and instruction by Reformed communions worldwide."[12]

The Westminster Standards have been recognized for more than three centuries as setting the correct pattern for covenant theology. The Catechism describes the two-covenant schema (*arrangement*) as follows:

Q. 20. *What was the providence of God toward man in the estate in which he was created?*

A. **The providence of God toward man in the estate in which he was created, was the placing him in paradise**, appointing him to dress it, giving him liberty to eat of the fruit of the earth; putting the creatures under his dominion, and ordaining marriage for his help; affording him communion with himself; instituting the sabbath; **entering into a covenant of life with him, upon condition of personal, perfect, and perpetual obedience**, of which the tree of life was a pledge; and forbidding to eat of the tree of the knowledge of good and evil, upon the pain of death.

Q. 30. *Doth God leave all mankind to perish in the estate of sin and misery?*

A. God doth not leave all men to perish in the estate of sin and misery, **into which they fell by the breach of the first covenant,** commonly called the covenant of works; but of his mere love and mercy delivereth his elect out of it, and **bringeth them into an estate of salvation by the second covenant, commonly called the covenant of grace.**

Q. 32. *How is the grace of God manifested in the second covenant?*

A. The grace of God is manifested in **the second covenant**, in that he freely provideth and offereth to sinners a mediator, and life and salvation by him; and requiring faith as the condition to interest them in him, promiseth and giveth his Holy Spirit to all his elect, to work in them that faith, with all other saving graces; and to enable them unto all holy obedience, as the evidence of the truth of their faith and thankfulness to God, and as the way which he hath appointed them to salvation.

Q. 33. *Was the covenant of grace always administered after one and the same manner?*

A. The covenant of grace was not always administered after the same manner, but the administrations of it under the Old Testament were different from those under the New.[13]

Introduction Notes

1. Isaiah 49:8, God declares to His Son, "I will keep you and give you as a covenant to the peoples..."

2. *Ebenezer* means "stone of witness" or "stone of testimony," from 1 Samuel 7:12, "Then Samuel took a stone and set it up between Mizpah and Shen and called its name Ebenezer; for he said, "Till now the Lord has helped us." (1 Samuel 7:12)

3. Ephesians 2:12.

4. Myopia is "the inability to focus on distant object; seeing clearly things close to the eye only." As a metaphor, it means "a lack of foresight or discernment: a narrow view of something".

5. If we date the beginning of the new covenant to the Day of

Pentecost, the Gospels belong in the Old Testament. But if the new covenant began when the Prophet, Priest and King of the new covenant was anointed by the Spirit and began his ministry, then the Gospels rightly belong to the New Testament.

6. We should be thankful that there is not an historical book for each and every great missionary expansion of all the apostles and others in the first century; an entire lifetime would not be sufficient to read all of the books, and our Bibles would be too huge to carry!

7. This book will sometimes make reference to "the Reformed position" or "the Reformed view." This refers to the view presented by Reformed theology over the centuries, especially summarized in the Reformed creeds, such as the Westminster Confession of Faith, the Belgic Confession of Faith, the Heidelberg Catechism, and the Canons of Dort.

8 . Homer Lemuel Paine, "Contemporary Amillennial Literature." *Bibliotheca Sacra 106*, no. 422 (April 1949): 204-205, Logos e-book.

9 . S.M. Baugh, "Covenant Theology Illustrated: Romans 5 on the Federal Headship of Adam and Christ." *Modern Reformation 9*, no. 4 (2000), 16, http://www.modernreformation.org/default.php?page=articledisplay&var1=ArtRead&var2=496&var3=authorbio&var4=AutRes&var5=247 [1] (accessed June15 , 2011).

10. Especially Calvin, because NPP authors say that the Reformers misunderstood Paul. The leading Reformers were Calvin and Luther. Therefore, to represent early Reformed covenant theology, in this chapter on the covenants we will draw mostly from Calvin, and from the Reformed Creeds and their authors.

11. These two covenants will be capitalized, as proper nouns, through later chapters.

12. Baugh, "Covenant," 16.

13. *Westminster Confession of Faith.*

Part One:
An Overview
of the
Divine Covenants

One

The Garden Paradise

Genesis 1:26, the first mention of mankind in the Bible, presents two incredible facts about man that are apparently tied together. The first is that mankind has *an inherent right to rule over God's creatures*—over the earth itself—simply because of the second fact, that man is *created in God's own image*. To be fashioned in the likeness of the Creator is in itself an amazing thing. But God anchored the rule of the earth and its creatures to that image. This is tantamount to saying that lordship over the natural world belongs only to beings made in the very image or likeness of God. It is fascinating that God would design a creature who would rule over the earth as a perfect reflection of God's own rule! To be made like God, and to rule like God, implies that God intended a very close relationship with man, an intimate fellowship of Divine Spirit with human spirit.

The second chapter of Genesis reveals that man, though made like God in perfect righteousness and godly wisdom, is absolutely forbidden to regard himself *to be equal with God*. To make this absolutely clear, God established a rule for Adam, a law, with the threat of a severe penalty for any violation. This law represented God's covenant with man.

The law is not actually called a *covenant* in Genesis 2, but then the name wasn't necessary since it was the first such relationship between man and God in the new world. Every later pact between God and man, having some semblance of the pattern of the first one (in which God's demands and promises are presented to man) is thereafter named, *covenant*. When God gave a similar Law with much more detail at Mt. Sinai, He again threatened all violators with death and then He Himself *did* call it a covenant. A covenant is the terms for a relationship with God, such as a friendship with God or a pact between God the king and his subjects. From the *terms* God presented to Adam we may reasonably assume that these words do indeed reveal a covenant. A covenant consists of words, that is, the Word of God, presented to man with the obligation that the Word must be believed and obeyed.

With Adam, there were more covenant words from God than this one command not to eat from a tree. The terms of a covenant must describe much more than merely how to enter into or break off the relationship. Certainly there must be words teaching us how to live in covenant relationship, or specifying responsibilities that belong to those brought so near to God by covenant. In the Garden covenant, God assigned specific responsibilities to Adam. He commanded him to subdue the earth and rule its creatures, and being in God's own likeness, it was to be a just and caring rule. The same holds true for Adam's other responsibilities. He was to populate and fill the earth with children made in God's image and work in the soil of the earth to produce its harvest, showing that God's image must be seen in both home life and the workplace. He was given permission in a decree of the covenant, to enjoy the fruits of his labor, to eat of all green plants and fruits of trees. So Paul writes that "the hard working farmer ought to be the first to enjoy his share of the crops" (2 Timothy 2:6). Just as the first covenant was to last forever, these principles were meant to endure as long as the earth exists: fill the world with godly children who bear His image in everything they do, rule over the earth and its creatures as God's image and for God's glory, and be God's fellow laborers doing all work for the glory of God. So thousands of years later the principles still stand in the epistles of the new covenant, "Whatever you do, do your work heartily, as to the Lord rather than men," and "If anyone will not work, neither let him eat." (2 Thess. 3:10).

To the list of Adam's responsibilities mentioned above, should be added a day of rest every seven days. Only one day after Adam was made, God blessed the seventh day and made it a Sabbath of rest—before Adam's first day on the job. Can we believe that God forever blessed the seventh day on the second day of Adam's life, but waited until Moses came thousands of years later to reveal that blessing of rest to His people? God didn't want man to toil endlessly without resting; he was to take time from his activities to lead his family to remember who made the earth, and resting, worship God together with them.

We know that these responsibilities were presented to Adam in a covenant, because when God made the next covenant with mankind, through a new Adam named Noah (the new father of all mankind), he repeats the same list again: populate and fill the earth, rule the creatures, and *"just as I gave you the green plants, I now give you everything"* to eat, both plants and meats—these are all words of a new covenant.

The covenant God made with Adam has been most commonly known as the "Covenant of Works," although it has been assigned such names as, the "covenant of creation," the "covenant of nature," and the "covenant of life." In the "Covenant of Works," God made Adam in His own image, revealed to Adam the words of His covenant, then brought forth Eve from Him, making Adam the head of all mankind. It was because Adam was the head of the human race that God established the covenant first with him. As Paul writes in Rom. 5:14, "Adam was a type of Him who was later to come." Since this set the pattern for all later covenants, Adam's relationship with God was most certainly a covenant. Just like Adam, each great covenant that followed was established by God with only a single man at first (Adam, Noah, Abraham, and David). This first man was an imperfect new Adam, a type of the first Adam, a father to all of God's people who would come from him. Noah is truly the father of all peoples on earth. Abraham is the father of a new people, to be regenerated by the Holy Spirit from every nation, even from the Jews. David is father to all who would rule in God's kingdom. Each of these *patriarchs* foreshadowed different features of the Last Adam who was coming. Placing each new Adam before us in history, each crippled by the sin of the first Adam, God pointed to the need for a sinless truly-human Adam to come into the world, a Last Adam, who would fulfill all things that each imperfect Adam, including the first man, had failed to accomplish in their respective covenants. Because each covenant, beginning with Adam, was established with a type of Christ, every covenant included *the children* of that one man (as with Noah, Abraham,[1] and David) from generation to generation. With Christ's covenant, the new covenant, this means more than spiritual rebirths alone, as we shall see in later chapters.

There were not only *first Adam—later Adam* parallels. *Within* each covenant there were features that paralleled, or contrasted Adam's covenant.[2] We have already seen that God revised and reintroduced Adam's covenant to Noah commanding him to populate and rule the earth. With Abraham, God spoke promises that clearly reflected His Adamic blessings saying, *"This is my covenant with you, I have made you a father of many nations."* Similarly, the Sinai covenant contained a republication of a form of the Covenant of Works first made with Adam, "I place before you life and death," and "the soul that sins shall die." In David's covenant God promised a throne that would rule the world, an inheritance that rightly belonged to the first Adam before the fall. Anticipating the covenant of the last Adam God declared to Christ, His Son, in Psalm 2, "Ask of me, and I will give you the nations as your inheritance, the ends of the earth as your possession." This is a clear allusion to Adam's covenant in Romans 5:14, "Adam, who was a type of Him who was later to come."

But obedience to Adam's Covenant of Works was *not* the condition for fellowship with God after Adam's fall. Even though there are allusions to the Covenant of Works in every covenant it was for the last Adam alone, Jesus Christ, to fulfill the requirement of the Covenant of Works, *perfect obedience*. In this way the first Adam is more obviously the type of the last Adam. Romans 5 goes on to explain that Christ's one act brings justification and eternal life to all who are "in Him," just as Adam's one sin brought condemnation and death to all "in him." Christ's perfect obedience to the Father in all things commanded, including submitting Himself to be crucified, was a true and greater Covenant of Works.[3] Having perfectly fulfilled God's demands, He became the gracious way of salvation in the Covenant of Grace. Christ's obedience and his sacrifice were both entirely covenantal; it stands to reason that Adam's failure was covenantal, in the Covenant of Works.

Returning to the first Adam. God placed two trees before Adam's eyes in the center of the garden. One of these, the tree of life, symbolized the eternal life that would be Adam's reward for obedience. It was a symbol of the promise of life, the life of God (the life that comes from God alone), the tree is the first sacrament.[4] So common is this understanding, that many who are not Reformed have held it such as Samuel Farmer Jarvis (1787-1851), one of the original framers of Dispensationalism.[5]

Like every other sacrament in later history, this tree symbolized the life that is from Christ alone, the Living Word, the life that God forever shares with all who listen to His Word.[6] In the sixteenth century the Reformers understood this but Calvin wrote that the concept first came from the writings of early church fathers,

> "I am not dissatisfied with what has been handed down by some of the fathers, as Augustine and Eucherius, that the tree of life was a figure of Christ, inasmuch as he is the Eternal Word of God: it could

32

not indeed be otherwise a symbol of life, than by representing him in figure. For we must maintain what is declared in the first chapter of John (John 1:1-3), that the life of all things was included in the Word, but especially the life of men, which is conjoined with reason and intelligence. Wherefore, by this sign, Adam was admonished, that he could claim nothing for himself as if it were his own, in order that he might depend wholly upon the Son of God, and might not seek life anywhere but in him."[7]

The apostle John explains that the Word (Christ) was "in the beginning" with God when "all things were created by Him" (John 1:1-4). From the very beginning, when Adam was formed from the dust, the second member of the Trinity was God's Word to man, the Word who would come into the world as Jesus Christ, the Word that was to be made flesh to dwell among us. It is this Christ, "the Word of God" who was "in the beginning with God," that John speaks of when he writes, *In Him was life, and the life was the light of men."* (John 1:1-4). The eternal life promised by this covenant, the life that comes from God Himself, was symbolized by the tree of life in the center of the garden. Brighter than the beams of sunlight streaming through the canopy of branches, the Word was a lamp lighting not foliage and fruit, but the hearts of Adam and Eve with the hope of everlasting life. Whenever Adam partook of this sacramental fruit it was as if God was saying through the tree, *"Take, eat, this is my own life, shared with you."*[8] By keeping the Word (and thus the giver of the Word) always before him and obeying the Word from his heart, instead of laying his mind open to Satan's words, Adam could have lived forever.

There was another tree that stood beside the tree of life. God gave this tree an unusual name because it symbolized the terrible lesson that Adam would learn if he should disobey God and eat from it. Having perfect foreknowledge the Lord knew that Satan would test Adam and manipulate him to rise against his Creator. Calvin wrote of this: *"All, however, who think piously and reverently concerning the power of God, acknowledge that the evil did not take place except by his permission. For, in the first place, it must be conceded, that God was not in ignorance of the event which was about to occur; and then, that he could have prevented it, had he seen fit to do so. But in speaking of permission, I understand that he had appointed whatever he wished to be done."*[9]

So God determined the trial would come at that tree, where Adam would learn the bitter and painful lesson (or knowledge) that he had not done the "good" of loving God with all his heart and that his "evil" of disobedience and rebellion bore only the fruit of bitterness, misery, and death. So God called it *"the tree of the knowledge of good and evil,"* or in other words, simply that disobedience is the wrong way to learn the difference between good and evil. It was in fact, a forbidden and deadly way, the way that Adam would lose the life promised in the first tree; for God said of the forbidden tree, *"In the day you eat of it, you will surely die"* (Gen. 2:17).

The essential parts of the covenant were represented by these two trees. God promised that He would confirm eternal life to Adam and his descendants, giving him authority to rule over the world-kingdom forever with God (as God's image), if Adam would truly love God and prove faithful to Him and remain an uncorrupted likeness of God. For those who like few words it was *a simple test of obedience,*as Reformed theology, beginning with Bullinger and Calvin in the 16thcentury, has always described it.[10]

Heinrich Bullinger, successor to Zwingli, one of the first to set forth a system of covenant theology wrote, *"For God in saying, " Thou shalt not eat of the fruit of the tree of knowledge of good and evil," did simply require at his hands faith and obedience, and that he should wholly depend upon God: all which he had to do, not by compulsion or necessity, but of his own accord and free good-will."*[11]

Calvin states it more clearly:

"The prohibition to touch the tree of the knowledge of good and evil was *a trial of obedienc*e, that Adam, by observing it, might prove his willing submission to the command of God. For the very term shows the end of the precept to have been to keep him contented with his lot, and not allow him arrogantly to aspire beyond it."[12]

The reward for obedience was the *tree of life.* The penalty for disobedience was *death,* that is to be cut off from the *tree of life* or from the internally abiding life of Him who is our tree of eternal life, Christ Himself. Calvin continues:

"The promise, which gave him hope of eternal life as long as he should eat of the tree of life, and, on the other hand, the fearful denunciation of death the moment he should taste of the tree of the knowledge of good and evil, were meant to prove and exercise his faith."[13]

The proper name for this simple arrangement has become a sticking

34

point today. It has often been called the "Covenant of Works," because there was a law, a negative prohibition, and a threat of death upon breaking the law.

It has been proposed that this covenant should not be named with such a legalistic term as *works*. Some have pointed[14] out that God was being so especially gracious even in condescending to enter into a relationship with man, a friendship, that the covenant itself with its magnificent promise of eternal life was an exceptionally gracious act on the part of God. There is truth in this. This is the reason that theologians who have held to the concept of the Covenant of Works have suggested to us that we should view God in such a light of graciousness, even in the garden, *even at the Covenant of Works*. For example, Alexander Hodge wrote,

> "...it is called the "covenant of works," because perfect obedience was its condition, and to distinguish it from the covenant of grace, which rests our salvation on a different basis altogether. It is also called the "covenant of life," because life was promised on condition of the obedience. It is also called a "legal covenant," because it demanded the literal fulfillment of the claims of the moral law as the condition of God's favor. *This covenant was also in its essence a covenant of grace, in that it graciously promised life in the society of God as the freely–granted reward of an obedience already unconditionally due.* Nevertheless it was a covenant of works and of law with respect to its demands and conditions."[15]

Hodge's comment should have been followed by a detailed explanation. Yes, eternal life was a reward infinitesimally greater than the demand of obedience. Yes, God was gracious to offer such an incredible prize for Adam's conformity to a single rule. There's a great difference between God's motive and attitude in delivering a covenant and the actual wording, or terms, of the covenant itself. It is only the legal terms that continue binding covenant members, unchanged, as long as a covenant is in force. Though it is true that Adam's obedience was due unconditionally, the terms of the covenant set forth *a clear condition, a firm condition* on which Adam's life was to depend. The condition was part of the actual covenant; this idea that God was gracious in promising eternal life failed to make grace part of the words of the equation actually presented to Adam. Should Adam disobey, grace simply wasn't promised to him in the words of the covenant. Hodge understood this, so he counters his previous statement with a *nevertheless*, "Nevertheless, *it was a covenant of works and law* with respect to its demands and conditions."

Specifically, the name, "Covenant of Works," has been preferred by many because Adam was commanded not to break God's law. In a similar manner, the inspired author, Paul, uses the phrase, "works of the Law" to describe a long list of negative commands in the covenant of Sinai, such as *"do not murder," "do not commit adultery,"* and closer to Adam's garden home, *"do not eat"* a long list of unlawful foods (cf. Leviticus 11:1-41; Colossians 2:16, 20-22). In Paul, a command not to eat, such as was given to Adam, is properly called a "work of the law," so that the Covenant of Works has not been erroneously named. With this negative command, and its terrible threat of death, the Covenant of Works surely was a legal covenant. In other words, Adam's continued relationship with God and his very life depended on his keeping this one law perfectly (Gen. 2:17; 3:3). One violation would be the end, the end of his life, the end of the covenant, and the end of this special relationship with God. Disobedience would result in death and death would cut off everything. So much for God being gracious to sinners in this first covenant. He may have had gracious intentions in promising life to the sinless and righteous persons fashioned exactly in His own impeccable image; but this graciousness did not make a way *within Adam's covenant itself* to save Adam from being cursed when he sinned.

It should be clear even to a child that the covenant was a legal arrangement and not merely a mutual friendship between God and man. Just survey the carnage. Look at what became of Adam's entire family tree after he rebelled. Every twig of every branch is born already a sinner and alienated from God! His disobedience broke God's covenant with mankind, with its promise of eternal life, and heaped on his descendants a tragic mess of sin, corruption, separation from God, bondage to Satan, death, and condemnation—so that every human child, anywhere on earth needs salvation from sin (in the classic words of many of the early church fathers) *"even if his life is but one day."* These consequences do not result from a mere broken friendship, but from rebellion against the demands of the Lawgiver and Judge. Calvin concurs, *"As the act which God punished so severely must have been not a trivial fault, but a heinous crime, it will be necessary to attend to the peculiar nature of the sin which produced Adam's fall, and provoked God to inflict such fearful vengeance on the whole human race."*[16]

The answer to, *"Why?!"* that is, *why* these dreadful consequences came to "the whole human race," to Adam's children, belongs to a right understanding of the Covenant of Works. Just as deliberate rebellion in the Sinai covenant brings a long list of curses upon the life of the offender, the first sin in the garden was followed by a list of curses that haunted Adam's family line, curses that God vowed to bring upon both the rebels and their descendants (Gen. 3:14-19; Romans 8:20-22; Deut. 27:14-26; 28:15-68). Reformed theologians insist that every trail of evil, perversion, and violence, throughout human history can be followed back to Adam's one sin in the Covenant of Works. This is because we see Adam as both the physical head of mankind and the representative head of the whole human race. In theology, this is known as "federal headship," a central principle of the first covenant. The understanding of this concept wasn't formed simply by reading the book of Genesis, but by studying everything else that the rest of the books of the Bible reveal about sin, judgment, Christ, salvation, covenant, and of course, Adam. Simply, the "federal headship" model is like this: *To prove mankind's faithfulness to Himself, God tested the first man when he was perfect and sinless, making him the representative of all men before any were born. When Adam's disobedience broke this first covenant, he brought upon himself and all his descendants, death, God's curse, and bondage to Satan, because he was the representative of them all, the federal representative of the whole human race that would come from him.* The consequences that came to Adam, came to all. Calvin defends federal headship in his Commentary on Genesis, where he declares that God justly punishes the whole human race with death, condemning all in the one person of Adam. This may be easier to see when we understand that the entire human race, except Eve, was *in Adam* when he sinned, and even she came forth from him. The entire human race sinned when it numbered only two. And the human race continues to be charged with its original guilt. Calvin writes:

> "...that we are also lost and condemned, and subjected to death, is both *our hereditary condition*, and, at the same time, *a just punishment which God, in the person of Adam, has indicted on the human race.* Now, if any one should object, that it is unjust for the innocent to bear the punishment of another's sin, I answer, whatever gifts God had conferred upon us in the person of Adam he had the best right to take away, when Adam wickedly fell. Nor is it necessary to resort to that ancient figment of certain writers, that souls are derived by descent from our first parents. For the human race has not naturally derived corruption through its descent from Adam; but that

result is rather to be traced to the appointment of God, who, as he had adorned the whole nature of mankind with most excellent endowments in one man, so in the same man he again denuded it."[17]

Calvin is often hard to understand, and the same is true here. But this is what I believe he means. Calvin distinguishes between three important things: "our hereditary condition," imputation of guilt (which he describes as *"a just punishment that God, in the person of Adam, has indicted on the whole human race"*), and the "appointment" of "corruption" to every individual born to the human race. Calvin acknowledges all three elements at work in man's fallen condition. Guilt is imputed (p. 41) to the whole human race, because the entire humanity sinned in the garden when Adam sinned. In reality, two people sinned, but the Holy Spirit does not say that the sin of the two brought condemnation upon all, but the sin of only one (see Romans 5:16, 18). This is a very important point. It implies that there is not only inherited corruption from Adam and Eve, but imputation of guilt (p. 41) from one man who stood as the representative of all. Calvin also seems to say that the depraved mind that still exists in the whole human race is God's just punishment on mankind because of Adam's rebellion. The father of all mankind sinned and corrupted himself. That same sin, corruption and bondage to the devil belongs to every descendant born of Adam. The apostle, Paul, writes in Romans 1:28-29, that the Sovereign God had a part in sentencing mankind to depravity, *"Furthermore, since they did not think it worthwhile to retain the knowledge of God, he gave them over to a depraved mind, to do what ought not to be done. They have become filled with every kind of wickedness, evil, greed and depravity. They are full of envy, murder, strife, deceit and malice. They are gossips..."* (Romans 1:28–29, NIV84)

Some may think of taking Calvin to the carpet on how he has explained the corruption that plagues the human race, but before we tie him to the firing wall we should at least try to understand what he really means, and what is the Scriptural basis for his conclusions.

Calvin's intention is to answer those who object to federal representation, so he firmly insists that imputation of one man's guilt to all men is no blight on the justice of God.[18] Many ignore what he says here and focus on the following statement that Calvin makes at the end of this section, as if his last words are intended to cancel what the good doctor has already clearly stated. He writes, *"But now, from the time in which we were corrupted in Adam, we do not bear the punishment of another's offense, but are guilty by our own fault."*[19] When this is considered within its context,

Calvin simply means, that being corrupt creatures, we are justly condemned by Adam's one sin alone, but if anyone should protest against this, the many sins that have flowed from our corrupt nature is enough in itself to condemn each and every person. Calvin insists Paul himself makes the same point, in his comments on Romans 5:19, where he shows that Paul declares all men guilty in the one sin of Adam..." Romans 5:19 states, "...by the one man's disobedience the many were made sinners..." Calvin continues, "...but for those who object to this idea, the apostle adds that all are equally guilty for the sins springing from their own corrupt nature, "For [Paul] shows that *we are guilty through the offense of one man, in such a manner as not to be ourselves innocent. He had said before, that we are condemned*; but that no one might claim for himself innocence, he *also* subjoined, that everyone is condemned because he is a sinner."

It is Calvin's remark on Romans 5:17, however, that seems to be most at odds with his view already expressed above (I say, "seems," because a closer look indicates he's saying the same thing as in the references above): "...by Adam's sin we are not condemned through imputation *alone*, as though we were punished *only* for the sin of another; but *we suffer his punishment*, because we also ourselves are guilty; for as our nature is vitiated *in him*, it *is regarded by God as* having committed sin."

This has sometimes been taken as a denial of imputation, but that's not Calvin's intention because he has already made clear that the human race is not guilty by imputation *alone*. Calvin regards mankind as truly condemned in Adam (by imputation, as he has clearly stated above), but just as guilty and condemned by our sharing in Adam's corrupted nature, so that we also commit sins. In other words, we are condemned for Adam's sin, and we are also condemned for his corrupt nature in us. We were condemned in the imputation of Adam's guilt, but having inherited his depraved condition, that perverted nature itself is enough to condemn us, even before it begins to commit actual sin; so now we are not condemned by imputation *alone*.[20] Paul has a simpler way of saying this when he writes: "...we were by our very nature children of the wrath of God." (Eph. 2:3) God condemned mankind in Adam, and according to Paul, every man since, by his very nature, has been an object of God's wrath.

In Reformed theology, the doctrine of original sin includes the points found in Calvin's statements, above. The guilt of Adam's one sin is charged to all of us, as having participated in it with him—this is the *imputation* Calvin describes in his commentary on Genesis 3. But he closes with the second point, that all are also condemned for the sinful nature we have inherited from him. A sinful nature is just as offensive and guilty as any sins eventually committed by that evil nature. Conceived under the bar of God's justice, a sinful nature stands guilty before God from the moment it begins to exist.

This raises a number of questions not tackled in this brief overview of the covenants, so there's more to come in Part Two, on the Covenant of Works.

Immediately after Adam's fall God revealed His eternal plan to Adam in the form of a mystery, He vowed that "the seed of the woman" would one day be born to set man free from Satan. In covenant theology this is understood as the first promise of the "Covenant of Grace." The seed of the woman, a man truly sinless, would be born through the human race and overcome Satan by sacrificing His own life as a perfectly righteous man. The apostle Paul explains in Romans 5:18, *"Consequently, just as the result of one trespass was condemnation for all men, so also the result of one act of righteousness was justification that brings life for all men."* This is the context where the Holy Spirit says that Adam was "a type of Him who was later to come" (Rom. 5:14). Just as Adam's one act of rebellion brought condemnation to all who were born of Adam, the Redeemer's one sacrifice would provide redemption to all who trust in Him for salvation, and are born again through Him.

The Redeemer does this by becoming our representative before God. Therefore, when Adam was tested, he also represented every person who would be born of him, because he was a type of Christ—*"a type of Him who was later to come."* (Romans 5:14) This is one of the reasons that Eve had to be made from Adam.

Reformed theologians pondered all these things in Scripture until they saw that the demand of Adam's obedience was the essential point of the Covenant of Works. He was to obey God as the representative of all mankind, all who would be born of Him, just as Christ would come to serve as the representative of all who would be spiritually born of Him. Adam's failure to obey was the sin of all who were in him. When the human race was but one man, and one woman who came out of that man, God charged the whole human race with the sin and rebellion of that one man.

In the same way, Christ would come as the Last Adam, representing all the elect *in Himself*, all who would be born of His Spirit. *As the Last*

40

Adam, He had to obey perfectly for their sakes, all the commands and laws of the Father. The demand of Christ's perfect obedience, throughout His entire life and especially in His death at the cross, is the essential point that makes possible the Covenant of Grace, because in His obedience, Christ represents all the elect of God, so that His righteousness can be imputed to them. In His obedient death on the cross, all of their sins are imputed to Him because He is their representative, and He takes the sin and guilt away by paying the penalty in full. Without the perfect active and passive obedience of our representative, Jesus Christ, there can be no Covenant of Grace, no substitutionary atonement, no salvation, and no hope for Adam's lost children. In Adam, *all* die.

"You were dead in trespasses and sins," writes Paul (Ephesians 2:1,4). From that first sin of Adam, real life, spiritual life, the eternal life that comes from God alone, was taken away from the human race. Adam and Eve, dead in sin, were driven out of the garden, cut off from the tree of life.

The Covenant of Redemption

But then God came with His eternal plan, revealing the first clues that in Christ, man would be brought to life again—delivered from Satan's domain of spiritual bondage and death. This was an eternal plan of God determined within the Trinity before the beginning of time. This great mysterious agreement between God and Christ, called the Covenant of Redemption by many Reformed theologians,[21] is alluded to in many passages of Scripture, but never plainly stated. It is intended to be a hidden mystery.

It is a simple plan. *God demanded His Son take human form to become the Last Adam—one who would represent all people who would be spiritually born again through Him. To bring dead sinners to life, the Son of God must bear the full penalty of the sins of all persons God had chosen to give to His Son from human history. As Adam's one sin plunged the human race into death, corruption, and bondage to Satan, Christ's one act of righteousness would bring life to the dead, free them from corruption and set them free from Satan's slavery. As in Adam, all die; in Christ, all shall be made alive. Those in Christ would have a share in His perfect obedience, His suffering and death on the cross, and His resurrection as a perfectly righteous man unto newness of life. Just as God charged all "in Adam," with the sin of the human race; God credits all who will be brought to life through Christ with the righteousness of Christ Himself.* This ("charging" and "crediting") is called imputation. *(Isa. 49:4; Heb. 12:2; Isa. 53:10-11).*

Paul, describing the plan, writes that the elect were chosen "in Him." (Eph. 1:4-5) "In Christ" they would die with Him, be buried with Him, and be raised from the dead to ascend within Him into heavenly glory. "In Christ" they would share not only in His death and resurrection, but as members of His body, they partake of his life, his righteousness, his sanctification, his glorification, his exalted reign, and his eternal inheritance. Christ, writes Paul, "is all in all," emphasizing in another place, "and you are complete *in Him.*" Because none of us were actually *in Christ* at the precise point in time when He died and rose from the dead, to make Christ our representative and us sharers in His death and victorious life, God credits us with Christ's death, resurrection, righteousness and ascension into glory. He imputes Christ's righteousness to the personal account of each one of the elect.

When His imputed righteousness becomes clear, it is easy to understand what R. Fowler White and E. Calvin Beisner mean when they write that Christ is the archetype of Adam.[22] Christ is the model of federal headship already existing from eternity. He came before Adam, and certain characteristics in Adam, and in Adam's covenant, are patterned after the archetype.

Before time began, God the Father established a covenant of obedience with His Son. This covenant demanded that Christ humble Himself by taking the weakness of human form in order to be the head and representative of all the elect. Christ would represent them in His active obedience, so that, obeying where Adam disobeyed, in Him the elect might share in the righteousness of a perfectly sinless federal head and father. Christ's obedience, however, would be so much more than Adam's. Born under the Law to redeem those under the Law, He would obey every righteous commandment of the Sinai covenant to escape the curse of the Law Himself, and to deliver those who are cursed in both Adam and Moses. Additionally, to "fulfill all righteousness," Christ would have to obey every command the Father gave to Him personally, so that by His wholehearted sinless love for God, Christ would fulfill the essential requirement of the Covenant of Works. Through His active obedience (His entire life) and passive obedience (surrendering Himself to die at the hands of sinners) Christ demonstrates, and is, the very righteousness of God. Christ not only saves the elect from their sins by His death in their place, His life also saves them. "For if when we were enemies, we were reconciled to God through the death of His Son, how much more, having been reconciled, shall we be saved through His life!" (Romans 5:10) All who were chosen *in Him* before the foundation of the world have a share in that righteousness, and in every other spiritual gift that is in Him (Eph. 1:4-5); Christ truly is all in all (Col. 3:11; Eph. 1:23). In Him alone is all that is needed for righteousness and life and eternal inheritance, in all who belong to Christ.

Because Christ is the archetype of Adam, the first man formed of the dust of the garden enters into a covenant patterned after Christ's eternal covenant. In the Covenant of Redemption, God required the absolute obedience of His Son to every law and commandment of God. So God made a covenant in the garden demanding Adam's obedience. God's demands from Adam are a small mirror of His demands from Christ. As a sinless son of God, Adam represents all who were in him just as Christ does. God tested the human race in one man. Adam's disobedience is the disobedience of mankind. Every person he represents has an equal share in his unrighteousness, corruption, guilt, and condemnation. Every person born of that one man shares in his death, being spiritually dead from the moment of conception.

Plunged into the abyss of spiritual darkness and bondage to Satan by the fall of Adam, and thrust out of the garden of God's covenant, man lives out his days in the snare of the devil, "taken captive by him to do his will" (2 Tim. 2:26). The true God sent Adam out of the Garden, without any ability in himself to return to the Tree of Life. The serpent, the "god of this age," was determined that Adam's children would never learn God's way, the Covenant of Grace. Satan has engulfed the minds of Adam's descendants with a veil of spiritual blindness to this present day. He darkly "veils those who are perishing," blinding their minds from seeing the truth, confusing their understanding, leading them into a maze of spiritual deceptions, so they might never know the true God (2 Cor. 4:3-4) and the only way of salvation.

But God stood ready with "the plan". The "seed of the woman" would come into the world.

It was *God's plan* to reveal the mystery of Christ to His people in various stages, a series of covenants. Each covenant revealed more and advanced further toward the coming of the Redeemer. From the first revelation of the "good news" of Christ, immediately after the fall, nearly every supernatural work of God for man, and every covenant God made with mankind in history, was connected to His central purpose of fulfilling this one eternal plan. At the Last Supper with His disciples, Christ revealed that "the plan" was at last reaching its climax; He lifted the cup of wine saying, "This is my blood of the new covenant, which is poured out for many for the forgiveness of sins" (Matt. 26:28). The next afternoon, as His lifeblood streamed to the ground, He loudly cried out, "It is finished!" gave up His spirit, and died. The plan had been accomplished.

In this plan, unfolding through the ages and revealed especially in God's covenants with man, there were certain characteristics that stood out boldly in the Scripture testimony. These were things God surely meant man to notice in His Word, because they are details that are consistently the same, appearing again and again throughout the history of redemption:

a. **After Adam sinned, covenants could only be established over the shedding of blood.** An animal sacrifice always had to be slain as a symbol of the Last Adam who would obey the Covenant of Works in perfect sinless obedience, and die as a spotless Lamb for the sins of God's covenant people to fulfill the eternal Covenant of Redemption (cf. Gen. 8:20-9:17; Gen. 15:9-20; Exodus 24:3-8; Matt. 26:28).

b. **Every covenant had the purpose of glorifying Christ**, in keeping with God's intention that He must have first place in everything (Col. 1:16-19). God's love for His Son, and the Son's love for the Father, chiefly consists in wholeheartedly seeking the glory of the other. Therefore, in God's love for his Son, every covenant must be seen to be Christological, or in other words, Christ-centered (Col. 2:17; Heb. 10:1). Calvin understood this, and emphasizes it in his commentaries.

c. **Covenants always continued with the descendants of anyone who was made a true member of the covenant**, even with those who joined the covenant from the Gentiles. But only those descendants who were genuine believers experienced the full blessings, the complete forgiveness of all sin, and the gifts of righteousness and life, promised by the covenants (Gen. 9:8-9; Gen. 17:4-5, 7; Romans 4:12, 16; 9:8).

d. **In every covenant, righteousness was always a gift of God, given by grace through faith**, for it was impossible for fallen mankind to establish their own righteousness before God by any works of the Law. All were enslaved by their very nature to sinful lusts and pleasures (Noah, Heb. 11:7; Abraham, Gen. 15:5; David,

Rom. 4:6-8; Christians today, Rom. 3:22-24).

e. **Membership in covenant was absolutely vital to a person's relationship with God**. Paul explains in Ephesians 2:12, that anyone who did not have citizenship in God's covenant kingdom, anyone who was not a member of the covenants of promise God made with Abraham and Israel, was *"without Christ....without God, and without any hope in the world."* One of these "covenants of promise" was God's gracious pact with Abraham. From Abraham's time, until the coming of Christ two thousand years later, the only people God saved from the world were believers who were members of Abraham's covenant. It is easy to see from this that salvation and fellowship with the true God are provided only where He has established His covenant with man. Or we might better say, salvation restores man to the full privileges of covenant membership.

Covenant membership, however, didn't benefit those who would not believe God's Word. Only those with true faith were justified, not those members of the covenant who lacked sincere faith, even when by birthright they were entitled to membership, instead of gaining the justification by grace promised in the covenant, they perished as covenant breakers.

Chapter One Notes

1. The covenant with Israel is a further addition to the covenant first made with one man, Abraham, and with his children after him. It is established with the descendants of Abraham, "until the seed should come to whom the promise [of Abraham's covenant] was made." Gen. 3:19

2. Several of these parallel features are mentioned here. Others are described in later chapters.

3. It should be noted here that we are not suggesting that "Christ's one act" in Romans 5 is a different obedience than His death on the cross. Rather, his ultimate act of obedience, in offering Himself to die, after a lifetime of sinless perfection in the last Adam's "Covenant of Works," represents an entire life of perfect obedience now offered to God as the final act and the conclusion of his life.

4. The idea that the tree of life was a sacrament has been held by many theologians over the past five centuries. A sacrament is a sacred symbol of the life and blessing God gives to us through Christ, and always represents some aspect of Christ Himself. In the sacrament of the Lord's Table, the bread symbolizes his body broken for us all and raised up to newness of life; the wine represents the blood he shed unto death for the forgiveness of the sins of His people. In the sacrament of water baptism, the water symbolizes the blood of Christ that is sprinkled on our souls to cleanse our conscience of sin, and also stands for the Holy Spirit, poured out on God's people on the Day of Pentecost. John the Baptist said that Christ would "baptize you with the Holy Spirit and fire." Therefore, water baptism must be a sign of the real baptizing work of God which is done in the heart and by the Spirit. As the apostle Paul wrote, in Titus 3:5-6, "...He saved us through the washing of rebirth and renewal by the Holy Spirit, whom He poured out on us generously through Jesus Christ our Savior..."

5. It should be noted, however, that Jarvis' description of the "Dispensations" might be more akin to covenant theology than to 20th century Dispensationalism. See Arnold D. Ehlert, "A Bibliography of Dispensationalism," *Bibliotheca Sacra 102*, no. 405 (January 1945), 90. William Law (1686-1761), an Anglican who focused on his devotional and mystical writing when he was excluded from the Church of England, described the sacrament as a "tree of life" in a book he wrote against errors, "Be glad to know, that as the nature, office, and condition of our savior could not be made known to us, but by a variety of different names and titles ascribed to him; so the nature and end and effects of this holy sacrament could not be made known to us, but by a variety of different names and titles ascribed to it; that in one respect it is a propitiatory sacrifice, in another a commemorative sacrifice; in one respect it is the seal and renewal of the covenant between God and man, in another the food of immortality, the life of the soul, the bread that came down from heaven, the tree of life; that in one respect it is the holy eucharist, in another the holy communion. " William Law. "A Demonstration of the Errors of a Late Book," *The Works of the Reverend William Law*. (Brockenhurst: G. Moreton [1], 1893), 55, Logos e-book.

6. Wilhelmus Brakel wrote, "The Lord Jesus Christ, the Mediator of the covenant of grace, is called the tree of life (Rev. 2:7; 22:2)." *The Christian's Reasonable Service* (Simpsonville, SC: Christian Classics Foundation, 1996), vol. 1: 327, Logos e-book.

7. John Calvin. *Commentary on Genesis* (Albany, OR: Ages Software, 1998), 48.

8. Meredith G. Kline, *Kingdom Prologue*. (Overland Park, KS: Two Age

Press, 2000): 96.

9. Calvin, *Genesis*, 63.

10. Some have argued (such as Trinterud) that Zwingli, Bullinger and Oecolampadius developed a much different view of the covenant than Calvin and his successors. Lyle Bierma in "Federal Theology in the Sixteenth Century," WTJ. Vol. 45, demonstrates convincingly that a closer examination of more details in both schools of thought leads to agreement rather than incongruity between them. Bierma summarizes his comparative research, "It is our conclusion, then, that there were no substantial differences in the way the covenant was understood in the Zurich-Rhineland and Genevan theological traditions. That Zurich and Geneva were not in agreement on all points of doctrine and ecclesiastical practice is not to be denied, but these disagreements cannot be traced to fundamentally different views of the covenant."

11. Henry Bullinger, *The Decades of Henry Bullinger: The Third Decade*, ed. Thomas Harding (Cambridge: Cambridge University Press, 1850), 369, PDF e-book.

12. John Calvin, *Institutes of the Christian Religion*. (Bellingham, WA: Logos Research Systems, Inc., 1997), II, I, 4, Logos e-book.

13. ibid.

14. This has been especially proposed by advocates of "Federal Vision" theology and the "New Perspective on Paul." Within Reformed circles, "New Perspective" teaching has been picked up and promoted by those who adhere to "Federal Vision" ideas. Federal Vision has become one of the popular titles of a loosely organized group of Reformed teachers and pastors united by their preference for eclectic doctrine, by personal preferences more than by universal agreement. For example, some Federal Vision proponents promote the doctrine that there is an initial justification by grace through faith, but a final justification based on the works we have done as believers. For a description of additional "Federal Vision" views see the following resources:

a. The 2010 synod of United Reformed Church in N. America unanimously approved a detailed study report describing the errors of Federal Vision theology. The report is available online at:

https://www.urcna.org/urcna/StudyCommittees/FederalVision/Federal_Vis ion_Study_Committee_Report.pdf

b. An article in the Orthodox Presbyterian Church magazine, New Horizons, describes twenty errors of Federal Vision doctrine,

"Understanding the Federal Vision" written by Alan D. Strange

http://www.opc.org/nh.html?article_id=478

c. The Mid-America Reformed Seminary identifies and summarizes many more errors in their 2007 booklet, Doctrinal Testimony Regarding Recent Errors:

http://www.midamerica.edu/pubs/errors.pdf

The free booklet is also available from the seminary bookstore:

http://marsbooksonline.com/index.php?l=product_detail&p=38

d. An article describing the Presbyterian Church in America's rejection of Federal Vision, in the magazine, byFaith, can be found here: http://byfaithonline.com/page/in-the-church/federal-vision-the-issue-for-this-generation

e. The PCA report rejecting Federal Vision is summarized on page 12 of the following issue of the PCA publication, Equip. The article lists the rejected errors of Federal Vision theology:

http://www.pcacep.org/Publications/EquipArchives/2007/3rdquarter/Equip3-07web.pdf

15. A. Hodge and C. Hodge, *The Confession of Faith: With Questions for Theological Students and Bible Classes (Simpsonville SC: Christian Classics Foundation*, 1996), 122.

16. Calvin, *Institutes*, II, i, 4.

17. Calvin, *Genesis*, 86-91.

18. The absence of the term, imputation, means nothing. Imputation is to charge guilt, or to credit righteousness. The same concept is easily described in many ways, without reference to the term, *imputation*.

19. For example, Augustus Strong, in his Compendium of Theology, apparently understands Calvin in this manner. He contends that later adherents of Federal Theology are not truly Calvinists. Many, following Strong's misconstruing of Calvin, or the comments of others who have done the same thing, have interpreted Calvin the same way, and may need to look more closely at the context of his words.

20. Those who would stand Calvin against imputation would have a stronger case if he had written, "We are not condemned by imputation." But by adding the word, "alone," Calvin does lend support to imputation. It is just that he doesn't allow it to be the only guilt we bear before God.

21. Herman Bavink writes, "For dogmatics as well as for the practice of the Christian life, the doctrine of the covenant is of the greatest importance. The Reformed church and theology have grasped this fact more clearly than the Roman Catholic and Lutheran churches. Basing itself on Scripture, it consistently viewed the true religion of the Old Testament and the New Testament as a covenant between God and humans, whether it was established with unfallen humanity (the covenant of works), or with the creation in general in the person of Noah (the covenant with nature), or with the chosen people (the covenant of grace). But it did not even stop there; instead, it sought and found for these covenants in time a stable, eternal foundation in the counsel of God, and again regarded this counsel—conceived as aiming at the salvation of the human race—as a covenant between the three persons in the divine being itself (pactum salutis, counsel of peace, the covenant of redemption). This last-mentioned covenant occurs, briefly and materially, already in Olevianus, Junius, Gomarus, and others and was then further developed at length by Cloppenburg and Cocceius. It subsequently received a fixed place in dogmatics in Burman, Braun, Witsius, Vitringa, Turretin, Leydekker, Mastricht, Marck, Moor, and Brakel, in order finally to be opposed by Deurhof, Wesselius, and others and gradually to be banished from dogmatics altogether." Bavink goes on to explain how the covenant of redemption lost its place, but then explains why it is important for us to understand the pact between the Trinity as the foundation for God's covenant with the redeemed. Herman Bavinck, *Sin and Salvation in Christ*, vol. 3 of *Reformed Dogmatics* (Grand Rapids, MI: Baker Academic, 2006), 212–216.

22. R. Fowler White and E. Calvin Beisner, "Why the Covenant of Works is a Necessary Doctrine: Revisiting the Objections to a Venerable Reformed Doctrine." In *By Faith Alone: Answering Challenges to the Doctrine of Justification*, ed. By Gary L.W. Johnson and Guy Prentiss Waters. (Wheaton, IL: Crossway Books, 2006), 151, Mobipocket e-book.

Two
Noah, the Second Adam

In stark contrast to man's belief in his own goodness, the Holy Scriptures testify that man's nature is essentially evil, universally corrupted in Adam. The fifth chapter of the Bible describes man's wickedness spreading like a malignant cancer into the whole earth. In the dark scenes of this vast depravity, God's eternal plan made its next majestic appearance in a man named Noah. The great prophet Moses, writing the account of Noah's life, draws back the curtain of history in Genesis 6, revealing an angry and grieving God who has now come to the end of His patience; the judge of the earth stands ready to pour out His wrath upon all mankind. As Psalm 29:10 explains, "The Lord sits enthroned at the flood; the Lord is enthroned as King forever."

The scene unfolds in a terrifying display of God's righteous wrath. Its solemn record in the first chapters of the Holy Scriptures continues to testify that the entire world, corrupt as ever and enslaved to the same evil desires as that generation, lies under the same condemnation today as in Noah's time and only awaits a distant but far greater day of judgment. The sorrowful story of the worldwide flood shows how desperately the world needs the Savior before that day comes.

In the indictment of the entire human race, in Gen. 6:5-7, not only man's deeds, but his very nature and every motive of his heart is condemned and sentenced to death, *"The Lord saw how great man's wickedness on the earth had become, and that every inclination of the thoughts of his heart was only evil all the time."*

51

So the Lord said, "I will wipe mankind, whom I have created, from the face of the earth—men and animals, and creatures that move along the ground, and birds of the air—for I am grieved that I have made them."

But there was one man who found grace with God. People in all nations of the earth were swept along in the powerful flow of rebellion against the true God. Noah alone resisted. He struggled upstream against the flow of sin and rebellion to seek Yahweh (Gen. 6:8). But why? The reason is to be found in Christ alone. God chose one man out of the earth to keep His promise that the Redeemer will surely come into the world. Noah was God's new Adam, the second father of all humankind living today.

At the same time, Noah was an antitype of Adam, having the same fallen condition as the first father. Noah's sinful nature and weaknesses, inherited from Adam, made him unable to produce sinless children of God. Instead of bearing God's image of perfect righteousness and holiness, Noah's children were born with Adam's fallen and corrupted nature. This pointed to the need for a better and perfect Last Adam. So Noah was also a foreshadow of Christ, "a type of Him who was later to come;" God used him to reveal something about the Promised One to his descendants. In Noah's life and deeds of faith and obedience, God set into place many foreshadows of Christ for later generations who would read the account of the flood in God's Word. In Genesis 7:1, God declares that *only Noah* was righteous before Him (a picture of Christ, the only truly righteous man) therefore God would save Noah and his family through the ark, just as He saves Christ and His household through the gospel. Like Christ, Noah spent his life constructing the way of salvation. He did everything God commanded him to do, as Christ did more completely and perfectly. His obedience brought judgment upon the whole world, as does the obedience of Christ. Arthur Pink lists sixteen ways in which Noah symbolized Christ, stating that these are not the only foreshadows but are "the *most* striking points of correspondency between the type and the antitype."[1]

Both faith and obedience were demonstrated by Noah; the faith showing the way of the Covenant of Grace that Christ would prepare to give us salvation, and the obedience alluding to the Covenant of Works that Christ alone would fulfill to provide our righteousness. God's command to Noah most certainly pointed ahead to a greater more perfect Noah who would righteously fulfill the essential requirement of the Covenant of Works, *obedience*—"Go into the ark, you and your family, because I have found you righteous in this generation." Yet, Noah was *not* righteous in Himself, "for all have sinned and fallen short of the glory of God" (Rom. 3:23). He was an "heir of the righteousness that is by faith," the righteousness that God gives to sinners when they confess their sins, sincerely seek God's mercy, and believe His Word of promise. God Himself testifies of Noah, and his family after the flood, that *"every imagination of [man's] heart is evil from childhood"* (Gen. 8:21). Noah believed God and saved his family from the judgment of the world by obeying God's command to build an ark for their salvation. But only the perfect Noah, the Last Adam, would be truly righteous before God in His generation. He would save His children by obeying every command of God perfectly, fulfilling the requirement of the Covenant of Works, and then lay down His own life to save His children from God's wrath. Noah inherited a world washed clean of its perverse sinners, only to see it repopulated with the same. The perfect Noah, Jesus Christ, and His family will inherit "a new heaven and a new earth, the home of righteousness." We will not understand the story of Noah, until God lifts our eyes to see the True Noah, God's righteous Son, now seated in glory, and heir of the world to come. Calvin says, "As soon as ever we depart from Christ, there is nothing, be it ever so gross or insignificant in itself, respecting which we are not necessarily deceived."[2]

God drew Noah to Himself, while all of humanity slept under the heavy veil of Satan's illusions and the power of sin, so that "God's purpose in election" (Rom. 9:11; Eph. 1:11; 2 Tim. 1:9) might be clearly revealed. Like all descendants of Adam, Noah was "a man with a nature like ours," born a sinner, yet he came to know God and rejected the world. Christ's words, "Blessed are you…for this has not been revealed to you by man, but by my Father in heaven" (Matt. 16:17), are true not only of Peter but of Noah, and of all who, like our apostle Paul, can say with utmost confidence, "I know whom I have believed in…" (1 Tim. 1:12). Millions of worldly wise men perished in the floodwaters, grasping empty idols. They hopelessly pleaded for their deliverance from the rushing waters. Only Noah knew the true God, and in that fact alone his wisdom far surpassed them all.

Earlier, through Noah, God warned of the flood that was coming. The warning seemed at that time only the insane imagination of an old fool. Because Noah knew God was true and His word trustworthy he spent generations building the huge ark that would save his family. Heb. 11:7 says, "By faith he condemned the world and became an heir of the righteousness that comes by faith." A man who is sinless has no need for a free gift of righteousness, a "righteousness that comes by faith."[3] In His first covenant with man after Adam's fall, God graciously imputed righteousness as a free gift, through faith, thus establishing the pattern of justification by grace through faith that would continue through all future covenants.

Noah's Covenant: An Old Covenant with New Amendments

Genesis chapters 6-8 tells the tragic story of God's judgment, humankind's demise, and the worldwide flood. The curtain closes on the flood at the end of chapter eight with the shining rays of a new dawn streaming down from glory, a renewal of the world with a new "Adam," the patriarch, Noah. Because Noah was now the head of mankind, and the earth was off to a new start, God made the *new covenant* with him when he emerged from the ark, just as He made the first covenant immediately after Adam emerged from the soil.

It is important to note that God established the covenant when Noah sacrificed animals, a symbol of Christ's death for His people. Calvin comments on this event, "…when the holy fathers, formerly, professed their piety towards God by sacrifices, the use of them was by no means superfluous. Besides, it was right that they should always have before their eyes symbols, by which they would be admonished, *that they could have no access to God but through a mediator.* Now, however, the manifestation of Christ has taken away these ancient shadows."[4]

"God smelled the pleasing aroma" of the sacrifice and swore that He would never again destroy all mankind with a flood.[5] This reveals that the new covenant between God and man was based on the central hope of the coming Redeemer. The bloodshed on an altar shows that there was also a legal dimension to this covenant. God's Word consistently reveals that the penalty for sin is death and the shedding of blood is to make atonement for sin.[6]

Noah brought clean animals into the ark by sevens (Gen. 7:2; 8:20). In the distant future the clean animals would be commanded in the Law of Moses to serve as types of Christ. Surely, God taught Noah that *"without the shedding of blood, there is no forgiveness of sin"* (Heb. 9:22); otherwise, the killing of animals is senseless. Clean animals brought into the ark by sevens, stood for completeness or perfection, and thus were signs of the perfect sacrifice, Christ. When God saw a shadow of His own Son in Noah's animal sacrifices, "the LORD smelled the pleasing aroma, and He said in His heart, "I will never again curse the ground for man's sake"" (Gen. 8:21).

54

Then he spoke to Noah the comforting words of this new covenant. Thus with Noah the pattern began, a pattern repeated in every gracious covenant that followed, that of Almighty God swearing the oath and promises of the covenant over a symbol of the sacrifice of Christ.

God's first promise in the new covenant shone like sunbeams of a *bright hope* upon the Ark's weary passengers, a comforting hope that another disastrous flood would not overthrow their world again "as long as the earth exists" (Gen. 8:22). God's second word to Noah, in Gen. 9:1ff, reconfirmed responsibilities the Lord formerly gave to Adam. In this, it is easy to see that God's words to Adam had indeed been a covenant, a *kingdom-covenant*. It was only at the time He revealed the first covenant to Adam, and later when He made this new covenant with Noah, that God gave mankind the right to rule earth and its creatures (Gen. 1:26, 28; 9:2). Both covenants, at the time of their foundation, contain the explicit command to populate and fill the earth, giving the whole world as the home of humanity. There is a clear sense of continuity from the older covenant, "Just as I gave you green plants, I now give you everything." "Everything that lives and moves will be food for you." (Gen. 9:3b, 3a) More distinctly, God says that just as He gave plants for man's food in the first covenant, in this new covenant He gives animals to be eaten. With this permission to kill and eat "anything that moves" comes *a necessary qualification*, the blood of man may not be shed, and *a new law, "whoever sheds the blood of man, by man shall his blood be shed, for in the image of God has God made man."* (Gen. 9:6) Of all creatures made from God's hand, only the human race had been made in God's image and likeness. The animals were *"made after their own kind"* (Gen. 1:20-21, 24, 26). This revealed two important things. First, that the image of God does not consist in the visible and physical similarities that exist between humans and animals, but in the moral and spiritual qualities of the human soul, qualities that God breathed into Adam to make him truly alive; and second, that there is a vast distinction between the human soul and all other creatures and forms of life on earth. Animals were made to serve man, as gifts to man. Human souls were made to serve God and are of infinitely greater value than animals.

When God swore the words of this covenant over a sign of Christ's death, God promised to be patient with fallen man; He would never again destroy the whole human race with a flood (Gen. 8:21). "Never again" (Gen. 8:21) would God curse the ground nor destroy all living creatures; "as long as the earth exists" (8:22), and "for all the generations to come" (9:12) God would see His rainbow in the clouds and remember His "everlasting covenant between God and all living creatures of every kind on earth" (9:16). The Lord would permit sinful man to increase and fill His kingdom-world again so that out of the fallen human race, the children of God, the elect, could be brought forth in all nations, and the promised Redeemer would finally appear to save them. Like all divine covenants, this one continues from one generation to the next, *"unto a thousand generations as an everlasting covenant"!* (Deut. 7:9; 1 Chron. 16:15-17; Psalm 105:8-9)

We should not make the mistake of presuming that judgment *delayed* by the covenant is judgment *canceled*. This covenant had to be established over the sacrifice of a symbol of Christ, demonstrating that only those children of Noah who walk in the righteousness of the *faith* of Noah would be saved by the Redeemer from the judgment coming at the end of this age. This judgment of the whole world was foreshadowed by the worldwide flood. Moreover, just as Noah's family followed him into the ark of salvation, only those who follow the everlasting Noah, Jesus Christ, will be saved from the judgment and condemnation of the entire human race at the end of the world.

God's new covenant with Noah is a promise that extends to every generation of Noah's descendants, to the very end of the world. The covenant is also a warning, reminding sinful men in every generation that God, the Sovereign King of the world, is man's rightful judge. Just as He fulfilled His vow to judge the world in Noah's day He will most certainly do as He promised. He will bring the final day of judgment upon the whole world at the end of this age (2 Peter 3:6-16).

Chapter Two Notes

1. Arthur W. Pink. *Gleanings in Genesis*. (Chicago: Moody Bible Institute, 1922), 96.

2. Calvin, *Genesis*, 18.

3. Calvin comments on this in Gen. 6:22, "In a few words, but with great sublimity, Moses here commends the faith of Noah. The

unskillful wonder that the apostle (Hebrews 11:7) makes him "heir of the righteousness which is by faith." As if, truly, all the virtues, and whatsoever else was worthy of praise in this holy man, had not sprung from this fountain. For we ought to consider the assaults of temptation to which his breast was continually exposed. First, the prodigious size of the ark might have overwhelmed all his senses, so as to prevent him from raising a finger to begin the work. Let the reader reflect on the multitude of trees to be felled, on the great labor of conveying them, and the difficulty of joining them together. The matter was also long deferred; for the holy man was required to be engaged more than a hundred years in most troublesome labor. Nor can we suppose him to have been so stupid, as not to reflect upon obstacles of this kind. Besides, it was scarcely to be hoped, that the men of his age would patiently bear with him, for promising himself an exclusive deliverance, attended with ignominy to themselves. Their unnatural ferocity has been before mentioned; there can therefore be no doubt that they would daily provoke modest and simpleminded men, even without cause. But here was a plausible occasion for insult; since Noah, by felling trees on all sides, was making the earth bare, and defrauding them of various advantages."

4. Calvin, *Genesis*, 8:20.

5. Calvin comments on Psalm 66:15, "…although in themselves vile and loathsome, yet the rams and other victims, so far as they were figures of Christ, sent up a sweet savor unto God."

6. Several things that bring the event into clearer focus:

a. There can be no doubt that before the flood, God taught Noah about animal sacrifices, and that certain animals would be considered clean for the purpose of sacrifice.

b. Noah brought seven of each kind of clean animal into the ark, the very number that symbolizes the Mediator.

c. Immediately after the flood, Noah sacrificed these clean animals to God. On the same occasion, God grants Noah permission to kill and eat animals.

d. The Lord instructed Noah that the blood of animals must be poured out on the ground. Lev. 19 explains that the life of every creature is in the blood, God gave the blood to make atonement for our sins, therefore the blood must be poured on the ground.

57

Three
Heaven in Abraham's Heart[1]

After Noah's time, the world of sinners born of Noah's descendants gradually strayed from God, turning to gods created in their own image, crafted by human imagination. So God showed His "purpose in election" once more, revealing Himself to an idolater named Abram. God chose Abram and gave to him the Covenant of Grace, making him head of a new people of God.

They were people chosen out of the stock of fallen mankind to be purified and brought to life by God's own power and will. Abram was God's new Adam. Noah, as an Adam, had repopulated the world with children who were fallen, dead in trespasses and sins. But Abram was a new kind of Adam. As God did with the first two Adams, He established a covenant with Abram. His intention was to bring forth His own children, through Abram and the Covenant of Grace (see Romans 9:6-8). Like all people on earth, Abram was a sinner, and thus unable to produce sinless children of God on his own. His human attempt to fulfill God's promise through Hagar only brought forth a son "according to the flesh" and destined for slavery (see Galatians 4:23-24). Nevertheless, Calvin rightly called God's pact with Abram the "covenant of life," because the patriarch was "a type of Him who was later to come." Through His covenant, God would "revive the church" through one man, Abram, a type of Christ (see Galatians 3:7-9).[2] By *circumcision of the heart*, that is, spiritual rebirth, God Himself would bring forth a new race of mankind through Abram, a people freed from bondage to sin and Satan, a people alive from the dead to serve the true God. To understand this, we need to follow the steps of this great man's faith.

God called Abram to leave his "father's house" and his "father's country" to inherit "a great nation." This meant much more than the tiny kingdom established in Canaan after the Exodus from Egypt. The "great nation" is God's own eternal kingdom; He vowed to Abram, *"I will make you into a great nation…and in you all the families of the earth will be blessed."* (Genesis 12:1-3). The latter promise was the good news that a descendant, a Redeemer, would come from Abram, who would bless all families of the earth with salvation. The Lord repeated the promise more clearly in later years, saying, *"and through your offspring all nations on earth will be blessed."* (Gen. 22:18)[3]   Paul explains in Galatians 3:8, *"The Scripture foresaw that God would justify the Gentiles by faith, and announced the gospel in advance to Abraham: "All nations will be blessed through you."*

After Abram settled in Canaan, God spoke to Him again, promising to multiply his children as the heavenly stars in number. Taking him outside one night, God said, "Look up at the heavens and count the stars—if indeed you can count them." Then he said to him, "So shall your offspring be." Abram was very old when he heard this impossible promise, but like Noah, he simply believed God's Word, and God "credited his faith as righteousness" (Gen. 15:6; cf. Rom. 4:3, 5-6, 9, 11, 16, 22). When Abram believed that God would truly give him these children, God made him "the father of all who believe" (Rom. 4:11), announcing later, "…I have made you a father of many nations" (Gen. 17:5).

It is important to notice certain covenant details of Genesis 12 and 15. One thing that stands out is the sequence. In Gen. 12, the Lord revealed that He will bless Abram and also bless all nations through him. Abram has a central place in God's eternal plan to redeem people from all nations. It would be through the Patriarch, not without him or apart from him, that God will "bless" all nations with the good news of Christ (Gen. 12:3). In Galatians 3, Paul defines this "gospel" blessing in simple terms: God will justify the Gentiles by faith.

Another significant detail is in Gen. 15, where God fulfilled the promise He made to Abram in Gen.12:2, "I will bless you." He did this justifying Abram by faith alone (Gen. 15). Abram received this personal "blessing" with a promise kept in his heart (Gen. 12:3), that God will expand the blessing from him outward, to all the world. Abram is the father of all those God will bless with justification by faith, in every tribe, language, people, and nation.

Commenting on Genesis 12:3, the apostle Paul clearly identifies the gospel (Gal. 3:8). In the same breath, he defines that gospel as the "good news" of "justification by faith." "The Scripture foresaw that God would justify the Gentiles by faith, and announced the gospel in advance to Abraham: "All nations will be blessed through you." " (Galatians 3:8, NIV84)

Calvin had much to say about this free justification, as did Luther. Both men laid the foundations of the doctrine of justification, which Reformed theology would build on to the present day. For example, on Galatians 3:6, Calvin wrote:

> "As to the word *righteousness*, we must attend to the phraseology of Moses.[4] When he says, that "he believed in the Lord, and he counted it to him for righteousness" (Genesis 15:6), *he intimates that that person is righteous who is reckoned as such in the sight of God.* Now, since men have not righteousness dwelling within themselves, they obtain this by imputation; because God holds their faith as accounted for righteousness. We are therefore said to be "justified by faith," (Romans 3:28 5:1,) not because faith infuses into us a habit or quality, but because we are accepted by God."

> "But why does faith receive such honor as to be entitled *a cause of our justification*? First, we must observe, that it is merely an instrumental cause; for, strictly speaking, our righteousness is nothing else than God's free acceptance of us, on which our salvation is founded. But as the Lord testifies his love and grace in the gospel, by offering to us that righteousness of which I have spoken, so we receive it by faith. And thus, when we ascribe to faith a man's justification, we are not treating of the principal cause, but merely pointing out the way in which men arrive at true righteousness. For this righteousness is not a quality which exists in men, *but is the mere gift of God, and is enjoyed by faith only*; and not even as a reward justly due to faith, but because we receive by faith what God freely gives. All such expressions as the following are of similar import: We are "justified freely by his grace." (Romans 3:24.) Christ is our righteousness. The mercy of God is the cause of our righteousness. By the death and resurrection of Christ, righteousness has been procured for us. Righteousness is bestowed on us through the gospel. We obtain righteousness by faith."

Here we see that Calvin did not regard *faith itself* as righteousness, but as the instrument through which one receives the gift of righteousness from God. This "gift of righteousness" (Romans 5:17) is not defined as *our faith in God*, but is God's gift *to all who truly believe*. The Roman Catholic Church *of Calvin's time* insisted that justification infuses a quality of righteousness into a person, thus actually making one's nature to be righteous and capable of practicing true righteousness. Calvin clearly denied this, in the passage quoted above, where he argues, *"We are therefore said to be "justified by faith," not because faith infuses into us a habit or quality, but because we are accepted by God,"* adding in the next paragraph, *"this righteousness is not a quality which exists in men, but is the mere gift of God, and is enjoyed by faith only."* Let us take Abram as an example, in Genesis 15. In this text there is no suggestion that God infused righteousness into Abraham's character. He simply *declared* the patriarch's faith to be righteousness, so that as a gracious gift, he credited Abraham with a gift of righteousness that was not found in his human nature.

Returning to Genesis 15, Abraham received the promise *"by faith alone,"* the promise that God would multiply His children. To show that He would bring them forth by His own hand, God commanded Abram to bring animals, cut them in half, and arrange a pathway of blood, to establish His Covenant of Grace with the sinner, Abram. God's covenants were not merely "made," they were "cut" just as the animals were cut. The literal translation of Genesis 15:8 is, "On that day the Lord *cut a covenant* with Abram, saying..." Morton H. Smith comments:

> "Palmer Robertson in...*The Christ of the Covenants*, defines a covenant as "a *bond in blood sovereignly administered*. Where God enters into a covenantal relationship with men, he sovereignly institutes a life–and–death bond. A covenant is a bond in blood, or a bond of life and death, sovereignly administered."
>
> The terminology in the Old Testament translated "to make a covenant" is literally "to cut a covenant."...."The cutting procedure is seen in Genesis 15, where Abraham sacrifices the animals, and then cuts the pieces, laying them over against one another. Then, God symbolically passed through between the cut pieces. The result was the cutting of a covenant. The symbolism is that the persons entering into the covenant take upon themselves the pledge of death if they break the covenant...As a bond in blood, a covenant "involves commitments with life–and–death consequences."[5]

This wording is common when God introduces a covenant. Psalm

50:5 is literally translated, "Gather to Me my faithful ones, who *cut a covenant* with Me by sacrifice!" When Israel entered into the covenant at Mt. Sinai, Moses sprinkled blood on the people and said, "Behold the blood of the covenant that the Lord has *cut* with you in accordance with all these words." (Exodus 24:8). The covenant was *cut* by *cutting off the life* of sinless animals, as a type and shadow of Christ's death. That night, the second member of the Trinity, the One whose life would be "cut off" as the Redeemer, passed between the halves of the animals, swearing the words of a new covenant to Abram—in this way, demonstrating to Abram that He would even be made a sacrifice Himself, to keep His oath to multiply Abram's children, and to give them the land of their sojourning (Gen. 15:9-21).[6] This oath of the covenant began to be fulfilled in foreshadow on the night of the sacrifice of the Passover lamb, when the Jews came out of Egypt as a great multitude, and in type when Joshua (the name, Y'shua, or Jesus) conquered Canaan and the Jews settled in their homeland. These carnal blessings were the final goal for many Jews, but they were really only a shadow of better and greater things to come after long ages. Nailed to the cross, Christ literally became the sacrifice promised in covenant to Abraham. Still the promise waits for yet another future day when the passing of longer ages will bring its ultimate fulfillment, that great day when Christ will return from heaven and Abraham's seed will finally "inherit the world" (Romans 4:13).

Calvin calls this, *"the free covenant God made with the Patriarchs,"* explaining that the coming of Christ was the main promise given to Abraham:

> "As to the *free covenant* which God established with the Patriarchs in ancient times, the Prophets are much more distinct, and contribute more to strengthen the people's attachment to it; for *when they wish to comfort the godly, they always remind them of **that** covenant, and represent to them the coming of Christ, who was both the foundation of the covenant and the bond of the mutual relation between God and the people, and to whom therefore the whole extent of the promises must be understood to refer."*[7]

Note Calvin's words, *"the whole extent of the promises"* given to Abraham were of Christ. This is his way of saying that the entire Abrahamic covenant was Christological—a *Christ covenant*.

Calvin saw (see quote above) what Abram discerned as a prophet, that these promises of "children like the stars in number," a "great kingdom"

(Gen. 12:2) and a descendant who would "bless all nations," were closely related. The Spirit from heaven was moving Abram's heart, prompting him to lift up his eyes not only to the stars, but to that great unseen kingdom that lay beyond them, until at last, with eyes of faith he began to perceive far away, in the distant future, the heavenly domain that would forever be his homeland. He saw that the blessing God promised to bestow upon people of all nations was to put the same Spirit within them that He had given Abram, the Spirit that would fill their hearts with longing for things above and make them citizens of that gracious country. Abram saw that the One who would fulfill all these promises was a Son who would come from his own body, and yet one who would also come from heaven into our world. "...Abraham rejoiced that he would see my day," declared that promised Son two thousand years later, "He saw it and was glad!"[8] And so the pilgrim wandered in the land of Canaan, *"looking forward to the city with foundations, whose architect and builder is God."* (Heb. 11:10) Calvin understood this is heaven, as we can see from his comments on this passage,[9]

> "He gives a reason why he ascribes their patience to faith, even because they looked forward to heaven. This was indeed to see things invisible. It was … a great thing to cherish in their hearts the assurance … of the land …; yet as they did not confine their thoughts… to that land, but [saw through it] into heaven, it was … a clearer evidence of their faith."
>
> Calvin calls heaven a ***city that has foundations*** ...."[10]

> The Holy Spirit testifies of both Abraham and Sarah, that *"they admitted that they were aliens and strangers on earth"* because, by faith, *"they were longing for a better country—a heavenly one. Therefore God is not ashamed to be called their God, for he has prepared a city for them"* (Heb. 11:8-16).

Calvin explains that Abraham's faith was focused on Christ's coming and on Christ's kingdom, the kingdom of heaven,

> "...the fathers had a distant view of the spiritual kingdom of Christ, while we at this day have so near a view of it, and that they hailed the promises afar off, while we have them as it were quite near us...."[11]

> "By another country, then, they meant, that which is beyond this world."[12]

"...when the holy fathers aspired to a celestial country, God on the other hand counted them as citizens. We are hence to conclude, that there is no place for us among God's children, except we renounce the world, and that there will be for us no inheritance in heaven, except we become pilgrims on earth; moreover, the Apostle justly concludes from these words, — "I am the God of Abraham, of Isaac, and of Jacob," that they were heirs of heaven, since he who thus speaks is not the God of the dead, but of the living."[13]

To Abraham the wanderer, peering at the distant promises through God's telescope, his sojourning in Canaan was no longer a question of merely changing an earthly homeland. Abraham no longer belonged to the world. The covenant God established with him was not of earth, but heaven. The city God was preparing for him was not of this world. Paul explains that Abraham's wife, Sarah, symbolizes this heavenly city, in Galatians 4:26, *"But the Jerusalem above is free; she is our mother."* The beloved apostle understood, and points out to us in Galatians 4, that the city of heaven, or heaven itself, is the mother of all of Abraham's true covenant children, both Jews and Gentiles. Just as the temple of the new covenant is constructed of living stones, of God's holy people, so the souls of believers are the stones that construct the city of God. The city is the dwelling-place of God and the King, Jesus Christ. It is the bride of Christ (Rev. 21:2) which will come down to earth in Christ's second coming. The bride of Christ is the children of Abraham who are members of the body of Christ. Paul writes on one hand that every believer is *"seated in heavenly places in Christ Jesus"* (Eph. 2:6), and on the other hand, *"If you belong to Christ, you are Abraham's seed..."* (Gal. 3:29). Heaven is the very *"bosom of Abraham"* (Luke 16:22). Long before Abraham's children ascend to their heavenly homeland at death, the apostle writes of them all, *"Our citizenship is in heaven"* (Phil. 3:20).

Some have suggested that God made at least two covenants with Abraham. The Baptist scholar, John Gill, wrote that the covenant described in Genesis 17 is different than the one in chapter 15. This interpretation is based on the meaning of one Hebrew word, וְתֵן , often translated, "I will make," in Gen. 17:2. The denotation, "make," is certainly one of the most common definitions, but there is a wide range of meaning to this verb in Old Testament usage, including *"to give, bestow, grant, permit, ascribe, employ, devote, consecrate, dedicate, pay wages, sell, exchange, lend, commit, entrust, give over, deliver up, yield produce, occasion, produce, requite to, report, mention, utter, stretch out, extend; to put, set, put on, put upon, appoint, assign, designate; to make, constitute."* With such a range of possibilities to the Qal stem alone (a class of verb stem that this word belongs to), what will determine the correct translation? Only a careful study of the context. John Gill probably knew this. But he paid attention to the immediate context of Genesis 17 and went off track because he thought he saw differences in these two chapters. So he concluded that God made two distinct and separate covenants with the patriarch.

The NIV translation of Gen. 17:2 conveys the sense more accurately, "I will *confirm* my covenant," that is, God will confirm the covenant He has already established with Abraham. This more accurately represents the original Hebrew and seems to be a translation based on studying the context of Genesis together with the entire Bible (comparing Scripture with Scripture). There are other passages in the Bible that shed light on the meaning of Genesis 17 because this text refers to a major event in Abraham's life which many inspired authors comment on, including Paul.

For example, Moses repeatedly mentions only a single covenant God made with Israel's forefathers, Abraham, Isaac and Jacob. The same is true of all other prophetic writers of the Old and New Testaments. Paul mentions only one covenant God made with Abraham. In Galatians 4, where he writes, "these women are the two covenants," he specifically refers to two covenants God made with Abraham's descendants. The covenant Israel entered into at Sinai was a form of bondage. It was eventually put aside, just as God commanded Abram to cast out the slave wife, Hagar, and her slave son. The other covenant was made with Abraham and Sarah. She represents the heavenly city that gives birth to the children of God set free from sin and Satan. This latter covenant was established with Abraham, but was not completely fulfilled until the Son of God came from heaven to be the sacrifice of the new covenant.

John Gill's two-covenant view of Abraham may still leave some wondering if the Genesis 15 covenant later becomes the Sinai Covenant, and the Genesis 17 covenant becomes the New Covenant in Christ Jesus. Paul answers this clearly enough for anyone with an open mind to listen. Consider the words of Gen. 17:4-5, where God confirmed His covenant, declaring Abram *"the father of many nations,"* and renaming him, *"father of many."* Paul demonstrates that these "many nations" of Gen. 17:4-5 are the same children of Abraham who would number as the stars in Genesis 15:5. Paul, a Jew, explained the connection of these two references, in his letter to

Gentile Christians in Rome, in Romans 4:16b-18, *"Abraham is the father of us all* [Jewish and Gentile believers], *as it is written, "**I have made you a father of many nations**"... Abraham in hope believed and so became **the father of many nations** (Gen. 17) just as it had been said to him, "**So shall your descendants be**"* (Gen. 15). To the Gentile believers in the churches of Galatia, Paul adds in Galatians 4:28, *"We, brethren, just like Isaac, are the children God promised"* to Abraham, clearly referring to the children who would number as the stars, in Genesis 15.

The "children God promised" as Paul points out in Romans 4 (above) are "promised" both in Gen. 15 and 17. Paul mentions them again to the Gentile Romans, saying, *"It is not the natural children who are God's children, but it is the children of the promise who are regarded as Abraham's seed,"* Romans 9:8. This did not mean that there were no true children of Abraham from his natural descendants, but that many who were born in the natural way were not the children God had promised to him. The promised children of Abraham would be known by their sincere faith, both Jews and Gentiles from many nations, including the nation of Israel.

Notice also, in Galatians 4:29, that Paul makes a distinction between "the son born in the ordinary way," Ishmael, and "the son born by the power of the Spirit," Isaac, through whom God promised that Abraham's descendants would come. If the son of Abraham was spiritual, what about the father? In Romans 2:28-29, there is a similar contradistinction, *"A man is not a Jew if he is only one outwardly, nor is circumcision merely outward and physical. No, a man is a Jew if he is one inwardly; and circumcision is circumcision of the heart, by the Spirit, not by the written code. Such a man's praise is not from men, but from God. "* (Romans 2:28–29, NIV84). This is an important point. If a man is not a true Jew without circumcision of the heart by the Holy Spirit, then Abraham, the father of all true Jews must have experienced this himself. This would explain why God gave him the outer sign of circumcision, to point all of his children to the need for the inner reality, which Abraham had when He believed.

This is the reason that there is a direct connection between *the blessing* God promised to Abram when He called Him in Gen. 12, and the sign of circumcision He gave to Abraham, the believer, in Gen. 17. When God said, *"My covenant is with you,* I have made you a father of many nations," He had already given the blessing to Abraham, making him a child of God *by regenerating his heart through the Holy Spirit.*[14] To show that He would keep His promise to "bless all nations" and give the same Spirit of life to regenerate the hearts of promised sons and daughters from "many nations," God gave Abraham the sign of circumcision. This is the seal of God's covenant, to mark the patriarch's descendants with His promise. Romans 4:11 says that he "received the sign of circumcision, a seal of the righteousness that he had by faith while he was yet uncircumcised."

As a sign, circumcision symbolized that there is a thick veil of blinding darkness and spiritual bondage over the hearts of all men; this veil is in the flesh, in man's very nature. Man is able to cut away the symbolic veil of flesh, marking the sign on the body, but only God, by His Spirit, could remove the real veil of darkness from the heart of man, to bring forth righteous, believing children of God for Abraham, and for the kingdom of heaven. Real circumcision is this work done by the Spirit within the heart of true Jews, those who are believers like Abraham (see Romans 2:28-29). Jehovah had promised to be God to Abraham's physical descendants, in their generations, but God makes very clear that Abraham is father "to those who not only are of the circumcision, but who also walk in the steps of the faith which...Abraham had while still uncircumcised." (Romans 4:12) God's pact with Abraham is known as the covenant of circumcision. It is not the covenant of *the sign of circumcision*, it is the covenant of what the sign represents, the covenant of the gift of the Holy Spirit who circumcises the heart to make sons and daughters of Abraham who are true believers and children of God.

A comment from Calvin, on Romans 4:12, wraps up this section,

> "[Paul] touches the carnal descendants of Abraham, who, having nothing but outward circumcision, confidently gloried in it. The other thing, which was *the chief matter, they neglected*; for *the faith of Abraham*, by which alone he obtained salvation, they did not imitate. It hence appears, how carefully he [Paul] distinguished between faith and the sacrament; not only that no one might be satisfied with the one without the other, as though it were sufficient for justifying; but also *that faith alone might be set forth as accomplishing everything*: for while he allows the circumcised Jews to be justified, he expressly makes this exception —provided in true faith they followed the example of Abraham..." (Italics mine)[15]

Calvin saw that Paul "distinguished between faith and the sacrament," insisting that faith alone is enough to justify, but that the Jews wrongly gloried in the sacrament, the badge of covenant membership, "as though it were sufficient for justifying." Jewish covenant members could be justified, but only by faith, only if "in true faith they followed the example of Abraham." This many could not do, for they had "nothing but outward circumcision." (For an expanded treatment of these and other themes, see "Volume 2" of this series, titled, *Camp of the Saints*)

Chapter Three Notes

1. John Calvin, "The Preface to the Prophet Isaiah." *Commentary on the Prophet Isaiah 1*, of *Calvin's Bible Commentaries*. (Albany, OR: Ages Software, 1998), Ages e-book. John Calvin wrote that the promise of the coming of Christ, through whom God would bless the Gentiles, was the main point of Abraham's covenant, and that Christ is the one in whom all the Abrahamic promises have their fulfillment. This section, therefore is primarily summarizing the understanding of Abraham's covenant Christo-centrically, and not from the perspective of Judaism, nor by comparing temporal promises with eternal, nor by closely examining the literal fulfillment of Abraham's covenant in the material geo-political Jewish nation, and separating a later spiritual fulfillment among the Gentiles. Guided by Paul's words, that Abraham is "the father of the circumcised (the Jewish nation) who are not only circumcised, but who also walk in the steps of the faith of their father Abraham..." thus regarding the true seed of Abraham to be those circumcised in heart by the Spirit, and true believers, from the physical descendants of Abraham before Christ's coming, and from all nations, Jew and Gentile. I realize in taking this approach that Reformed theology has noted both the material and spiritual aspects and rightly so, because the Jews were God's covenant people. But desiring to present what I believe is the more Pauline stream in Reformed covenantal theology, in this brief summary I'm focusing primarily on the light Paul sheds on understanding these ancient covenants. My apologies if a comprehensive summary more generous to the carnal Jew is preferred, but after all, this is a book especially highlighting the comments of Paul, within the context of the inspired statements of the entire Word of God.

2. Calvin, *Genesis*. In his commentary on Gen. 12:1, Calvin writes this, "...it is wonderful, that a man, miserable and lost, should have

the preference given him, over so many holy worshippers of God; that the covenant of life should be placed in his possession; that the Church should be revived in him, and he himself constituted the father of all the faithful. But this is done designedly, in order that the manifestation of the grace of God might become the more conspicuous in his person. For he is an example of the vocation of us all...."

3. Calvin comments, "Therefore God (in my judgment) pronounces that all nations should be blessed in his servant Abram because Christ was included in his loins....Now Paul assumes it as an axiom which is received among all the pious, and which ought to be taken for granted, that the whole human race is obnoxious to a curse, and therefore that the holy people are blessed only through the grace of the Mediator. Whence he concludes, that the covenant of salvation which God made with Abram, is neither stable nor firm except in Christ. I therefore thus interpret the present place; that God promises to his servant Abram that blessing which shall afterwards flow down to all people." (Genesis, 12:3)

4. When Calvin refers to "the phraseology of Moses" he means that Moses wrote the book of Genesis. Moses composed the phrases written in Genesis 15.

5. Morton H. Smith, *Systematic Theology* (Simpsonville, SC: Christian Classics Foundation, 1997): 278, Logos e-book.

6. This may be the Father or the Holy Spirit speaking to Abraham, even the Trinity. But it makes good sense to see Christ here, "when He predicted the sufferings of Christ and the subsequent glories..." (1 Peter 1:11). The members of the Trinity can often be distinguished from each other in the writings of the prophets. In Isaiah 4:2-6, and 9:7, the Holy Spirit mentions the Son and the Father. In Isaiah 49:1-6, the Son speaks through Isaiah. The Father speaks in 49:8-12 and 52:13-15. In 53:1-10, the Holy Spirit mentions the Father and the Son, but in vv. 11-12 the Father describes the Son.

7. Calvin, *Isaiah*, 24, Ages e-book.

8. John 8:56 (ESV)

9. Some words are dropped from this quote to enable speakers-of-English-as-a-second-language to grasp the meaning easier.

10. John Calvin, *The Commentary on the Epistle of Paul the Apostle to the Hebrews.* (Rio, WI: Ages Software, 2000), 11:10, Ages e-

book.

11. Calvin, *Hebrews*, 11:13.

12. Calvin, *Hebrews*, 11:15.

13. Calvin, *Hebrews*, 11:16.

14. For questions regarding spiritual rebirth before the incarnation of Christ, see volumes 2 and 4 of this series. Some insist that the Holy Spirit was not given at all until the Day of Pentecost, based on the Gospel of John 7:39. But there are many examples of the presence of the Spirit with God's people in the Old Testament. Therefore, it is better to understand that the full blessing and power, with many new gifts of the Spirit, was withheld until the Day of Pentecost. By withholding His teaching about the Spirit, God rightly associated the gift of the Spirit with the redemption provided by Christ. But 1000 years before Christ, David said, "Take not thy Holy Spirit from me." If it is insisted that this can only mean that David was a prophet, and that priests, prophets and kings were the only ones who had the Holy Spirit, then how do we explain passages that describe the work of the Holy Spirit in or among ordinary people prior to the crucifixion?

15. Calvin, *Romans*, 4:12.

72

Four
Sinai's Foreshadow Kingdom

Before the Law of Moses could be given, the covenant of Abraham had to clearly establish that righteousness is only by grace through faith. In Galatians 3:17, Paul explains that "the law, introduced 430 years" after Abraham, "does not set aside the covenant previously established by God and thus do away with the promise." The promises to Abraham were not evicted by Moses. *Justification* would continue to be *by grace alone through faith alone.* So Paul says plainly in Romans 3:20, *"Therefore no one will be declared righteous in his sight by observing the law; rather, through the law we become conscious of sin."*

Gary D. Long writes, "It is no understatement to say that Paul's understanding of the law is an interpretive problem that encompasses one of the most intricate doctrinal and practical issues in New Testament theology."[1] On one hand, he is right. Peter explains that Paul "wrote some things hard to understand." This is one reason why books giving "fresh appraisals" of Paul's teaching, from a myriad of angles, are being paraded out endlessly. But is Paul's understanding of the *Law* really so hard to figure out? Didn't God intend for the Gentile church in Rome or the Gentile churches of Galatia, both lacking Jewish understanding of the Law, to be able to put the pieces together right out of the box?

An older pastor, after reading much of *this* series, commented that the series' size and details make it difficult to keep everything in order mentally. I thought that might happen, readers might lose the path and fail to see the connections between various parts. This is the reason that the first

73

part of Volume One is a summary, or synopsis, of covenant theology. It's placed at the starting gate of the book to help the reader get a handle on what could be confusing or "intricate," by pointing all our flashlights on main things first, to avoid getting lost in the details. Once the house is set in order, and things are arranged in their proper "rooms," any discerning reader can put the details into the rooms where they belong. In other words, by referring to this synopsis when confused, the reader will see where to fit subjects addressed by various chapters of the four volumes. If feeble-minded authors like me carefully compose their writings, planning each detail with concern that the reader should understand, surely the all-wise God and His inspired prophets arranged the material of the Bible in a much more wise and perfect order, an order designed to hide God's truth from the wicked who will misuse it, while revealing it through the Holy Spirit's illumination to God's chosen children. The Bible is composed of sixty-six different books written by many authors, most of whom never consulted with each other. Yet, those who devote their lives to its study remain fascinated by the intricate connections between its many parts.

Therefore, we cannot handle the Bible simplistically, taking only what is readily revealed by first glance, or by light reading. The Bible was designed so that the writings of a prophet from one period contain cryptic statements that shed light on the meaning of passages written by another prophet from a different era. Scripture must be compared with Scripture. The entire Bible should be studied carefully, and thoroughly read again and again, so that the student becomes familiar with every detail. This is also the reason that the study of the covenants must cover the breadth and depth of Scripture. The covenant God made with Abraham cannot be understood only by studying Genesis chapters 12-22. In fact, God intentionally designed that those chapters alone cannot give the complete picture. The spiritual meaning of this covenant is not explained at all in that part of the Bible. To grasp the true meaning of the Abrahamic Covenant we must start with those portions for the basic foundation, but also learn the overall themes of the entire Bible, and study Adam and Christ and the covenants God established through both of these men, and read from many of the Bible's authors, especially, but not only, when they are specifically commenting on the Abrahamic Covenant. The same is true of the Sinai Covenant. It is not enough to read only the five books of Moses. These provide the background, the history of the covenant's establishment, and the structure and principles. But we need to look into Joshua to see that God expected even the greatest prophets to meditate on the book of the covenant night and day. And we need to read David to learn that there was, even for those in the Old Testament, a spiritual side to the Law covenant experienced only by those who, like David, meditated on the Law and loved both God and His commands. Sincere worshippers are "like a tree planted by streams of water, whose leaf is always green and which always grow their fruit in season. Whatever they do prospers." Solomon, in Proverbs, teaches us that in our study of the Law we must search for truth and knowledge like a man searching for *hidden* treasures. From the books of the prophets, we understand that the covenant was to continue unchanged from generation to generation until the coming of Jesus Christ. The comments of Paul and other New Testament authors are especially illuminating. They uncover the true spiritual dimensions of these important covenants, revealing what Old Testament prophets may have hidden from the ungodly but taught privately to those who were truly faithful and spiritually minded.

The apostles also help us to see that after the fall of Adam, God never provided a way to establish self-righteousness. This is one of the important lessons about the Sinai Covenant, usually understood only after we are familiar with the entire Bible story—or never learned at all. Before the Mediator should pay the price to send grace into all nations, Abraham's family was the first that had to understand why grace is the only possible way to life. The Law of Moses became their tutor, teaching them the seriousness of sin, the curse of the Law on all sinners, the condemnation of the whole human race, the certainty of God's final judgment, and the reality of hell. The believer can't stop there, however, and see the entire covenant of Law as only negative. The Law threatens curse and doom to show how desperately every sinner needs redemption through the Mediator. He applies the grace that restores us to peace with God so that we can enjoy life indeed, and the immeasurable treasure of gracious love as members of God's kingdom.

God made His Law the tutor of Israel by writing a textbook through His servant Moses, who calls it "the book of the covenant" in Exodus 24. This new covenant, presented to Abraham's family at Mt. Sinai, introduced a new feature into their relationship with God. It formed Abraham's family into a *kingdom* ruled by God. The details and structure of the written Words that defined the kingdom were vital to the very existence of every citizen. *This* citizenship, writes Paul, and this covenant membership, is what brought them near to God, and established their only hope, giving them access to the grace that Christ alone provides to repentant sinners, by faith alone. This is little understood today, but Paul states it simply and clearly in the New Testament, speaking to Gentiles in Ephesians 2:12, "remember that at that time you were *separate from Christ, excluded from citizenship in Israel and foreigners to the covenants of the promise, without hope and without God* in the world. "

The Sinai covenant revealed the only way anyone could be saved. Paul says of the Sinai covenant, "The law was put in charge to lead us to Christ that we might be justified by faith." (Gal. 3:24). These words clearly show that the Sinai covenant is Christo-centric; its main purpose was to lead the Jews to Christ alone for justification by grace through faith. Accepting this as true, we're well on the way to being correctly tutored by the Sinai covenant. How it actually works must be considered next.

First, the covenant revealed the unyielding standards of God's law, pressing upon all men the same threat of judgment and death that was set before the eyes of Adam in the first covenant, as a kind of republication of the Covenant of Works for utility sake. That primitive covenant had only one law, threatening the disobedient with death. But in the Sinai covenant, this same demand for obedience is multiplied by many commandments that threaten death, so that by seeing the condemnation of sin on every side, the sinful nature of every person might be fully exposed and it may be plain to see that it is impossible for such depraved human nature to be justified by a Covenant of Works. Calvin, explaining the purpose of the Law, wrote that it is this very realization that drives sinners to seek justification through the mercy of God, rather than through keeping the rule list of the Law,

"...the same Apostle declares, that "God has concluded them all in unbelief;" not that he might destroy all, or allow all to perish, but that "he might have mercy upon all," (Rom. 11:32); in other words, that divesting themselves of an absurd opinion of their own virtue, they may perceive how they are wholly dependent on the hand of God; that feeling how naked and destitute they are, they may take refuge in his mercy, rely upon it, and cover themselves up entirely with it; renouncing all righteousness and merit, and clinging to mercy alone, as offered in Christ to all who long and look for it in true faith. In the precepts of the law, God is seen as the rewarder only of perfect righteousness (a righteousness of which all are destitute), and, on the other hand, as the stern avenger of wickedness. But in Christ his countenance beams forth full of grace and gentleness towards poor unworthy sinners."[2]

By placing life and death, blessing and cursing, before man's eyes, as God had once done in the garden of Eden, the need for the Covenant of Grace was more easily understood. This covenant was revealed first to Adam *after the fall*, then to Noah, and finally to Abraham, providing righteousness (or justification) as a free gift from God. The same justification by faith continued in the Sinai Covenant. This one point made the covenant of Law vastly different than Adam's covenant. The Covenant of Works had *no provision* for mercy, nor was it able to take away sin. The Law of Moses *promised* God's forgiveness through ceremonial laws that demanded repentance, bloodshed and *especially*, faith. An innocent animal had to be sacrificed, dying in the place of the sinner, whenever God's law was broken by any kind of sin. *"Then the priest is to take some of the blood with his finger and put it on the horns of the altar of burnt offering and pour out the rest of the blood at the base of the altar… **In this way the priest will make atonement for him, and he will be forgiven**"* (Leviticus 4:30-31). Moses explains God's purpose in Leviticus 17:11, *"For the life of a creature is in the blood, and I have given it to you to make atonement for yourselves on the altar; **it is the blood that makes atonement for one's life**."* Hebrews 9:22, summarizing the entire temple service of the Old Testament, declares to all who might seek some other way, that *"without the shedding of blood, there is no forgiveness of sin."* This forgiveness is called *remission of sin*. Hugh Martin describes remission,

> "For, when the inspired writer affirms that without shedding of blood is no remission, it is as if he had said: You may imagine a forgiveness without shedding of blood, if you will; you may conjecture, or conjure up, some other scheme or principle of pardon; you may conceive of God as dealing with the sinner, and delivering him from the punishment due to his iniquities, without these iniquities being expiated, without the penalty incurred by them being exacted, without the law of which they are transgressors being relieved from the stain of dishonor which they had cast upon it, without any costly sacrifice, any solemn propitiation, any priceless ransom. But whatever this transaction might be, it would not be remission. Granting that it were quite possible for God to let the sinner off; to wipeout, by a mere arbitrary decree, and without any satisfaction to divine justice, the debt which the sinner had contracted; to cease from His anger toward His enemies and return

77

to a state of friendship; to say, Your sins be forgiven you, you have nothing now to fear; all this, 'without shedding of blood,' without any sacrifice, or atonement, or expiation: still all this, whatever it might amount to, does not amount to remission. Call it what you please: be it what it may; it is not remission. It may be held up as an equivalent for it; it may be in room and lieu of it; it may be all that multitudes care to inquire after, or have ever felt the need of, or troubled themselves to seek. But, however possible it might be on God's part, however satisfactory it might be on their part, it is not remission. It may look like it. It may seem to carry with it all that the unenlightened have any thought of when thinking of remission; but real remission it is not. *Without shedding of blood it is not remission.*

"What the enlightened conscience of an anxious inquirer longs for is 'remission' — remission of sin. And what is that? It is removal of guilt; removal of liability to the wrath of God; removal of Criminality or ill-desert. It is a sentence of 'Not Guilty.' It is a recognition of blamelessness before the Holy One of Israel; a position and relation toward God, therefore, in which His wrath would be undue, unrighteous, impossible. That would be Remission."[3]

It is this remission that God repeatedly promises to sinners who believe and repent, in Lev. 4:26, 4:31, 4:35, 5:10, 5:13, 5:18, 6:7, etc. These were not empty words to Jewish believers, but were God's genuine promises that had to be received by faith or they would never be fulfilled.

The Law was given so that sinners, hardened in heart, insensitive to God, unable to sense their own depravity, may, by the sword of justice hanging always over their heads, at last see the wickedness of their sins, and being convicted, repent. Animal sacrifices were commanded in the Law that we might learn that God is merciful to those who believe His Word; He was willing to accept the death of the innocent animal as a shadow of Christ, dying in place of the sinner, for the wages of sin is death, if sinners would only humble themselves before Him, confess their sins to Him, and trust in the promises of forgiveness that are repeated so many times in the book of Leviticus. Calvin says of this:

"The threatenings ... pressed and entreated them to seek refuge from the wrath and curse of God, and gave them no rest till they were constrained to seek the grace of Christ.

78

"Such too, was the tendency of all the ceremonies; for what end did sacrifices and washings serve but to keep the mind continually fixed on pollution and condemnation? When a man's uncleanness is placed before his eyes, when the unoffending animal is held forth as the image of his own death, how can he indulge in sleep? How can he but be roused to the earnest cry for deliverance? Beyond all doubt, ceremonies accomplished their object, not merely by alarming and humbling the conscience, but by exciting them to the faith of the coming Redeemer. In the imposing services of the Mosaic ritual, everything that was presented to the eye bore an impress of Christ. The law, in short, was nothing else than an immense variety of exercises, in which the worshippers were led by the hand to Christ."[4]

It should be clear that Calvin saw in the entire pattern of the demands of moral law, that is, in confession of sin, repentance, sacrifice of the substitute, and the sprinkling of the blood of atonement—he saw the "schoolmaster to lead us to Christ." The sacrifices, demanded by the Law, were the type and "shadow of the good things to come" through Jesus Christ (Heb. 10:1-2). Through the death of animals, Abraham's descendants, those Jews who were truly believers, participated ahead of time in the grace that comes by the sacrifice of the Lamb of God, Jesus Christ. The sprinkling of the blood of every sacrifice before the closed veil bore witness to the need for a perfect sacrifice which would at last tear open the forbidden chamber. The need for the atoning sacrifice of the Mediator is the main thing revealed in the ceremonial laws, for the Sinai covenant, and the kingdom of Israel, was all about Christ. This is the reason that God told Moses to warn Pharaoh with these words, *"Israel is my first-born Son, and I say to you, 'Let my Son go that he may serve Me. If you refuse to let him go, behold, I will kill your firstborn son.'"* (Exodus 4:22-23). For these were to be a people *"called by God's own Name,"* as it is written, "If my people, who are called by My Name, humble themselves and pray and seek my face and turn from their wicked ways, then I will hear from heaven and will forgive their sin and heal their land..." (2 Chron. 7:14). It is the pleasure of the Father that Christ must have *first place in everything*, and this is true of the nation of Israel and the covenant of Sinai. Christ's Old Testament nation and covenant foreshadowed everything that Israel, the King, would do in His incarnation for His people.

He who must have first place in all of God's purposes, truly was the literal King of the Old Testament nation. It is His kingdom; it bears one of

79

His many meaningful Names, *Israel.* This is the reason that Christ appeared to Moses as the Angel of Jehovah on Mt. Sinai, and told him, "I am the God of your fathers: Abraham, Isaac and Jacob." Today it is clear that Moses was called and sent by Christ. The people were delivered from Egypt, in the sacrifice of the Paschal[5] Lamb, on the same day that Christ would be crucified. Christ was the angel of God's presence, who was with them when they came out of Egypt. When they came to Mt. Sinai, the Word of the covenant—the Word that fell down on the mountain in fire to proclaim the ten commandments—was Christ, the living Word. And the people became members of the Sinai covenant when Moses sprinkled a shadow of the blood of Christ on every person. Afterward, when seventy elders of Israel ascended the mountain with Moses and Aaron, they sat down for a fellowship meal on the mountain and looked upon Christ their King, ate and drank in His presence, and did not die. (Exodus, chapters 3, 20, 24).

Christ was also the Spirit in their ancient prophets, who predicted the sufferings of Christ, and the glory that would follow (1 Peter 1:10-12). He spoke through Jeremiah and said that He would make a new covenant, in which all His people would finally know Him, from the least to the greatest. (Jer. 31:31-34).

A covenant is established between two parties. At Mt. Sinai, the Infinite and Glorious One, high above the heavens, reached down to give Israel His covenant. It was a national constitution, composed for the citizens of an earthly kingdom of God. In the kingdom of Israel, Christ is the invisible first man, the King, the One who represents God's party in the Sinai covenant. Later, in his incarnation, He would become the perfect Mediator, for being fully God, He perfectly represents God's party before man, and being fully human in the incarnation, He also perfectly represents man's party before God, the human head and representative of all who trust in Him, who are members of His spiritual body.

The *symbolic* design of the Sinai covenant, for an earthly kingdom, was threefold.

First, to foreshadow the things of the eternal kingdom of heaven, promised to Abraham, that Christ would later establish in His incarnation, such as the one true acceptable sacrifice, the High Priesthood in heaven, and citizenship in the heavenly city. This will be considered in Volume Three.

Second, to reveal that the King of Israel, Himself, would become the sacrifice and Redeemer for the citizens of His kingdom, to fulfill the promise of His death represented by all the sacrifices commanded in the Sinai covenant.

Third, to introduce the mystery that the citizens of the kingdom of heaven, foreshadowed by citizenship in national Israel, would all be contained within one man, Jesus Christ, the Last Adam. In the new covenant, only those regenerated unto life by the Holy Spirit and baptized by Him into the spiritual body of Christ, have a share in the physical death of Christ, the physical resurrection of Christ, the physical ascent of Christ's body into heaven, and eternal citizenship in heaven in Christ. In a sense, the new covenant kingdom is Christ Himself. Therefore, when God appointed Moses to bring His Old Testament people out of slavery in Egypt to form them into a kingdom of Christ at Mt. Sinai, He said to Moses, "Israel is My Son, My first-born Son," then after the exodus of the nation from bondage, He declared, "Out of Egypt I have called My Son."[6] Calvin comments on these two verses, explaining that "what is said of the whole people," Israel, is actually "limited to Christ" in whom alone the elect from the nation are "adopted" as God's "son":

> "…we must come to Christ, the only head, in order that the adoption should be sure. For we must hold fast to that statement of St. Paul, that the blessing of Abraham was not promised to his seeds, but to his [single] seed (Galatians 3:16); because not all that sprang from his flesh are accounted to be children, but those that were called; as Isaac, Ishmael being rejected, and as Jacob, Esau being passed by. (Romans 9:6) But Christ is the root of our calling. Therefore, *what in Hosea is spoken, as here, of the whole people,[7] Matthew limits to Christ; and justly, since upon Him alone the grace of adoption is founded.* (Hosea 11:1 ; Matthew 2:15 .)[8]

In his Commentary on Hosea, Calvin further explains that the nation is the body, the church or assembly, where the head of the body is Christ Himself:

> " the first place, it must be remembered that Christ cannot be separated from his Church, as the body will be mutilated and imperfect without a head. Whatever then happened formerly in the Church [OT Israel], ought at length to be fulfilled by the head…

The covenant that created the kingdom of Israel had one significant difference from former covenants; those former were each established with a new Adam, *one man* from whom all the children of God shall come. The new Adams came in the weakness and image of the first Adam, being sinful and imperfect like him in his fall. Each new Adam was also "a type of Him who was later to come," showing the need for a perfect Adam to fulfill every foreshadow acted out by the types.

But with the Sinai covenant the *one man* was not. The Sinai covenant was a pact between God and the people of His earthly kingdom. However, the *one man* who should have been standing in front, at the head, was visibly absent.

The last man who could have been the *"one man"* from the family of Abraham was Jacob. His name, Israel, given after he wrestled with God all night, was the name of God's own Son, effectively making Jacob "a type of Him who was later to come."[9] He is the last patriarch that *all* the covenant people were born from. Patriarch means "father over all."

Jacob was not present when the Sinai covenant was instituted, and the nation was not named the "kingdom of Jacob." God formed the descendants of Jacob into a nation centuries after his death, so that the kingdom of people who would be brought to life only through the Son of God would forever be named after Him alone. "Thus says the Lord, "Israel is my firstborn son.""[10] Because the citizens of the kingdom of heaven are contained in one man, the earthly kingdom which foreshadowed the heavenly symbolizes that one man. The former corporate covenants were each made with a father and his descendants after him. The Sinai Covenant differed in one very conspicuous way. The person or father at the head of this covenant was absent at its inauguration, yet it is a covenant in which nearly every detail is a sign, symbol, allusion or foreshadow of that one man. Therefore, White and Beisner describe Christ as the "True Israel" and the kingdom as "the national Son of God."[11] Kim Riddlebarger concurs that Christ is the "True Israel," and adds that He is the fulfillment of both the earthly city of Jerusalem, and the temple it contained.[12] J. Gresham Machen concluded that "the ideal Israel is Christ."[13]

Everything in Israel pointed to the one true man, the true Israel of God, who is conspicuously invisible, until the incarnation at last reveals Him to His people.

Hebrews 8:5 reveals that the priests of Moses' covenant "served the copy and shadow of the heavenly things." According to Hebrews 9:23-24, the earthly Holy of Holies was only a copy of the true Holy Place in heaven, which Christ would enter one time on behalf of His people, to remain there forever making intercession for their sins with His own blood. Therefore, everything in the earthly temple signified Christ, as Gregory of Nyssa (330-c.395) wrote in the fourth century, "The ark, my brethren, was that man of God; an ark containing in itself the Divine and mystic things. There was the golden vessel full of Divine manna, that celestial food. In it were the Tables of the Covenant written on the tablets of the heart, not with ink but by the Spirit of the living God. For on that pure heart no gloomy or inky thought was imprinted. In it, too, were the pillars, the steps, the chapters, the lamps, the mercy-seat, the baths, the veils of the entrances. In it was the rod of the priesthood, which budded in the hands of our Saint; and whatever else we have heard the Ark contained was all held in the soul of that man."[14]

All of the annual ceremonies of Israel were shadows of Christ's work in the new covenant. For example, on the Day of the Passover Feast every family slew a lamb for their entire household, and sprinkled the blood on the wooden doorframe. Together, they passed through that bloody doorway into the house, then closed the door to shut out the wrath of God.

There, the family feasted hastily on the body of that sacrificed lamb and then rose from the table to be set free, immediately, that very night, from their Egyptian slavery. Israel was commanded to celebrate this feast every year, as a memorial, on the very day when Christ would be crucified as our Paschal Lamb. The church passes through the doorway of the bloody cross to escape the wrath of God that is coming upon the fallen world.

The remaining annual festivals of Israel, such as the Day of Atonement, the Feast of Pentecost, and the Feast of Tabernacles, are considered in the third volume of this series, *The Lighthouse Kingdom*, where more attention is given to the meaning and purpose of that important covenant, the Law as the schoolmaster, justification under the Law, and the revelation of Christ in all the ceremonies and temple service of the nation of Israel.

Chapter Four Notes

1. Gary D. Long, "The Grace of God and Departures from It." *Reformation and Revival 3*, no. 1 (Reformation and Revival Ministries, 1994), 80, Logos e-book. Gary D. Long writes, "Differences (within Reformed theology in particular) over the Christian's relationship to the law and the gospel are not a willful departure over the nature and design of the cross-work of Christ; rather they are a departure resulting from misunderstandings of God's law as it relates to the flow of redemptive history, especially the meaning of "law" in the Epistles of Paul."

2. Calvin, *Institutes*, II, vii, 8.

3. Martin, Hugh. *The Atonement.* (Edinburgh: James Gemmell, 1882), 173-174.

4. Calvin, Galatians, 3:24.

5. "From "Pascha," a Latinized spelling of the Hebrew word Pesach, meaning Passover."—Wickipedia. Paschal refers to the annual Passover Feast, celebrated in Israel on the 14th day of the month Nisan, to remember the sacrifice of a Lamb for each household on the very night the Hebrews were set free from their bondage in Egypt. The blood of the lamb was sprinkled on the doorframe. The family entered, closed the door, and set down at the table. In the middle of the night, the angel of the Lord went forth to kill the firstborn in every household in Egypt. Wherever he saw the blood on the doorframe, he "passed over" that house and did not kill anyone inside. Thus the name, Passover.

6. This is often thought to be only a prophecy of the return from Egypt to Judea of Joseph and Mary, with their holy infant, Jesus. It certainly was that event that was later to come. But at the time it was revealed it was also an allusion that the Son is synechdoche for the entire nation, which means that He represents all because all are contained in Him.

7. "When Israel was a child, I loved him, and out of Egypt I called my son." Hosea 11:1

8. John Calvin, *Harmony of the Law* (Albany, OR: Ages Software, 1998), vol. 1, 80, Ages e-book.

9. The first father of God's people, Adam, "is a type of Him who was later to come," and Christ is called "the last Adam." The second father

of all, Noah, is also a type of Christ. Noah's name means "rest," pointing ahead to the One who would "give us rest from the land the Lord has cursed." Abram's name was changed to Abraham when he was made a type of that "everlasting father," Jesus Christ, mentioned in Isaiah 9:7. David, the man after God's own heart, is a type of that David who was later to come, mentioned in Ezekiel 37:24-25. The names of types of Christ are also the names of Christ. The same is true of Jacob, who returned with a quiver full of sons who would become the twelve tribes of God's people. He is a type of Christ. So the Lord wrestled with him all night and gave him the Name of the man who would truly "wrestle with man and with God and prevail." Christ is the true king of the nation of Israel. It is His kingdom. And Israel is His Name. Therefore, in reorganizing spiritual Israel, He chose twelve spiritual fathers, the apostles.

10. Exodus 4:22 (ESV)

11. White, *Covenant*, no page numbers, Mobibook e-book.

12. Kim Riddlebarger, *A Case for Amillennialism: Understanding the End Times.* (Grand Rapids: Baker Books, 2003), 68-80.

13. J. Gresham Machen, *A Rapid Survey of the Literature and History of New Testament Times* (Oak Harbor, WA: Rose Tree Press, 2000), 33, Logos e-book.

14. Gregory of Nyssa, *The Nicene and Post-Nicene Fathers*, Second Series, ed. Philip Schaff (Albany, OR: Ages Software, 1996), 5: 978, Ages e-book.

Five
David and the Coming Messiah

A s the time drew nearer to the Redeemer's birth, God made another new covenant, this time with a shepherd whom He anointed to be king of His holy people. David, who was a man "after God's own heart," was another "type of Him who was later to come". God made a covenant with David, promising the throne of God's kingdom, Israel, to his sons forever, until a King should be born in David's family whose reign would never end and whose rule would extend from Palestine "to the ends of the earth." It is important to note, just like the other covenants, the covenant of David continued along family lines, from generation to generation. Those descended from David had a birthright to the throne, or at least to royal prestige, but each and every descendant did not enjoy God's covenant blessings as David did. These were promised to those who had faith in God and His Word, loved the Lord, and in that faith and love, sought to keep God's commandments in humble submission to Him.

As the father of all the kings who would rule God's earthly kingdom, David was a type of the first Adam, of whom God said, "Let us make man in our own image, in our likeness, and let them rule..." But also having a sinful nature like that first Adam, at best he was only a shadow of the greater David, the perfect David, who must come into the world to fulfill the need for a final Adam who would reign forever in God's image and would bring forth sons and daughters to reign forever with Him in perfect righteousness. So David's covenant promised that the Messiah, Christ, would one day come from David's family line, from the king's family—to reign over all the earth forever and ever. The "one who was later to come" would be the true David, "a man after God's own heart" without the corruption of the first David.

David's terrible failure is soon well known by anyone who becomes a Christian and is common knowledge even to many who otherwise have little contact with the stories of the Holy Bible. David's sin has already been mentioned in connection with Abraham's covenant. In describing the covenant God made with David himself, there are significant things to note from the story. David ascended to the throne as God's chosen man, because he was "a man after God's own heart" from the days of his youth. But when he became preoccupied by the daily business of running a kingdom and the important matters of state, the daily devotional lifestyle that marked his earlier years faded into history and his flesh became the dominant leader of his actions. Soon he no longer walked in the power of the Holy Spirit, but as one enslaved to the flesh, "fulfilling the [sinful] desires of the flesh and of the mind" (Eph. 2:3), he served the Tempter instead of God. Walking on his roof one day, he looked down into the courtroom of the house of one of his most loyal officers, Uriah the Hittite, to see the beautiful wife of Uriah, Bathsheba, bathing. Moved by desire for her, David sent for her. Both David and Bathsheba were guilty of adultery: she for bathing where he could see her, for coming when he called her, and for willingly yielding to his advances. Her lack of resistance testifies that she sought his attention and welcomed it when it came.

But the weight of guilt was heaviest upon David. He was king of Israel, a type and shadow of the true, invisible, heavenly Lord of righteousness and justice. David's calling was to lead the nation to love God and obey His laws. He pushed aside the Holy Spirit's promptings and seared his own conscience to follow his selfish desires! To quote his own words of king Saul, "How the mighty have fallen." The evil one, who has thousands of years of experience in using "desires that wage war against the soul,"[1] overcame and took David's will captive. There would be no covering of this sin; Bathsheba discovered she was pregnant. David's attempts to hide it drove him deeper into the will of the Evil One. When David's faithful servant came home from a distant battle, he sent Uriah home to sleep with his wife. Uriah would not go to her while the army was at war and stayed at the palace in the servant's quarters. Too proud to expose himself, David sent Uriah to the frontline of battle to die. He went from adulterer, to deceiver, to betrayer, to murderer.

God's hand became heavy on David for his wickedness, as upon any adulterer or murderer under God's conviction. David rightly expected God to take his life for sins that were certainly unto death.[2] The Law commanded that adulterers and murderers must die. David's soul tasted hell already, until he came to his senses and realized that God is merciful to those who truly repent, and he confessed the wickedness of his crimes.

Paul writes very little of David. But desiring to help the Jews understand man's sinful nature, God's gracious forgiveness, and justification of sinners by grace through faith as a free gift, Paul sees in David the very same justification God gave to Abraham, and writes, "... to the man who does not work but trusts God who justifies the wicked, his faith is credited as righteousness. [6]David says the same thing when he speaks of the blessedness of the man to whom God credits righteousness apart from works: [7]"Blessed are they whose transgressions are forgiven, whose sins are covered. [8]Blessed is the man whose sin the Lord will never count against him" (Romans 4:5-8).

David's words, after the tragedy of his fall into sin, are simple enough for any child to understand. No one can deny David's sin, nor the fact that when God credited righteousness to David it was most certainly apart from works. He was truly justified by grace, restored from sin to righteousness, or right-standing with God.

Calvin's comments here are most helpful. He writes:

"...the Prophet not only declares that our sins are covered, that is, removed from the presence of God; but also adds, that they are not imputed. How can it be consistent, that God should punish those sins which he does not impute? Safe then does this most glorious declaration remain to us — "That he is justified by faith, who is cleared before God by a gratuitous remission of his sins."[3]

Calvin learned from Paul and David that God's free righteousness is not an occasional blessing or a one-time gift, but is bestowed upon repentant believers whenever they seek God's mercy throughout their entire lifetime. He adds:

"We may also hence learn, the unceasing perpetuity of gratuitous righteousness through life: for when David, being wearied with the continual anguish of his own conscience, gave utterance to this declaration, he no doubt spoke according to his own experience; and he had now served God for many years. He then had found by experience, after having made great advances, that all are miserable when summoned before God's tribunal; and he made this avowal, that there is no other way of obtaining blessedness, except the Lord receives us into favor by not imputing our sins. Thus fully refuted also is the romance of those who dream, that the righteousness of faith is but initial, and that the faithful afterwards retain by works the possession of that righteousness which they had first attained by no merits."[4]

Calvin's final comment is very important. When God forgives sin, He not only ceases to hold the sin against the sinner, He no longer charges or imputes that sin to the offender's record. The charge is removed on one hand and perfect righteousness is credited to the sinner on the other. This then, Calvin insists, completely cancels all thought of an initial but incomplete justification, followed by a final justification at life's end based on good works.[5]

There may be some for whom grace is not so simple.[6] So we will look at God's grace in David's life again. In the next chapter, "The Covenant of the Kingdom of Heaven," and in the second volume, *Camp of the Saints*, there are still some important things to consider.

David was a type of the greater and perfect David, who was later to come. God refers to this later David through Ezekiel, saying, "My servant, David, will be king over them, and they will all have one shepherd...David my servant will be their prince forever. I will make a covenant of peace with them; it will be an everlasting covenant" (Ezek. 37:24-28). Ethan the prophet, in Psalm 89, writes that God said of David, "[26]He will call out to me, 'You are my Father, my God, the Rock my Savior.' [27]I will also appoint him my firstborn, the most exalted of the kings of the earth." Calvin understood that "It was ... a privilege peculiar to only one king in this world, to be called the Son of God .... for a time, [David] represented the person of Christ."[7] It is in this role that David, representing Christ, described the Messiah's suffering on the cross of death to provide redemption to His people (Psalm 22). The Spirit of the Redeemer often sang, prayed, and spoke about Himself through King David, who was a prophet, since David was a symbol of the Son of God who would take upon Himself human form to live with God's people, and rule over them forever.

90

Chapter Five Notes

1. 1 Peter 2:11, "Dear friends, I urge you, as aliens and strangers in the world, to abstain from sinful desires, which war against your soul."

2. 1 John 5:16b, "… There is a sin that leads to death. I am not saying that he should pray about that."

3. Calvin, *Romans*, 4:6.

4. ibid.

5. Initial justification followed by final justification on the day of judgment is a concept held for centuries by Roman Catholics. A modified but similar form is advocated in NPP and Federal Vision teaching.

6. Marketing advocates of consumer church theory insist that it is passé to preach about sin and judgment; that old way of thinking isn't popular and doesn't sell. New Perspective adherents argue that the terms, "righteousness" and "justification" were misunderstood by Calvin and by all other Reformed theologians and exegetes over the past five centuries. And Emerging Church teachers insist that even in this passage we cannot determine Paul's meaning with certainty, and if we can't, neither could Calvin.

7. Calvin, *Psalms*, 89:26

Six
The Covenant of the Kingdom of Heaven

After the time of David, the Lord promised often that He would make yet another New Covenant with Abraham's children. In the New Testament, Christ is declared "Mediator" (Heb. 8:6) of a "better covenant" (Heb. 7:22). He is much greater than the prophet Moses, because He is the Son of God. So also His new covenant, the full revelation of the Covenant of Grace, is vastly superior to the covenant of Moses.

This has often been misunderstood to mean a completely different way of salvation. Calvin makes haste to correct this in his Institutes, writing, *"it must now be clear, that all whom, from the beginning of the world, God adopted as his peculiar people, were taken into covenant with him on the same conditions, and under the same bond of doctrine, as ourselves ... the Fathers were partakers with us in the same inheritance, and hoped for a common salvation through the grace of the same Mediator..."*[1]

Calvin means that from the time of Adam's fall, God promised only one way of salvation through "the seed of the woman," the Mediator, who was to be born to Adam's fallen posterity. Every person saved in human history is redeemed by this one man, Jesus Christ, even those who found grace and forgiveness of sin ages before Christ was crucified on the mountain of God. Calvin emphasizes that this is very important to understand, and then goes on to explain[2] that the differences between the older and the new covenants have nothing to do with the means or the grounds of our salvation, which is through Christ alone. Calvin is quite right; the good student will search until this is well understood and the mystery of how redemption was applied before Christ died is no longer a mystery.

Nevertheless, to say that the new covenant is "vastly superior" is no exaggeration. The "better covenant" is the covenant of the kingdom of heaven. It's true members are God's own children and eternal citizens of heaven, already part and parcel of the new heavens and earth that are yet to come.

The old covenant established the people as God's kingdom at Mt. Sinai, the nation of Israel. That kingdom was earthly, with a city prominent in this present world and a geographical boundary among the nations of the earth. The new covenant gathers its citizens out of the world, establishing them as the kingdom of heaven. The remarkable manner it does this is by sending Christ, the man from heaven, who descended into the fallen world, to triumph over Satan as the last Adam. Perfectly obedient to the will of Yahweh His entire life on earth, the Law of Moses at last had to declare him the only righteous man to rise among Adam's depraved family. Being the first human to obey God in the history of the world, He became the means of salvation for all who trust in Him. As God once declared through Moses to Pharaoah, when He was determined to set His people free from the house of slavery, "Israel is my son, my first born. Let my firstborn son go, or I will kill your firstborn son," so now Yahweh opened the heavens to declare to Satan, the slavemaster of the world, "This is my Son, with whom I am well pleased"—displaying Him as the True Israel of God, in whom would be numbered all the citizens of the Kingdom of heaven, snatched from the domain of darkness. On that day the Evil One, still keeping vigilance for the One who would bruise His heel, saw the seed of the woman had come and began the contest in the wilderness in earnest. This Last Adam emerged victorious from the test, displaying himself the rightful keeper of the Covenant of Works and heir of the world lost by the first man. All the types and shadows contained in the old nation were now to be fulfilled in a single man. His body was the temple prefigured by the tabernacle. The Levitical order was a mere shadow of His holy priesthood. Now God offered Him as the sinless Lamb, the sacrifice of the new covenant, replacing the countless animals of the old order with a single propitiatory (or, satisfaction) offering. Though He never sinned, at that cross He died for sin, the sins of His people being *imputed* (p. 41) to Him. When at last He triumphed at the cross, slaughtered by him who had the power of death, His incorruptible righteousness rose victoriously over His enemy, casting off death's bonds to emerge from the dark tomb in the brilliant light of the life-giving Spirit. In that Spirit, His people, though never having righteousness, arose from the dead with a righteousness not their own, His own righteousness imputed to them, raising every one of them from death to glory with him. As Jews in bondage passed through the doorframe stained with death-blood of the passover lamb, so this cross of the True Paschal Lamb was now the only door out of the cruel land of Satan's slavery into the new life in the Spirit, and the freedom of the kingdom of the children of God. Ascending again into the glory above, He carried within Himself all those who had been chosen in Him for salvation from the foundation of the world—for He was the kingdom of heaven that had finally come to His people. Only those *in Him* see the kingdom and have life. Only by sharing in His righteousness are they ascended into heavenly glory in Him. His own Spirit is the life of His citizens. From this day forward, the Lamb would be their only light, and His Word, their food. Having received all authority over heaven and earth He was caught up to God and the throne of the Most High. His final triumph over the serpent of old was to cast out the accuser of His brethren, having obtained eternal redemption, abolishing the power of sin and death through the blood of His cross. There being no place found for Satan to accuse them before God's throne any longer, Satan and his angels were hurled down to the earth, fulfilling at last the ancient prophesy, "and he shall crush your head" (Gen. 3:15).

Here is the real Noah, who alone was righteous before God, Savior of His own household. His children alone will live to inherit the new world cleansed by fire. The whole world, the inheritance of Abraham's seed, will be "the home of righteousness."

Here walks the "father of many nations" before Yahweh blamelessly, to whom God swore that He, and His seed, shall be the heir of the world.

Now "your eyes shall gaze upon the King in His beauty" and behold the true David, whose children shall reign forever with Him, dressed in white garments.

At last the True Israel[3] began to gather His children to Himself from all nations, grafting them into His own body by His Word, His blood, and His Spirit as branches of the vine, stones of a holy temple *in the Lord*, the church of the Firstborn, whose names are enrolled in the heavenly Jerusalem, citizens of the everlasting kingdom.

95

Not only do all types find their fulfillment in Him, not only do all shadows cast down through the ages extend from the brazen feet where He now stands glorified, but the Lord God also described virtually every detail of His new covenant ages before it was finally confirmed by Christ's incarnation, death and resurrection, described beforehand by the many prophets who wrote the books of the Old Testament.

When He finally ascended into heaven to mediate the covenant and share it's promised blessings with His people in the world, much of the Word of His *new covenant* had already been written, sprinkled like yeast among the writings of Old Testament prophets, waiting for this new age when the whole lump would at last be rolled and kneaded by the apostles until all was leavened. The Old Testament that contained these prophetic teachings about the covenant is the only Bible that was available to the church on the day of Pentecost, when the new covenant was finally established in the lives of God's people and taught to the first Jewish believers.

It is important to understand this, because many evangelicals today believe all Christian teaching must come from the New Testament only. But this results in a distorted new covenant theology, since the things already written about the new covenant in the Old Testament, did not have to be rewritten in the New Testament. Each New Testament book was added to the already existing collection of Old Testament books, one book at a time—to form the complete Bible. Its like studying medicine or computer science, in which every year some new progress is made. Where would the medical profession be if students in medical schools learned only the knowledge that was gained this year? How would computer science make any progress if all past knowledge was ignored? It should be emphasized often. The new covenant apostles trained the church in the new teachings using only Old Testament Scripture backed up by apostolic revelation. The New Testament would not be written and assembled for many years after the new covenant had already begun to function as the governing principles of Christ's kingdom.

It was the covenant of Sinai that established the kingdom of Israel. The new covenant would usher in the kingdom of heaven. The covenant was not established merely by proclaiming it from the ancient Scriptures, nor by the birth of Christ, though that was the most significant event the Jews had seen up to that time. The covenant was not yet ratified when Christ was anointed by the Holy Spirit to be the Prophet, Priest and King of the New Covenant. There is a sense that the first step of inauguration began at that moment. But other steps must follow. Christ began to prepare for it, preaching as the Great Prophet, bringing the Word of the Father from heaven to His people. But the covenant still waited when Jesus laid down His life for the sins of His people. The blood must be sprinkled on the mercy seat. First, the Messiah had to be glorified, the Last Adam must ascend to the throne of the kingdom. He would be a High Priest on His throne, mediating the covenant. After fulfilling the meaning of the Feast of Passover (by sacrificing His own body on the cross of death), and the Day of First Fruits (by rising from the dead as the first fruit of the resurrections of the new covenant), He had yet to fulfill the Day of Atonement (by ascending bodily through the veil into heaven itself, the true Holy of Holies), and His intercessory prayers there would begin sprinkling the throne of grace with His own blood. Ten days after Christ's ascension, the Holy Spirit of promise was poured out upon the disciples from heaven to fulfill the Day of Pentecost, and only then the new covenant was confirmed in their hearts and through their lives and testimony. By the power of the Spirit they began to witness about Christ with words the Spirit put into their mouths. K.E. Brower comments, "Fundamental to all N.T. theology is the shift in eschatological perspective brought about by the coming of Jesus Messiah, *and the coming of the Holy Spirit*." (emphasis mine)[4]   The covenant cannot have only one party, even if the Mediator has begun His work. There must be a people who enter into the covenant. The people who gathered around Peter on the Day of Pentecost were like those who stood before Sinai with their families to enter into covenant with the Lord their God. It was the Holy Spirit who began to apply the benefits of Christ's death to His people, internalizing the covenant in life-giving reality within each one. Andrew Murray says, "Just as Christ is the visible revelation on earth and in heaven of the invisible God, so the Holy Spirit again is the communication of the life and redemption of the unseen Christ. The Holy Spirit is the power of the inner life."[5] The Day of Pentecost brought the fullness of that Spirit into the people God established the covenant with, and three thousand souls were made alive from the dead and ushered into the new covenant kingdom. The new covenant was ratified to God's people.

This very description of the new covenant, that it would come with the Holy Spirit, was already available in Isaiah 59: 20-21, before the Day of Pentecost, *"The Redeemer will come to Zion, to those in Jacob who repent of their sins," declares the Lord. "As for me, this is my covenant with them," says the Lord. "My Spirit, who is on you, and my words that I have put in your mouth will not depart from your mouth, or from the mouths of your children, or from the mouths of their descendants from this time on and forever," says the Lord.*

Here, God plainly declares that His new covenant in Christ will be characterized by two important features: first, that the Holy Spirit will be upon true members of the covenant from generation to generation, the Spirit poured upon the disciples on the Day of Pentecost; and second, that the words of the covenant would continue to be spoken and taught by the children's children of those who trust in Jesus the Redeemer. Since the covenant consists of *words*, this implies that the covenant itself would continue along family lines, as the Holy Spirit helps parents teach the Word to their children, and opens the hearts of the children to understand and believe. This is exactly the pattern God had established in all the covenants that were foreshadows of Christ in the past ages; for the covenant made Jehovah to be the God of believers from Noah's descendants, and also to Abraham God swore, "I will be God to you, and to your descendants after you in their generations..." On the day of Pentecost, Peter proclaimed to Jewish parents who were waiting for this promise of the Holy Spirit, ""*For the promise is for you and for your children* and for all who are far off, everyone whom the Lord our God calls to himself" (Acts 2:39, ESV).

This passage from Isaiah shows that external covenant membership is not enough. The covenant must be internalized; the covenant is words, *"This is my covenant with you,"* but they cannot be empty, lifeless or dead words, *"My words, which I put into your mouths..."* Therefore, the real work of the covenant is in the Holy Spirit applying the Word of God to the heart, transforming the inner man. The Spirit of promise, the promise given to Abraham (Gal. 3:13-14), must be upon us, and in us (in our mouths when we speak and teach), and upon our children after us, *"This is my covenant...My Spirit who is on you...and My words...shall not depart from your mouths, nor from the mouths of your children, nor from the mouths of your children's children..."* The fruit of this internal work of the Spirit is described by Paul, when he says that Abraham is the father of the circumcised, *"who are not only of the circumcision, but who also walk in the steps of the faith of Abraham"* (Rom. 4:12), as it was once described by Moses in different words, *"God Himself will circumcise your hearts, and the hearts of your descendants after you, to love the Lord your God with all your heart and all your soul, and live."* (Deut. 30:6)

Such faith was displayed by parents who brought their little children to Jesus to ask Him *to bless them*; they were Jews, members of the covenants of promise God made with their fathers, and now *they were believing* that the promised Messiah had come, the One who establishes *"the new covenant with the house of Israel and with the house of Judah"* (Jer. 31:31ff). Jesus took the infants *of these parents* in His arms and declared that the kingdom of heaven belongs to children such as these; because the parents' hopes were in the Messiah, and they were leading their children to the same hope, the True Israel, and to the only Gate into the kingdom of life. John the Baptist had taught all the people that Christ is the One who baptizes in the promised Holy Spirit. Peter strengthened the Jewish parents hopes for their little ones when he declared to them at Pentecost, "The promise *is for you and for your children...*" (Acts 2:39). In Gal. 3:14, Paul explains that this "promise" is "the gift of the Holy Spirit," the blessing promised to Abraham. It is this gift of the life-giving Spirit that God was promising when he swore the words of His covenant to Abraham, "In you, I will bless all the *families* of the earth" (Genesis 12:3).[6] "Families" is the Hebrew, המשפחה. Some translations have wrongly rendered this term, "nations," but the word, in Scripture, almost always means, "clan," or "family," a *"group in which the sense of blood relationship is still felt."*[7] Gordon Wenham suggests even a more specific sense in his commentary on Romans 12:3, where he writes that this term *"translated "clan" in* [Gen.]*10:5, 18, 20, 31, 32,* [המשפחה] *is a grouping intermediate between a tribe and a father's house (cf. the rarer term* מולדת, *12:1), Josh 7:14–18."*[8]

Is this emphasis on *families* a mere coincidence in Isaiah 59:21? It is repeated whenever a new covenant is established. These promises, in both the Old and New Testaments should not be ignored, as some have done. They can be easily misunderstood; therefore, they must be taken with a good appraisal of the entire covenant history. The failure of the Jews is a case in point. Many Jews believed that their children were eternally secure because they were physically descended from Abraham, and the promises and privileges of the covenant were presented to them from infancy. They failed to understand that there must eventually be genuine faith to confirm that the blessing of the covenant truly has been received by the next generation. Faithful parents were to do as Timothy's grandmother, Lois, and his mother, Eunice, had done, for true faith, if it will come, argues Paul, "comes by hearing, and hearing by the Word of God" (Rom. 10:17). Because of their patient daily instruction, Paul could say to him, "from infancy you have known the Holy Scriptures, which are able to make you wise for salvation through faith in Christ Jesus" (1 Tim. 3:15). To those covenant Jews who did not believe in Him, Jesus plainly said, "You are children of your father, the devil, and the desires of your father you want to do (John 8:44).....You want to kill me (John 8:40)..." They believed YHWH is God. They had the sign of covenant membership marked on them from infancy. But they did not believe in Him of whom the Scripture testified, so they did not truly believe what God said or trust in His Word. In the end they perished, and their family lines did not continue in covenant with God. Though rightful heirs of the covenant by birthright, many Jewish families were broken off because of their unbelief, while Gentile branches were grafted into their place (Romans 11:16-24).

In both Abraham's covenant and the Sinai covenant, and especially the new covenant in Christ Jesus, external membership in the covenant was never enough, there must be the work of the Spirit in the heart. Genuine faith is the evidence that there is a transformed heart. This is faith that repents of known sin, embraces Christ wholeheartedly as Savior *and* Lord, and follows the teachings of the apostles in Scripture as a sincere disciple of Christ.

Throughout the Old Testament, many who were members of the covenants simply perished in the wrath of God because they never embraced God and His promises with true faith. The generation of parents that came out of Egypt, the first members of the Sinai covenant, died in the wilderness because they would not believe God's Word (Hebrews 3:19). Within their respective covenants, Noah and Abraham were heirs of the righteousness that is by faith; in the first generation of the Sinai covenant, only Joshua and Caleb followed their example of faith, and lived to receive the promised land. They were men with a nature like all their brethren, born in trespasses and sins. Their justification was not their acceptance in the covenant, those who perished also had covenant membership, but it was the demonstration of genuine faith that came from their hearts. Those who would not believe perished for their own sins when, because of their unbelief, they deliberately rejected God together with His laws and commands; but believers who humbled themselves under the mighty hand of God, though sinful like the rest, found forgiveness of sins, eternal life, and peace, as well as the fulfillment of every other gracious promise. The Epistle to the *Hebrews* exhorts us to be "imitators of those who *through faith* and patience inherit the promises" (Hebrew 6:12).

It is in the new covenant in Christ Jesus that this justification of sinners by grace through faith comes to its fullest expression. Paul describes sinners who look to God for the gift of righteousness in Romans 4:5, *"...the one who does not work but believes in him who justifies the ungodly, his faith is credited as righteousness."* When Paul uses the term, "ungodly," in this verse, he's not referring merely to Gentiles who did not yet have covenant membership with the Jews. Paul uses David, a Jew in the covenant, as an example of what "ungodly" means. As a prominent member of God's covenant, a covenant leader, David was *ungodly* when he turned from God's moral law and committed adultery with Bathsheba and sent her husband, Uriah, to his death. But David, the ungodly sinner, was later justified again by God's grace. The very worst of sinners even in the world's eyes, he humbled himself in prayerful repentance until by faith he received the gift of gracious forgiveness. In Romans 4:6, David testifies of the "blessing of the one to whom God credits righteousness apart from works: *Blessed are they whose transgressions are forgiven, whose sins are covered. Blessed is the man whose sin the Lord will not take into account."* It is so very clear, from this, and many other passages, that God justifies sinners by taking away their sins and crediting a righteousness to them that is not earned by their own works of the Law, or by deeds of righteousness, or by their mere membership in the covenant. David says their *"sins are covered."* Here is the pure lamb's wool with which God covered the sin-stained nakedness of Adam and Eve, displaying a shadow of Christ. Or more directly in the words of Paul, in Gal. 3:27, *"As many of you as were baptized into Christ have put on Christ."* Christ is the robe of spotless righteousness in which sinners can stand justified before the Judge of the earth. It matters not who wears this robe; all who do have the very same righteousness and acceptance with God, whether Jew or Gentile, male or female, slave or free man. Romans 5:17 declares that *"those who receive...the free gift of righteousness* [will] *reign in life through the one man, Jesus Christ."* In fact, there is no other way to "reign in life," nor, for that matter, to come to life in the first place. Believers are crucified with Christ because of the sins that condemned our souls. Having died in Christ's death, our stains of wickedness are removed. But we are still left without any righteousness of our own to rise from the dead and ascend into heavenly glory. If we shall be raised to life, it must be in Christ's resurrection. Paul writes, "...even when we were dead in our trespasses..." God "...made us alive *together with Christ*—by grace you have been saved—and raised us up *with Him*, and seated us *with Him* in the heavenly places *in Christ Jesus"* (Ephesians 2:5-6) To live *with Him,* we must have a share in His righteousness and His life. So the apostle writes, "He was delivered over to death for our sins and was raised to life *for our*

101

justification" (Romans 4:25).

This "free gift" is received by faith; those who learn from God's moral laws that they are guilty and ungodly sinners, separated from God by their sins, must repent and confess those sins and *"believe in him who justifies the ungodly,"* that is, they must believe in *"Christ Jesus* [who] *came into this world to save sinners"* (1 Tim. 1:16b).   This is stated in no uncertain terms by Paul, who was, before his conversion, the foremost persecutor of the church in the first century, the man responsible for the imprisonment and murderous execution of many godly Christians. He was later chosen by Christ to be the chief apostle to the Gentiles and the author of many books of new covenant doctrine. Paul was a covenant member who sinned greatly, even more than David, a murderer condemned by the Law of Moses, who desperately needed the free gift of justification. In his own words from 1 Timothy 1:15-16, *"Here is a trustworthy saying that deserves full acceptance: Christ Jesus came into the world to save sinners, of whom I am the worst. But for that very reason I was shown mercy so that in me, the worst of sinners, Christ Jesus might display his unlimited patience as an example for those who would believe on him and receive eternal life."*

In this brief consideration of justification, it is enough to say that even the very worst of sinners, murderers of righteous people such as David and Paul were, can be saved from their sins and justified by God through Jesus Christ alone. But not by merely joining the church or by taking a sign of membership in the covenant (old or new); in the words of Paul, the "unlimited patience" of Jesus Christ, the grace that fully pardons all sin and justifies the ungodly, is for those who "believe on Him and receive eternal life." It is by faith.

To anyone familiar with the current debate on justification, this brief presentation will hardly seem adequate. So many books have been written in recent years approaching the subject from various new angles that the doctrine of justification has become, for some, a dark and tangled swampland with no solid path to step out of the mire. If you're trying to hack a trail through that dense jungle, a chapter on *justification* and *imputation* (pp. 41, 128), in Volume 2 of this series, *Camp of the Saints*, may help make sense of the muddle. Volume 2 is a closer look at the covenant of grace God made with Abraham.

The Cultivated Olive Tree

In Romans 11, Paul explains that all the Gentiles who are now being joined into Christ are grafted into an already-existing cultivated family tree that began with Abraham. Abraham, he points out, in Rom. 11:1 and v.16, is the root, and gentiles, who came from a wild tree, have been grafted into the cultivated family tree, to become partakers of the root. Christians in the new covenant share in the blessings and promises of Abraham's covenant (Rom. 11:17).

So Paul writes this assurance to Gentiles, "If you belong to Christ, you are the seed of Abraham, and heirs according to the promise" (Gal. 3:29). Christ is the branch of Abraham that will branch out into all the earth and become glorious (Zechariah 3:8; 6:12). In the covenant, believers are born of God through Christ's Spirit, and by participating in the one Spirit, are grafted into Christ by faith. God has given all who belong to Christ, the members of Christ, to Abraham, fulfilling His promise to give Abraham children from many nations; so that now, if you are a believer, you are literally an heir of the covenant promise given to Abraham your father, for an heir inherits what belongs to his or her father. The only way to receive the inheritance, the promise given to Abraham, is to be a member of the covenant God made with Abraham. This implies that Christ's covenant is a greater continuation or expansion of Abraham's covenant. Through the work of Christ, Abraham's covenant has now been expanded into all nations, fulfilling God's promise to make him the father of many nations.

Hagar and Sarah: The Two Covenants

Paul has a good analogy that connects the Abrahamic covenant *to heaven* (and thus to Christ and the kingdom of heaven), and the Sinai covenant to the *earthly kingdom*. The apostle describes these two covenants in Galatians 4:24-26, representing them by the two wives of Abraham, as follows: *"These things may be taken figuratively, for the women represent two covenants. One covenant is from Mount Sinai and bears children who are to be slaves: This is Hagar. Now Hagar stands for Mount Sinai in Arabia and corresponds to the present city of Jerusalem, because she is in slavery with her children. But the Jerusalem that is above is free, and she is our mother."* This passage has already come to the forefront in the brief chapter on Abraham's covenant, but there are additional aspects to consider in our discussion of the new covenant in Christ Jesus.

Calvin keeps us on the right track when he says of these two women, "Doctrine is the mother of whom we are born, and is [both] legal and evangelical... for the legal covenant makes slaves, and the evangelical covenant makes freemen."[9]

Hagar, a slave woman, symbolizes the legal covenant of Mt. Sinai and the earthly city of Jerusalem. As Hagar was the slave mother of a child born to slavery, so Jerusalem under the Sinai covenant produced children to be slaves. But, says Paul, the Jerusalem above is free; and she is our mother, *the mother of true Christians*. The "Jerusalem above," the heavenly city, is Sarah, the free wife of Abraham, and she represents the "evangelical covenant," the free covenant of justification by grace through faith, the same justification God gave to Abraham. By analogy, Paul shows us that this is the covenant of the kingdom of heaven.

The covenant of the Law of sin and death, and of the earthly city, ie., Hagar, could not by any works of Law produce children of heaven for Abraham. God established the heavenly covenant through Sarah, so the first of the children born to Abraham from this covenant, Isaac, was foreknown and promised by name beforehand, and then brought forth by the power of the Spirit rather than by the works of the flesh. Paul says to Galatian believers, "Now you, brothers, like Isaac, are children of promise." This means that the same heavenly covenant that gave birth to Isaac is the mother of Christian believers today. God promised children like the stars to Abraham, to be produced from all families of the earth.

There is a different analogy in Genesis 22, where Isaac is portrayed as a type of Christ, a shadow of the promised son who was later to come. God said to Abraham, *"Take your son, your only son Isaac, whom you love, and go to the land of Moriah, and offer him there as a burnt offering on one of the mountains of which I shall tell you"* (Genesis 22:2, ESV). Christ, is the true Isaac, God's Son, His "only Son," whom He loves. God later brought Him to the very same mountain to offer Him there as a sacrifice for all of Abraham's children.

The Scriptures portray Isaac as a type of Christ, the man from heaven, and Isaac's mother as the heavenly Jerusalem. Just as Isaac came from Sarah, not from Hagar, Christ literally came from the heavenly city (cf. Rev. 12:1-2, 5), not from the earthly city. He is the promised Son of Abraham through whom God would *"bless all the families of the earth"* (Genesis 12:3). God began to establish the covenant of the heavenly city with Abraham and Sarah in Genesis 15 and 17. It is the same evangelical

104

covenant of the kingdom of heaven later fulfilled and brought to fruition through Jesus Christ. Abraham's seed, those who belong to Christ today, have now come to the heavenly city (Heb. 12:22), for all are included in Jesus Christ (Eph. 1:13) who Himself has ascended into heaven to reign within that city as the King and Priest of the new covenant, the covenant of the kingdom of heaven. When Christ ascended, He took his physical body with Him. This was done as a sign that all who are members of His spiritual body were already carried to heaven in Him (Eph. 1:20; 2:6).

Returning to the analogy of the two women in Galatians 4, Paul writes that Hagar "corresponds to the present city of Jerusalem because she is in slavery with her children." The old covenant was mediated by Moses at an earthly mountain and it commanded a priesthood that served in an earthly temple, at an earthly city of Jerusalem, a city enslaved to worldly powers. Calvin says, "I agree with Chrysostom and Ambrose, who explain it as referring to the earthly Jerusalem, and who interpret the words, "which now is," τῷ νῦν ἱερουσαλὴμ, as marking the slavish doctrine and worship into which it had degenerated. It ought to have been a lively image of the new Jerusalem, and a representation of its character."[10]

But those who belong to the new covenant "are the temple of the living God." (1 Cor. 6:19; 2 Cor. 6:16). The holy of holies within the Jewish temple was the symbol of heaven. When the Holy Spirit came like a rushing wind at Pentecost the disciples became the new covenant temple. The glory fire was over the head of each one. All true believers in the new covenant today are the temple of God. Built together as "living stones," they have become the Holy of Holies. Therefore the prophet writes, *"You have come to Mount Zion, to the heavenly Jerusalem, the city of the living God. You have come to thousands upon thousands of angels in joyful assembly, to the church of the firstborn, whose names are written in heaven. You have come to God, the judge of all men, to the spirits of righteous men made perfect, to Jesus the mediator of a new covenant, and to the sprinkled blood that speaks a better word than the blood of Abel."* (Hebrews 12:22-24).

The old covenant belonged to an earthly kingdom of God. In Christ, we have not come to Sinai, that terrible mountain that can be touched and was burning with fire. Christ mediates the new covenant in the true Mt. Zion, the heavenly Jerusalem. We have come to the kingdom of heaven, established by Christ, the eternal covenant kingdom of the Messiah whose throne is in heaven. This is the true city of Jerusalem, where, in the words of Paul, God has raised Christ far above the heavens, *"above all rule and authority and every name that can be named,"* and has *"placed all things beneath His feet...not only in the present age, but also in the age to come."* (Ephesians 1:20-22) This is a covenant between God and the citizens of heaven, together with their households. The church, composed of believers in this world, is the *"church of the firstborn, whose names are enrolled in heaven"* (Heb. 12:23). This assembly gathers before the throne of Christ in every nation, tribe and language. Wherever we meet in this world, there He is among us, ruling in Spirit as King, serving as High Priest to bring the church into the Holy of Holies through His own blood, into heaven itself. (see Hebrews 10:19-25). Here is a precious handful of gold that should be taken out of the treasure box and gazed upon in wonder again and again, *"He raised us up with Him, and seated us with Him in the heavenly places in Christ Jesus"* (Ephesians 2:4ff), and he comforts the believers with these words, *"our citizenship is in heaven..."* (Philippians 3:20).

Believers need to understand that they are already citizens of heaven, living as pilgrims in the earth. Christ has already awarded us with citizenship in His country, His holy nation. Those who understand this are to *"set their minds on things above, and not the things that are in this world."* (Colossians 2:2). This is simply a way of saying that if we belong to heaven, let us live and speak as citizens of heaven. We may not follow the corrupt ways of this world, or the wicked practices of the nations of the world any longer. *"For all that is in the world, the lust of the flesh, and the lust of the eyes, and the boastful pride of life, is not of the Father, but is of the world, and the world is passing away, and also its lusts..."* (1 John 2:15-16).

It was necessary for Christ, as a human High Priest and King, to enter into heaven. He must serve in the capitol city of the heavenly country as the mediator of the covenant, the high priest of the covenant, the testator of the covenant, the great prophet who now speaks from heaven, the King of the kingdom of heaven, and the acceptable sacrifice of the covenant. He is the very covenant of heaven, as the Father says to His Son (the Man from heaven) through Isaiah, *"I will keep You and will make You to be a covenant for the people..."* (Isaiah 49:8). The completed book that we call the Holy Bible, *"the faith once delivered to the saints,"* is the Book of His covenant. Thus we have *"the letter,"* the Word written, even as they did at Sinai. But our letter has come to life to dwell with us, and now tabernacles among us. Because Christians are grafted into Christ, and are His very body, we have the Word made flesh with us whenever we read, and hear, and proclaim the precious words of revelation in this book.

106

Chapter Six Notes

1. Calvin, *Institutes*, II, 10, 1.

2. Ibid, II, 11.

3. "Jesus is the genuine Son of God, and, as Israel's Messiah, is the true Israel (see John 15:1); therefore, He gives fuller meaning to the prophecy of Hos. 11:1." E.D. Radmacher, R.B. Allen, and H.W. House, "Matthew 2:15—Note." *The Nelson Study Bible: New King James Version* (Nashville: T. Nelson Publishers, 1997), Logos e-book.

4. D.R. W. Wood and I.H. Marshall, *New Bible Dictionary*, 3rd ed. (Leicester, England: InterVarsity Press, 1996), 1058, Logos e-book.

5. Andrew Murray, *The Holiest of All: An Exposition of the Epistle to the Hebrews* (New York: Anson D.F. Randolph, 1894), 304, DJView e-book.

6. This does not mean that the blessing of Abraham is only the gift of the Holy Spirit and nothing else.

7. Ludwig Koehler et al., *The Hebrew and Aramaic Lexicon of the Old Testament* (Leiden: E.J. Brill, 1999), S. 651, Logos e-book.

8. Gordon J. Wenham, *Genesis 1-15*, vol. 1 of *Word Biblical Commentary*, ed. John D.H. Watts and Ralph P. Martin (Dallas, TX: Word Books, 1987), 278, Logos e-book.

9. Calvin, *Galatians*, 4:24.

10 . Calvin, *Galatians*, 4:25.

Part Two:
The Covenant of Works, Paul, and History

Seven
Old Theology, New Questions

The famous evangelist George Whitefield preached to great multitudes in the Great Awakening of the 18th century, a fiery revival that swept through the American colonies. In a sermon on Jeremiah 23:6, "The Lord Our Righteousness," he said, "...being once born under a covenant of works, it is natural for us all to recourse to a covenant of works for our eternal salvation."[1]

During that revival Jonathan Edwards, another instrument of God, in the year 1745 stayed at Crossweeksung. There he ministered both to native Americans, which he called, Indians, and to white colonists. Drawn to the spiritual needs of the "Indians" he gave himself to preach to them as often as he was able with the happy result that many repented and trusted in Christ for salvation. But Edwards wrote that some were hard hearted:

> "There were several Indians newly come, who thought their state good, and themselves happy, because they had sometimes lived with the white people under gospel-light, had learned to read, were civil, etc., although they appeared utter strangers to their own hearts, and altogether unacquainted with the power of religion, as well as with the doctrine of grace. With those I discoursed particularly after public worship, and was surprised to see their self-righteous disposition, their strong attachment to the covenant of works for salvation, and the high value they put upon their supposed attainments. Yet after much discourse, one appeared in a measure convinced, that "by the deeds of the law no flesh living can be

111

justified," and wept bitterly, inquiring "what he must do to be saved!"[2]

Edwards didn't mean that these natives, who were "strangers to their own hearts"[3] and had no knowledge of the true God, had any conscious "attachment to the covenant of works for salvation," but that they were very much like those who seek to establish their own righteousness through good works or works of the law. This entry from the famous preacher's diary, mentioning the "covenant of works" as a concept common to all, demonstrates the place that it held among the theological views of the early American settlers nearly three centuries ago. Yet three centuries before Edwards there was no mention of a "covenant of works" in any doctrinal treatise. This is one of the reasons that many of today's scholars question the validity of this covenant, or the title given to it, "Covenant of Works." This issue has been most prominent in recent years in arguments advanced by adherents of the New Perspective on Paul, by proponents of "Federal Vision" ideas, and by certain well known professors, such as John Murray, Herman Hoeksema, and Anthony Hoekema. Morton H. Smith comments, "The question of whether the Adamic relation should be called a covenant has occasionally been raised especially in this present generation. Professor John Murray preferred to call it the "Adamic Administration."[4] Murray himself writes:

"Towards the end of the 16th century the administration dispensed to Adam in Eden, focused in the prohibition to eat of the tree of the knowledge of good and evil, had come to be interpreted as a covenant, frequently called the Covenant of Works, sometimes a covenant of life, or the Legal Covenant. It is, however, significant that the early covenant theologians did not construe this Adamic administration as a covenant, far less as a covenant of works. Reformed creeds of the 16th century such as the French Confession (1559), the Scottish Confession (1560), the Belgic Confession (1561), the Thirty-Nine Articles (1562), the Heidelberg Catechism (1563), and the Second Helvetic (1566) do not exhibit any such construction of the Edenic institution. After the pattern of the theological thought prevailing at the time of their preparation, the term 'covenant,' insofar as it pertained to God's relations with men, was interpreted as designating the relation constituted by redemptive provisions and as belonging, therefore, to the sphere of saving grace."[5]

At first glance and backed by such an impressive array of early 16th century documents, Murray's comments are quite convincing. But Bible students trained to examine context will look at the environment of the early 16th century. It was the age of Protestants breaking off their shackles and coming out of the spiritual darkness of past centuries to study the Scriptures with new freedom. The creeds mentioned were written primarily to correct the deep abyss of doctrinal error that the church had descended into over the past millennia. This is illustrated by the brief life some of the above Creeds had as each creed was replaced by a better creed, and the better creed by one better yet, in step with the increasing knowledge. It was the century of discovery in God's Word and all things that were to be learned by carefully and prayerfully comparing Scripture with Scripture were not uncovered comprehensively at first, in a nice neat bundle. The entire century was marked by *gradual* progress in understanding the Word of God in successively deeper levels. We should expect that some things would *not* become fully realized until several generations of scholars running the race to learn had passed the baton to their students to carry farther than they had been able. Since the age of the printing press had begun, it could be expected that this would *indeed* be the century that would make the greatest advances in understanding the mysteries of God's Word. Whoever was given any insight into the truth could now arrange with the local publishing house to share their thoughts with others, more quickly and easily than any generation before their time.

By the seventeenth century, theologians comparing notes with each other had become so convinced that God made a covenant with Adam, that Wilhelmus Brakel wrote that this understanding was key to interpreting the rest of the Bible soundly. He believed that neither Scripture nor the Covenant of Grace revealed throughout the Word could be properly understood by anyone who denies the Covenant of Works. Brakel wrote these words that are now famous, *"Acquaintance with this covenant is of the greatest importance, for whoever errs here or denies the existence of the covenant of works, will not understand the covenant of grace, and will readily err concerning the mediatorship of the Lord Jesus. Such a person will very readily deny that Christ by His active obedience has merited a right to eternal life for the elect. This is to be observed with several parties who, because they err concerning the covenant of grace, also deny the covenant of*

113

works. Conversely, whoever denies the covenant of works, must rightly be suspected to be in error concerning the covenant of grace as well."[6]

The chief concern of this chapter is to set in order the apostle Paul's understanding of this ancient pact called the "Covenant of Works." Was he aligned to those who hold to a Covenant of Works or like some today, would he disagree with the concept?

Since Paul is cited on both sides of this debate, to determine his position on this question demands a good understanding of his epistles. Before attempting to get a handle on Paul, It is first necessary to define the *Covenant of Works*, then examine the place Paul's epistle's have held in the history of its doctrinal development. This will lead into a discussion of some important questions, such as the legitimacy of the Covenant of Works. Such a study would be incomplete without considering further details of the covenant beyond the scope of Paul's comments.

Toward the close of the 16th century, the century marked by many fresh or renewed discoveries in Scripture, many scholars, prompted by mention of Adam's covenant in the early church fathers,[7] and seeing the elements of a covenant in their own musings of Genesis, were undertaking studies to define this pact God established with the first man. There were some who regarded it primarily as a promise of life, represented by the tree of life, thus denominated it to be a covenant of life. There were others who believed that the purpose of the covenant was related to Adam's responsibilities to rule the world, populate it, and bring forth its fruits for God's glory, and so named it a "covenant of creation" or "covenant of nature." There were others who perceived that the purpose of the covenant, while indeed promising life and assigning earthly responsibilities, was chiefly summarized in the sovereign rights of the Creator and the subjection of His chief creation, man, whom He had appointed over all His works, but not over His own person. Therefore, the rule of God's Law was central to the covenant, with a particular law introduced purely as a test of obedience. In this simple test, Adam was the representative of the whole human race. This view was known as the "Covenant of Works" because a "work of the law," a simple test of obedience, was to be the means of confirming man's righteousness and everlasting access to the tree of life, or of his rebellion and unrighteousness, resulting in death and exclusion from the tree of life forever. Dewey D. Wallace provides this general definition in The Westminster Handbook to Reformed Theology: "According to this view, God made a covenant of works with Adam, the "federal head" of all humanity,

114

enjoining obedience to a perpetually binding moral law identified variously with the Ten Commandments (known to Adam before being given to Moses) and the law of nature. After Adam and his posterity with him fell, salvation was no longer available through the first covenant, so God established the covenant of grace, in which Christ fulfills the Law and atones for its breach, becoming the "federal head" of believers."[8]   In *federal headship,* Adam represents before God all who are in him or came from him and Christ represents before God all who are chosen in Him or came through Him.

The definition of the Covenant of Works that rose to prominence, and has been widely-held for more than four centuries, includes these features: a test of obedience, a promise of eteral life for obedience, a threat of death for disobedience, and this concept of "federal headship." For example, this was expressed by Robert Rollock (1555-1598), and after him, Amandus Polanus, in the latter part of the 16th century. Rollock wrote, "The covenant of works, which may also be called a legal or natural covenant, is founded in nature, which by creation was pure and holy, and in the law of God, which by creation was engraven in man's heart. For after that God had created man after his own image, pure and holy, and had written his law in his mind, he made a covenant with man, wherein he promised him eternal life, under the condition of holy and good works…"[9]

A century later, sometime before 1692, puritan expositor Thomas Watson was preaching, "When God had created man, he entered into a covenant of life with him upon condition of perfect obedience, forbidding him to eat of the tree of knowledge upon pain of death."[10]   Regarding "federal headship," Watson held the view that "This covenant was made with Adam and all mankind; for Adam was a public person, and the representative of the world.[11] Thomas Boston (1676-1732) promoted similar concepts in his writing on the Covenant of Works. John Dick, an eminent Scottish theologian in the early 19th century, provides a definition reflecting the same ideas, "The Covenant of Works has been defined to be, a convention between God and man concerning the method of obtaining eternal happiness, accompanied with a threatening of death in the case of disobedience; or the covenant which God made with Adam as the representative of his posterity, and in which he promised eternal life upon the condition of obedience, not only to the moral law written on his heart, but to the positive precept respecting the tree of knowledge."[12]

There were often disagreements over the the meaning of certain elements of the covenant, but the view that it truly was a *Covenant of Works,* usually including the concept of Federal Headship, quickly outdistanced other interpretations and became a fixed idea from the end of the 16th century into the 21st century. This view still receives affirmation from many modern theologians, such as Wayne Grudem, "Although the covenant that existed before the fall has been referred to by various terms (such as the "Adamic covenant," or the "covenant of nature") the most helpful designation seems to be the "covenant of works," since participation in the blessings of the covenant clearly depended on obedience or "works" on the part of Adam and Eve."[13]

Chapter Seven Notes

1. George Whitefield, "The Lord our Righteousness," *Selected Sermons of George Whitefield*. Sermon 14. (Oak Harbor, WA: Logos Research Systems, 1999), Logos e-book.

2. Jonathan Edwards, *Works of Jonathan Edwards* (Albany, OR: Ages Software, 1997), 5:388. Ages e-book.

3. That is, their fallen condition and need of a spiritual remedy.

4. Smith, *Systematic Theology*, 280.

5. John Murray, *Studies in Theology*, vol. 4 of Collected Writings of John Murray (Edinburgh: Banner of Truth, 1982), 217-218.

6. Brakel, *Christian's*, 1:355.

7. Herman Bavinck writes, "The relation in which Adam originally stood vis-à-vis God was even described by Augustine as a covenant, a testament, a pact [Augustine, City of God, XVI, 27.]; and the translation of the words kĕ'ādām by "like Adam" led many to a similar view." Bavinck refers the reader to J. Marck, Historia Paradisi (Amsterdam: Gerardus Borstius, 1705), 2: 6–7. Herman Bavinck, , John Bolt, , & John Vriend. *God and Creation*. Vol 2 of *Reformed Dogmatics* (Grand Rapids, MI: Baker Academic, 2004), 567.

8. Dewey D. Wallace, Jr. "Federal Theology," in *The Westminster Handbook to Reformed Theology*, ed. Donald K. McKim (Lousiville:

Westminster John Knox Press, 2002), 82. This definition is good, but I would suggest changing the word, "salvation," to "eternal life," even though there were theologians who used salvific language with Adam. Adam did not need salvation before he sinned, and soteriology is a concept introduced after he sinned. And second, though there were early Reformers who thought the ten commandments, or the whole moral law, were known to Adam, it is sufficient to say that the moral law was an ingredient in the composition of the image of God in man. Adam was created with exactly the same moral sense reflected in his Creator. But we do not know that God made known, viz, mentioned, any moral commandments to him before Adam sinned and before the power of sin began corrupting the human race to defy the moral image of God.

9. Robert Rollock, *Select Works of Robert Rollock* (Edinburgh: Wodrow Society, 1849), 1:34.

10. Watson Thomas. *A Body of Divinity.* (Grand Rapids: Christian Classics Ethereal Library, 2002), Q.12, PDF e-book.

11. Ibid

12. John Dick, *Lectures on Theology* (New York: Robert Carter and Brothers, 1851), 455.

13. Wayne A. Grudem, *Systematic Theology: An Introduction to Biblical Doctrine* (Grand Rapids: Zondervan, 1994), 517.

Eight
The Covenant of Works Doesn't Belong Here Anymore?

This chapter peers back into the mist to the beginning of the long road that Reformed covenant theology has traveled from the 16th to the 21st century. Nearly five hundred years is a long journey. But on the distant horizon behind us, the marks of the origin of covenant theology are still clearly seen along the trail emerging from the great landmark of that age, the Reformation. What began as a narrow path through the Scriptures in the early 16th century was so frequently traversed by an ever increasing number of wise pilgrims, that the Westminster Assembly in mid-17th century already saw a highway straightened and paved. Looking so far into the past, what is not so easy to discern are the footprints at the precise point on the trail that early trailblazers first perceived the Covenant of Works in the broad fields of prophetic revelation that lay on all sides of their journey.

By the time of Jonathan Edwards, the famous pastor of pioneers and early Americans, the Covenant of Works was a firmly established commonplace. Nearly every spiritual pilgrim hunting a square meal of grace frequented the "Inn of the Broken Covenant." It was common knowledge that the trail of the covenant of grace, leading throughout Scripture history to the Redeemer, begins where Adam broke the Covenant of Works that God made with him. This was the fruit of the earnest pursuits of 16th century Reformers who cast off the ignorance of past centuries, pursued truth with unflagging zeal, and unceasingly plumbed the depths of Scripture in their

119

thirst for the wisdom and knowledge of God. Their primary instructor, pointing out to them the *Covenant of Works* in the sacred pages, was the apostle Paul. Paul was the same master instructor whose lamp guided the church along the path of many earlier centuries, through Roman swords and lions to far off mountains and isolated islands, until the fires of Roman persecution were replaced by the victory chair of the Papacy. That great authority, the Roman Church, claiming to know all mysteries and all knowledge, buried this sacred foundation stone, the Covenant of Works, beneath mountains of superstitious traditions and rituals. It remained veiled in Scripture for centuries and was only finally uncovered when the generation of Reformers arose in the 16th century who left no stone unturned in the quest to discover every branch and twig of knowledge that God had hidden in His holy writ. This is the reason that Louis Berkhof comments: "The history of the doctrine of the covenant of works is comparatively brief. In the early Church Fathers the covenant idea is seldom found at all, *though the elements which it includes, namely, the probationary command, the freedom of choice, and the possibility of sin and death, are all mentioned...*"[1] For example, many today regard original sin to be the consequence of Adam's rebellion against the *Covenant of Works*. Early church fathers also held firm views on *original sin*. Their writings frequently describe the sin, condemnation, and need of salvation that all of Adam's fallen children have inherited, "even if their life is but one day."[2]

Berkhof *continues*, "In the scholastic literature and in the writings of the Reformers, too, all the elements which went into the construction of the doctrine of the covenant of works were already present, but the doctrine itself was not developed. The development of the doctrine of the covenant of grace preceded that of the doctrine of the covenant of works and paved the way for it."[3]

A Tree by Any Name is Still a Tree

Like the sacred Scriptures he studied, Paul himself never used the term, *Covenant of Works*, in any of his letters to the churches. Nevertheless, it is Paul's comments on the five books of Moses (the Torah) and his explanations of certain points of doctrine, which led the Reformers to eventually conclude that God established this pact with Adam which should be most properly titled, the *Covenant of Works*.

Huldrich Zwingli and Heinrich Bullinger were among the earliest theologians of the Reformation. Zwingli died in 1531, in a battle defending

120

Zurich from Roman Catholic aggressors. Both in his theological writings and in his correspondence he expressed ideas that would later be known as the federal headship of the two covenant fathers, Adam and Christ. "Federal headship" was coined to describe how Adam in the first covenant represented all humanity before God (in Romans 5:12ff) and how Christ represents in the new covenant all who are born of Him. According to Mark W. Karlberg, Zwingli taught "that in Adam all stand guilty. But what is lost in the first Adam by his transgression is restored in the second Adam, Jesus Christ, by way of his full and perfect obedience to the law of God. It is this obedience, viz., the righteousness of Christ, which is imputed to the believer as the ground of his justification."[4]

These two concepts are germane to any discussion comparing the "Covenant of Grace" and the "Covenant of Works:" first, that "what is lost in the first Adam by his transgression is restored in the second Adam," and second, that this restoration is accomplished through the "the righteousness of Christ, which is imputed to the believer as the ground of his justification." Its easy to see that Zwingli didn't invent these ideas, but they flowed from his studies of Scripture; for example, they are the center of Paul's discourse in Rom. 5:12-21, a passage which many regard to be a presentation of "federal headship". Herman Bavinck wrote that the Covenant of Works began to be understood by studying this very passage,

> "Paul with his parallel between Adam and Christ gave rise to thinking of the *status integritatis* [state of integrity] as a covenant. In distinction from the *foedus gratiae* [covenant of grace], then, this was named the *foedus naturae* or *operum* [covenant of nature or works]. It was called the covenant of nature not as if it sprung, of itself and naturally, from God's nature or that of man. Rather, it was called that because the foundation on which the covenant rested, that is, the moral law, was known to man by nature, and because it was established with man in his original state and could be kept by man with the capacities given to him by creation, without supernatural grace. When, later, this designation gave occasion for misunderstanding, it was replaced preferably by that of *foedus operum*, covenant of works; it bore this name because in this covenant eternal life was only to be gained in the way of works, that is, from keeping God's commandments. As parallel with the *foedus gratiae*, this covenant was now taught and developed by the Reformed with particular preference."[5]

121

To see how Romans 5:12-21 reveals the covenant of works, it's necessary to look into Paul's words in this passage. In v. 12, he writes "through one man sin entered the world, and death through sin, and thus death spread to all men, for all sinned." Adam, the "one man," sinned by disobeying the law of God in the garden and from him sin came to all mankind. To sin is to disobey the law of God. Death is the penalty for such sin, just as God said to Adam, "For in the day you eat of it, you will surely die." Paul writes that death reigned even over those who did not sin in the likeness of the transgression of Adam; in other words, they did not deliberately disobey a known law of God, *yet they all died*. According to Paul, this was the unhappy situation of all who were born from the time of Adam's fall to the coming of Moses, when the Law of Moses was given. There is a doctrinal paradox here that the apostle presents to his readers, summarized in these points:

1. Death is the penalty for breaking the Law. (6:23)

2. The Law was not established until Moses came. (5:13-14)

3. "Sin is not imputed where there is no law." (5:13)

4. Yet death reigned from Adam to Moses. (5:14)

Paul shows us this enigma so that we might ask the following question, "Well then, why *did* people prior to Moses die, if there was not yet a written law to condemn them for their many sins?" Verses 15-21 are his answer. By the use of a simple dichotomy, repeated several times, he shows the consequences that came to *all* the children of Adam by their father's *one sin* and the benefits that are bestowed on *all* those who are in Christ because of Christ's *one act of righteousness*. In Adam's one sin: "many died" (v. 15), "judgment" and "condemnation" came to all (v. 16), "death reigned" over all (v. 17), "judgment came to all men resulting in condemnation" (v. 18), and the "many were made sinners" (v. 19). On the opposite side of this equation stands Christ and all those who are in Him and are born of His Spirit. Paul declares that "through one Man's righteous act:" "the gift...by grace...abounded to many" (v. 15), "*the free gift*...resulted in justification" (v. 16), "those who receive abundance of grace and of *the gift of righteousness* will reign in life through the One, Jesus Christ" (v.17), "*the free gift* came to all men, resulting in justification of life" (v.18) and the "many will be made righteous" (v. 19).

These benefits that are communicated to all of His own because of the *"one righteous act"* of Christ refer to His death for the sins of His people to remove their guilt, but more than this, clearly describe his personal righteousness which is *imputed* directly to them all as "the free gift [that] came to all men." This *"free gift"* is not Christ's *"one righteous act,"* but is the reward the Father promised to give to the elect in the Covenant of Redemption. This name, *Covenant of Redemption*, is used by many theologians for the mysterious pact between the Father and the Son, established before time began, for the redemption of sinners. It is alluded to often by Christ:

> "… the works that the Father has given me to accomplish, the very works that I am doing, bear witness about me that the Father has sent me." (John 5:36; ESV)

> "… *My sheep hear my voice, and I know them*, and they follow me. I give them eternal life, and they will never perish, and no one will snatch them out of my hand. *My Father, who has given them to me*, is greater than all, and no one is able to snatch them out of the Father's hand." (John 10:27-29; ESV)

> "For I have not spoken on my own authority, but the Father who sent me has himself given me a commandment—what to say and what to speak. And I know that his commandment is eternal life. What I say, therefore, I say as the Father has told me." (John 12:49-50; ESV)

> "…but I do as the Father has commanded me, so that the world may know that I love the Father. Rise, let us go from here." (John 14:31; ESV)

In the covenant of redemption, God demands that His Son must die, in human form, bearing the guilt of His people as their representative. Upon fulfillment of this demand, God promised He would raise Christ from the dead, together with all who were "chosen in Him before the creation of the world" (Ephesians 1:4), granting them to share in Christ's life and resurrection, just as they had a share in His death, "If we died with Him, we shall also live with Him" (2 Tim. 2:11). Because they participate in Christ's righteousness, as members of Him, they truly live by faith in Christ alone. None of the elect were actually present locally, physically, or even spiritually at that real moment in history when the Lamb of God died for His own, so God credits all believers with the death of Christ as if they truly had been in Him at the cross. He bestows "the gift of righteousness" upon them as if they were actually part of Christ's own carnal nature and were present in Him when, as a perfectly sinless human, he rose from the dead, "because it was

123

impossible for death to keep its hold on him" (Acts 2:24, NIV84). Imputation first occurs in Christ bearing our sins. He was not actually present with the sinner, committing each lawless deed with them, but God charges His Son as truly guilty, imputing our sins to Christ as if He had committed each and every crime. Without imputation of our guilt upon Christ, His death would not benefit us. In the same way, in raising Christ from the dead, He continued to be our representative. But now the shoe must be on the other foot. As Christ could not die for us unless our sin was imputed to Him, making Him truly guilty with an alien sin, a sin not his own, so too, we could not be "raised up together with Christ" unless His righteousness was credited to us. As our representative, and the head of His body, the church, Christ was raised from the dead. As sharers in His righteousness and life, we were raised up with Him that "we may live a new life" (Romans 6:4b). "He was raised to life for our justification" (Romans 4:25b). But all believers were not physically with Him when He was resurrected, nor were they spiritually present. The benefits of His death, righteousness and resurrection must be credited to all of us who came along later. All those who freely receive "the gift of righteousness" (Romans 5:17) share in this justification. It is granted to all who are in Christ by virtue of His federal headship.

Let us look at imputation with respect to Christian baptism. In the New Testament, Christ represents His people before God. As the Lamb of God, He stood in their place, took their sin on His own head, and was nailed to the cross bearing their sentence of death. Paul indicates that this legal representation is symbolized by baptism. Baptism is a sign of the believer's unity with Christ at the cross of death, as Paul writes in Romans 6:3, "As many as were baptized, were baptized into His death." But water baptism doesn't truly unite a believer with Christ. Baptism is a visible sign of the work of the Holy Spirit, "By One Spirit you were baptized into one body." It is the Holy Spirit that truly unites believers with Christ, and literally makes us members of His spiritual body. He does this in our salvation thousands of years after Christ died and was raised. Yet from God's perspective believers are united with Christ in baptism at the very point of Christ's death, where He is nailed to the cross and hangs there bleeding, dying, and sprinkling with His blood all who are joined to Him. His bleeding is our bleeding. His death is our death. God credits it to us, regarding us from that point as if we had truly died. When this One Representative died, His death was credited to all who are spiritually in Him now, as if each one of them had actually been present in Christ and died at the cross with Him. Therefore, Paul comments, "One died for all, therefore all died." (2 Cor. 5) In Romans 6, Paul says, "Therefore, you are buried with Him, through baptism into His death." This is logic. If He represents us in His death at the cross, He also represents us in His burial. But dying and burial is not enough. There are nations which practice capital punishment, but when a criminal is put to death, no one declares that, because justice is satisfied, the dead man now has righteousness. Death does not make an unrighteous man righteous. This is the reason that Paul writes in Romans 5 of "the gift of righteousness" (v. 17) by which many who were not righteous were "made righteous" (v. 19), resulting in "justification that brings life" (v. 18).

Let us go a step further with the analogy of Christ representing us in baptism. Paul writes, "If we have been united with Him (the word is "baptized" in v. 3) like this in His death, we will certainly also be united with him in His resurrection" (Romans 6:5). If baptism means that Christ represented us when He died on the cross and represented us in His burial in the tomb, then He continues to represent us in His resurrection. Now the sin has already been paid in full. But there is this problem that we completely lack righteousness. We who were dead in sin have no inherent right to live again, or ascend into heavenly glory, even though our guilt has been washed away by His blood. We would still be like criminals who died, never having done anything truly worthy of life. But God who crucified us, imputing our sin to Christ, would not leave us lifeless in the cold tomb. It is His will to raise us from the dead together with Christ.

Continuing this analogy, let us gaze upon this crucified Christ. He has died for no sin of his own. There He lies, truly dead, a man who by His active obedience under the Law proved Himself worthy of eternal life. He is dead, but He is a sinless, righteous, worthy man who deserves to live and not be dead. It is only in this righteousness that the Father raises Him from the dead.

Now, let us consider again those united with Him in baptism. God the Father regards them as having died with Christ. Ephesians 2:4 states, "Because of the great love with which He loved us, even when we were dead in our transgressions, God made us alive together with Christ, it is by grace you have been saved." Christ's resurrection is the resurrection of all who died with Him, but none of us were actually present in Christ when God raised Him to life. If we will live with this righteous man, Jesus Christ, God must impute Christ's righteousness to us, in the same way that He imputed

125

our sin to Christ. This righteousness can come from nowhere else but Christ, He alone is our representative before God's bar of justice. He alone is raised from the dead. We are raised by God "together with Him" only if we are sharers in His righteousness and life. Yes of course, for we are *members* of His body.

Paul often describes the imputation of righteousness as a free gift. In Romans 3:21-24, he writes of the "righteousness of God, through faith in Jesus Christ, to all and on all who believe...being justified freely by His grace..." Later in the same letter, he makes clear that the "free gift" that comes to us "by the grace of the One Man, Jesus Christ" (Rom. 5:15), is "the gift of righteousness" (Rom. 5:17). To the Ephesians, he writes that salvation by grace through faith is "the gift of God, not of works, lest anyone should boast..." (Eph. 2:9). In his epistle to the Philippians, he rejoices that he is "found in [Christ], not having my own righteousness, which is from the law, but that which is through faith in Christ, the righteousness which is from God by faith..." (Phil. 3:9).

The idea that God reckons the righteousness of Christ *directly* to all who trust in Him is called "immediate imputation." Imputation is *immediate*, viz, direct, even to those who live thousands of years after Christ's death.

"Mediate imputation," would imply biological transmission of Christ's righteousness from one generation to the next generation. But there can be no thought of this with Christ and His people. The righteousness of Christ's children is imputed to them immediately, directly from the cross to the person who believes. Therefore, the guilt of Adam must also be imputed to His children immediately, otherwise the Romans 5 equation breaks down.

Several of the earlier 16th century Reformers expressed that the condemnation of Adam's descendants came by the mediate transmission of Adam's corruption. Adam was corrupt, he passed this corruption to his children, his children being corrupt were sinners, and thus they were guilty and were condemned for their personal sinfulness. But as Biblical scholars continued poring over Paul's words in Romans 5:12ff, they saw the concept of immediate imputation of Adam's guilt, and began to express this in their writings.

When we say that Adam's guilt was immediately imputed to his children, we mean that God charges every member of the human race with the guilt of Adam's one sin; in other words, the whole human race was condemned in Adam's rebellion because he was our first representative before God. All of Adam's children are pronounced guilty and condemned in the disobedience of this one man.

But God sent hope and life into the world. Christ, the Last Adam, now represents all believers before God. Every person who trusts in the One Man who died on their behalf, Jesus Christ, is declared righteous in the obedience of the One Man. Because He is our representative, our sin is imputed to Him, and His righteousness is imputed to us.

It has often been proposed that the justification which is granted to believers through sharing in the death and resurrection of Christ is communicated *only* through Christ's spiritual union with His people, rather than by imputation. It has already been shown that imputation is necessary, but exploring this further may strengthen this argument and clear some lingering doubts.

In 1 Cor. 15:21-22, Paul again compares the headship of Adam and Christ. The context has the spiritual union within view, when he writes, "Since by man came death, by man also came the resurrection of the dead. For as in Adam, all die, so also in Christ, all shall be made alive." This death, for all who are in Adam, came from Adam's one sin in a similar way that life for all who are in Christ came by Christ alone. Because the whole human race is "in Adam," every person faces the certainty of death. The authors of Holy Scripture, especially Paul, describe death as both spiritual and physical, and the apostle John additionally distinguishes between a first death and a second death. In Ephesians 2:1, Paul reveals that all who are in Adam are spiritually dead from conception to infancy, writing to all mankind, "And you were dead in your trespasses and sins..."[6] This is not a death of the physical body, but of the spiritual nature, for all who are alive bodily are dead spiritually. Those who are spiritually dead follow "the ways of this world," which are further described as the ways of "the prince of the power of the air, the spirit who now works in the sons of disobedience." Merely to be born with a sinful nature makes us spiritually "dead ... children of wrath, like the rest of mankind" (Eph. 2:3; ESV) When unsaved children of Adam die physically they are only passing from death to death.

But all who are in Christ shall be made alive. "For as in Adam, all die, so also in Christ, all shall be made alive" (1 Cor. 15:22). Incorporation into Christ's spiritual body is a life-giving union. It is the "first fruits of the Spirit" described by Paul in Romans 8:23, in which our spiritual nature, our inner man, is brought to life by Christ. But Romans 8:23 goes on to reveal that those who have been spiritually resurrected from death to life are still "waiting" for the "redemption of our bodies" to occur on that glorious day when we shall enter into "that which is life indeed". "If the Spirit of Him who raised Jesus from the dead dwells in you, He who raised Jesus from the dead will also give life to your mortal bodies through His Spirit who dwells in you" (Romans 8:10). More will be said of Romans 8:23ff later. But for now, it is necessary to understand that there is a *coming alive* for all who are joined to Christ. This is learned from Paul, "But because of His great love for us, God, who is rich in mercy, made us alive with Christ even when we were dead in transgressions, it is by grace you have been saved" (Romans 2:4-5). Understand that the spiritual union with Christ, and resurrection with Him, is *not* what is meant by *imputation*. The Biblical word, to *impute*, or to *reckon*, is to charge someone with guilt or credit someone with righteousness. Those who are spiritually joined to Christ are credited with righteousness, and thus justified, long before the union with Christ has finished its work of complete and eternal purification. When Paul says that all who are in Christ shall live, he adds that this will take place "at his coming." That is the day when all who are in Christ shall be made sinless, and therefore, literally no longer subject to physical death which is the wages of all sin.

To describe "imputation," Paul uses the examples of Abraham and David. In Romans 4:22, he quotes the Greek version of Gen. 15:6, where Abraham "believed in the Lord," and God "accounted it to him for righteousness." (Romans 4:22, NKJV) The word, *accounted,* is the Greek, ἐλογίσθη (from λογίζομαι) which means in this context, "to *charge* or *credit to* someone's account."[7] Paul employs the same term in the next verses, "Now it was not written for his sake alone that it was *imputed* to him, but also for us. It shall be *imputed* to us who believe in Him who raised up Jesus our Lord from the dead, who was delivered up because of our offenses, and was raised because of our justification." (Rom. 4:23-25) The apostle uses the term, *impute,* to describe the crediting of an alien righteousness to Abraham. In the same way, righteousness will be credited to all who believe in Him who raised Christ from the dead. He was raised, Paul says, for our justification. So it is seen that justification involves Christ rising from the dead because He is sinless, and the imputing of Christ's righteousness to the account of all who believe that Christ both died and was raised again for their own sake. Abraham, writes Paul, was not justified by works, but by a gracious gift (Rom. 4:1-3). Nor was David justified by works. According to his works David was unrighteous and worthy of death. Yet Paul says of him, "…David also describes the blessedness of the man to whom God imputes righteousness apart from works: *"Blessed are those whose lawless deeds are forgiven, and whose sins are covered; blessed is the man to whom the Lord shall not impute sin"* (Romans 4:6-8, NKJV).

It is important to see that this imputation of righteousness is not a *recognition* that someone is righteous or has become righteous. Through the imputation of righteousness, God is not justifying the self-righteous, but He does justify the ungodly and sinners, just as the apostle writes in Rom. 4:5, "…to him who does not work but believes in Him who justifies the ungodly, his faith is accounted as righteousness." (NKJV). Righteousness is imputed to the ungodly who sincerely repent, confessing their sins and trusting in Jesus Christ for salvation. On the basis of this imputed righteousness they are justified before God. They believe in Him who justifies the ungodly. Therefore, there must be conviction of sin, and acknowledgement of ungodliness.

Furthermore, it should not be thought that imputation makes someone inherently righteous any more than charging a person with guilt is what *made* him unrighteous. Christ was most certainly not *made* *unrighteous* when our sins were imputed to him, at least not in the literal sense of that word; His nature was incorruptible. When God credited Abraham with righteousness, he still had a sinful nature. When God imputes righteousness to those who trust in Christ, they continue to struggle with the sin that comes from their own hearts. In the same way, charging Adam's descendants with the guilt of Adam did not make them inherently unrighteous. They each inherited the corrupt nature from Adam.

When the first man's guilt was imputed to his descendants, that guilt already existed in Adam. With the imputation of righteousness, there must be a righteousness already existing in Christ, pure and free from sin, which can be credited to a person who lacks it. Spiritual union with Christ does not transform an individual from a sinful state to a perfectly sinless state, at least not *instantly*, but imputation of righteousness is instant. Those who are joined to Christ are saved in the hope of the redemption of their body, which God will raise from the dead incorruptible *on the last day*. Until that perfect day, those united with Christ are imperfect, struggling with sin and consciously aware of their inherent sinfulness. If they will be righteous in God's sight *today*, then a righteousness must be imputed to them, an *alien righteousness*. At the risk of being redundant, the term *alien righteousness* is

129

used because this righteousness is different than our natural sinful condition, it is the incorruptible righteousness of Christ, credited to the believer. Therefore, Paul frequently refers to it as the "righteousness of God." It is the righteousness that comes not from ourselves, but is given by God to us. This concept was broadly understood in the sixteenth century. Richard Hooker, appointed to preach at the London Temple in 1585, was in his day accused of expressing too weakly the doctrine of justification through the imputed righteousness of Christ. Yet he wrote,

> "...the righteousness wherein we must be found, if we will be justified, is not our own: therefore we cannot be justified by any inherent quality. Christ hath merited righteousness for as many as are found in him. In him God findeth us, if we be faithful, for by faith we are incorporated into him."[8]

Zwingli believed in righteousness by faith, but it was his successor, Henry Bullinger (1504-1575), who wrote clearly and extensively of justification based on the imputed righteousness of Christ. His understanding is expressed in the Second Helvetic Confession which he authored. When we read the Second Helvetic article on justification, it is clear that Bullinger had no problem understanding Christ's side of the comparison Paul sets up in Romans 5. He writes, "For Christ took upon himself and bore the sins of the world, and satisfied divine justice. Therefore, solely on account of Christ's sufferings and resurrection God is propitious with respect to our sins and does not impute them to us, but imputes Christ's righteousness to us as our own (II Cor. 5;19 ff.; Rom. 4;25), so that now we are not only cleansed and purged from sins or are holy, but also, granted the righteousness of Christ, and so absolved from sin, death and condemnation, are at last righteous and heirs of eternal life. Properly speaking, therefore, God alone justifies us, and justifies only on account of Christ, not imputing sins to us but imputing his righteousness to us."[9]

On the basis of Christ's one righteous act, believers are imputed with Christ's righteousness as a free gift by the grace of God and on this basis they are justified. They did not establish this righteousness themselves. They did not engage in any good works that might have merited it (if it were possible for sinners to merit righteousness). The Scripture declares that it is not by works of righteousness that we have done that He saved us (Titus 3:5, 7).

Bullinger didn't carry this concept of imputation over to the other side of the Romans 5 equation. He writes of our inclusion in Adam and of the transmission of his corruption along familial lines, but comes short of plainly stating that Adam's guilt was imputed to his children in the same way that Christ's righteousness is imputed to his. In Romans 5, however, Paul has set up a balanced equation, five times declaring the consequences that Adam's single sin has communicated to all his descendants and five times describing the blessings that Christ's one act, alone, has accomplished for all of *his* children.

It might be argued that early Reformers, such as Calvin, Zwingli, and Bullinger, were too close to the edge of that great gulf of spiritual darkness that lay behind them. They were really not far from expressing the "Covenant of Works" idea themselves, for they had seen and understood many features (of Adam's relationship with God) that would soon bring the *Covenant of Works* out of hiding. For example, Bullinger understood that there was one eternal plan of salvation, one Covenant of Grace, which was presented in successive stages of revelation, first to Adam immediately after the fall and then to Noah, Abraham, Israel, David, until it was finally fulfilled in its entirety with the coming of Christ.[10]

With respect to Adam, he understood that the law, restricting him from eating from one of the trees, was a plain test of obedience,[11] Adam being the best example that the chief thing God looks for in man is faith and obedience.[12] Disobedience plunged all mankind into death under the curse, and subject to spiritual bondage.[13] He saw that the fall of Adam is the original cause of sin that has been communicated to the entire human race.[14]

At this earlier stage of covenant studies, both Bullinger and Zwingli are thought to have used the the terminology, "original sin," only of Adam's *corruption afflicting all mankind*, for which all stand personally guilty. They were not using this expression as Reformed Theology did later in the 16th century, to describe the imputation of Adam's guilt to his descendants. Bullinger presents Zwingli's position as follows: "...the learned and godly man of famous memory, Ulderick Zuinglius , did diligently distinguish betwixt sin and disease or infirmity, when once he had occasion to dispute of original sin, which he chose rather to call a disease than sin: because by the name of sin all men do understand the naughty act committed by our own consent and will against the law of God; but by the name of disease or sickness they understand a certain corruption and depravation of the nature that was created good, and the miserable condition of bondage whereinto it is brought: even as also we read before, that Augustine did call this original sin *peccatum alienum*, another's sin, that thereby he might give us to understand that it is hereditary, and doth descend from others into us; and yet he denied not but it is proper to every several one of us. In like manner Zuinglius denied not original sin, as some did falsely slander him..."[15] So it can be seen that Zwinglius regarded "original sin" as the cause of man's personal "corruption," "deprivation of...nature," and "bondage," agreeing with Augustine that it is "alien sin," the sin of another. It is not completely clear that his understanding of the "sin of another" included the guilt of Adam imputed to all.

Bullinger does mention "original guilt" in his own theological writings, but the context surrounding his use of this term suggests that the guilt he refers to has resulted from the *natural corruption* of original sin, rather than by immediate imputation. He wrote, "For what is he that hath not some whiles felt concupiscence? Yea, what is he, that is not every hour and moment pricked with the sting of fleshly concupiscence? What man is there, I pray you, that is not diseased with the natural sickness common to us all, *and spotted with the blemish of original guiltiness*? Being wherefore convinced of sin before the Lord, we are not able to excuse our fault, nor escape the sentence of the judge that doth condemn all flesh. For the just Lord doth expressly condemn our natural corruption and wicked inclination, which is a continual turning from God, and rebellion against the sincerity which he requireth at our hands."[16]

Karlberg explains that it was Bullinger's understanding of the *Covenant of Grace* that paved the way for others after him to comprehend the *Covenant of Works*:

> "Did Bullinger conceive of the special command not to eat of the tree of the knowledge of good and evil to be part of an original covenant between God and Adam, wherein Adam was promised eternal life if he proved faithful to the commandment(s) of God and eternal death if he proved unfaithful? With one possible exception (what seems to be an *allusion* to an original covenant at creation), the idea of a prelapsarian covenant is not to be found in Bullinger's writings ... However, the underlying antithesis between the law and the gospel is crucial to Bullinger's exposition of the one and eternal covenant of grace. The historical-covenantal contrast between "letter" and "Spirit" provides ingredients for the ensuing doctrine of the two covenants, the covenant of works and the covenant of grace, that would eventually become the staple of Reformed dogmatics from the late sixteenth to the twentieth centuries."[17]

132

R. Scott Clark has highlighted another Swiss Reformer, Oecolampadius, an early Reformer whose understanding of covenant theology was more advanced than Zwingli, Bullinger, and others, "For the time, Oecolampadius taught a remarkably mature covenant theology including the doctrine of the covenant of redemption, the covenant of works and the covenant of grace. Indeed, the great Reformed theologian Amandus Polanus considered Oecolampadius the first Reformed covenant theologian."[18]

Oecolampadius died in 1531. Following close on his heels were the framers of the Heidelberg Catechism, Caspar Olevianus (1536-1587) and Zacharias Ursinus (1534-1583). Bullinger, mentioned above, reviewed their catechism. The *Encyclopedia of the Reformed Faith* attributes these two with *discovering* the Adamic covenant introduced earlier by Oecolampadius, "A new idea entered covenant thinking at the end of the sixteenth century with the appearance of a covenant of works separate from and antecedent to the covenant of grace. This view first appeared with the Heidelberg theologians Zacharius Ursinus, Caspar Olevianus, and Franciscus Junius (1545-1602), then with those who came under their influence, including the English Puritans Thomas Cartwright (1535-1603) and Dudley Fenner (c. 1558–1587). Later Reformed scholastic theologians further developed it."[19]

Olevianus and Ursinus understood that a sinner is justified, viz, "made right with God," purely as a gift of God's grace through faith in Christ. In the Heidelberg Catechism they pose the question, "How are you made right with God?" (q. 60) Their answer clearly shows their belief in the doctrine of imputation, "Only by true faith in Jesus Christ," adding , "…without my deserving it at all, out of sheer grace, God grants and credits to me the perfect satisfaction, righteousness and holiness of Christ, as if I had never sinned nor been a sinner, as if I had been as perfectly obedient as Christ was obedient for me."[20]

Building on the foundation of their predecessors, they were among the first to balance the scale by recognizing the Covenant of Works. For example, Olevianus saw contained in the Law of Moses, the reintroduction of a covenant God first established with Adam. Lyle Bierma writes, "The *foedus legale* for Olevian is really no more than a postlapsarian[21] renewal or reiteration of the *foedus creationis*, the obligation placed upon mankind at creation to conform to the righteousness and holiness of his Creator. This *pactum*, he says, was established at Mount Sinai following Israel's deliverance from Egypt and obligated the people of God to perfect obedience

133

of the law through the exercise of their own moral powers. Those who kept the commandments were promised eternal life; those who did not stood under the wrath of God's curse.[22]

It was Zacharias Ursinus who was "the first to clearly articulate the Covenant of Works,"[23] though not yet referring to it by that name. In his Larger Catechism (1562), published a year earlier than the Heidelberg Catechism (1563), he referred to it as "the Covenant of Nature," describing it first in Question 10, "What does the divine law teach? Ursinus answered, "It teaches the kind of covenant God established with man in creation, how man behaved in keeping it, and what God requires of him after establishing the new covenant of grace with him…"[24]

In Question 23 of his Larger Catechism, he writes, "The law contains the covenant of nature established by God with man in creation; that means, it is known by man from nature, it requires perfect obedience of us to God, and it promises eternal life to those who keep it but threatens eternal punishment to those who do not."[25]

His Commentary on the Heidelberg Catechism refers to this earlier catechism, where he mentions a Covenant of Works that demanded perfect obedience:

> "… we may say that the justice of God does not render good according to works which are imperfect, if he judges according to the covenant of perfect obedience to the law. But Christ, in rewarding the works of the saints, will not judge according to the covenant of perfect works,[26] but according to the covenant of faith, or of his own righteousness imputed and applied to them by faith ; and yet he will judge them according to their works, as according to the evidences of their faith, from which their works have proceeded, and which they, as the fruits of this faith, declare to be in them."[27]

The reference to "the covenant of perfect works" belongs to a time much earlier than the official publication of the Commentary in 1591, since the entire work was the culmination of notes he developed by expounding the entire Catechism annually until 1577. The commentary was first published by his students' from their notes soon after his death. Ursinus' close friend, Jacob Pareus, was elected to edit a more accurate official version, released in 1591.[28]

Ursinus' saw an integral unity in God's Law, expressed in Question Four of the Heidelberg Catechism, "What does the law of God require of us?"[29]   The answer, Christ's response in Matthew 22, reveals that the essence of the Law is genuine love for God and man: "Jesus said to him, *'You shall love the Lord your God with all your heart, with all your soul, and with all your mind.'* This is *the* first and great commandment. And *the* second *is* like it: *'You shall love your neighbor as yourself.'* On these two commandments hang all the Law and the Prophets." (quotation is from Matthew 22, NKJV)

Since every law depends on these two commands, there is a vital connection between them and the single law presented to Adam in Eden, "Of the tree of the knowledge of good and evil you shall not eat." This negative prohibition was, above all, a demand that Adam demonstrate his love for God by perfect obedience.

After the foundation had been laid by these Reformers, there were numerous attempts to pursue further details of the Covenant of Works. Amandus Polanus (1561-1610), a professor of theology at Basle; Francis Gomarus (1563-1641), a Reformed professor at Leyden; and Johannes Wollebius each taught a *Covenant of Works/Covenant of Grace* model. All three were important theologians. Gomarus began to oppose Arminius when the latter was a new colleague in the seminary, and arose to be the most virulent opposer of Arminianism at the Synod of Dort. Today, some propose it was Polanus who first coined the term, *Covenant of Works*, though he was a child when Ursinus proposed a Covenant of Works. A concise theology written by Wollebius, the "Compendium Theologies Christianae (1626), a volume of only 273 pages, was a textbook at Basle and other seminaries and was required study in early years of Yale and Harvard, being "a masterpiece of compact brevity, clear arrangement, and thorough comprehensiveness as respects all important doctrinal matters."[30]

With an ever-increasing number of theologians searching the Scriptures "to see if these things were so," the *Covenant of Works* began to settle down on solid ground much broader than only the first few chapters of Genesis.   Much more data had become relevant with the conclusion mentioned by Ursinus, that the Sinai covenant actually reintroduced the substance of the Adamic covenant while at the same time offering hope by presenting elements of the Covenant of Grace.

But there were some in this time period who disagreed. One such dissenter was the Dutch theologian, Jacobus Arminius (1560-1609). He rose in popularity near the end of the 16th century challenging certain points of the Reformed creeds, *The Heidelberg Catechism* and *The Belgic Confession of*

Faith. In retrospect, Arminius seems to have been appointed by the Sovereign God to provoke more cautious and earnest examination of Scripture from the Reformed churches, ultimately resulting in the superbly composed creed and refutation of Arminius, known as *The Canons of Dort.* Arminius also instigated debate over the doctrine of original sin, suggesting that the condemnation of the human race consisted only in the "absence of original righteousness," and not in anything else such as the imputation of original guilt to Adam's seed:

> "But because the condition of the covenant into which God entered with our first parents was this, that, if they continued in the favour and grace of God by an observance of this command and of others, the gifts conferred on them should be transmitted to their posterity, by the same divine grace which they had, themselves, received; but that, if by disobedience they rendered themselves unworthy of those blessings, their posterity, likewise, should not possess them, and should be liable to the contrary evils. This was the reason why all men, who were to be propagated from them in a natural way, became obnoxious to death temporal and death eternal, and devoid of this gift of the Holy Spirit or original righteousness. This punishment usually receives the appellation of "a privation of the image of God," and "original sin."

> "But we permit this question to be made a subject of discussion: Must some contrary quality, beside the absence of original righteousness, be constituted as another part of original sin? Though we think it much more probable, that this absence of original righteousness, only, is original sin, itself, as being that which alone is sufficient to commit and produce any actual sins whatsoever."[31]

Arminius' remarks demonstrate the growing conviction among all the Reformed churches that God had indeed established a covenant with Adam and his descendants. His remarks show that the most debated point was not the legitimacy of such a covenant but the extent to which Adam's guilt and corruption was communicated to all of his offspring. Arminius held that Adam's children share only in his corruption (thus depriving themselves of "original righteousness"), but have no part in the personal guilt of their father. Arminius was contending against a view that was already becoming popular, that Adam's guilt was imputed directly to all of his descendants. Imputation was one of the main points of the Covenant of Works, a teaching that was becoming widespread.

Wesley White demonstrates an example of this growing popularity. He writes,

"In 1575, the Prince of Orange established the University of Leiden which became the center of theological education in the Netherlands. One of the earliest theologians of that University, Franciscus Junius, explicitly and fully taught the covenant of works. Junius taught at Leiden from 1592 until his death in 1602. Junius, according to the regular custom of the time, set forth his teaching in various theses, which were delivered in the form of a discussion or disputation. In his Leiden Theses "On the Covenant and Testament of God," Junius stated that in Scripture there are two covenants corresponding to the "two states of men, namely, the state of integrity when he was created by God and the state of corruption arising from man's fall by his own choice" (Thesis 2, p. 183). He defines the first covenant as that which God "...entered into with our first parents in the Garden of Eden in which He promised to them supernatural life and bound them to reverence, worship, and obey Him, adding to it the threat of death if they did otherwise" (Thesis 3).[32]

It is significant that the Synod of Dort, which convened from 1618 to 1619 to address the spreading opinions of Arminius, wrote the following as the first words of their answer, "As all men have sinned in Adam, lie under the curse, and are deserving of eternal death, God would have done no injustice by leaving them all to perish and delivering them over to condemnation on account of sin..."[33] The words, "all men have sinned in Adam," indicate that all mankind participated in Adam's sin and thus in his guilt. Therefore, guilty of man's first sin they lay under the curse of condemnation and death. Although the Canons come short of stating that there was an actual covenant made with Adam, the synod wrote of him as if he was the representative of all mankind, preferring to describe him with the English term, "man," rather than by his particular name, "Adam":

"Man was originally formed after the image of God. His understanding was adorned with a true and saving knowledge of his Creator, and of spiritual things; his heart and will were upright, all his affections pure, and the whole man was holy. But, revolting from God by the instigation of the devil and by his own free will, he forfeited these excellent gifts; and in the place thereof became involved in blindness of mind, horrible darkness, vanity, and perverseness of judgment; became wicked, rebellious, and obdurate

137

in heart and will, and impure in his affections."[34]

In this text, the Synod of Dort declares that the sin of Adam, and its consequences, belong to "man," a term that is synecdoche for all mankind, the entire human race.

In the Synod's "rejection of certain errors" related to man's fall and corruption, the first paragraph appears to be particularly aimed at Arminius' opinions (expressed above): "The true doctrine having been explained, the Synod rejects the *errors* of those who teach: That it cannot properly be said that original sin in itself suffices to condemn the whole human race or to deserve temporal and eternal punishment".[35]

The Synod presented the apostle Paul as the chief representative of their position, insisting that those who hold to the mentioned error "contradict the apostle, who declares: *Therefore, as through one man sin entered into the world, and death through sin; and so death passed unto all men, for that all sinned.* (Rom. 5:12). And: *The judgment came of one unto condemnation* (Rom. 5:16). And: *The wages of sin is death.* (Rom. 6:23)."[36]

It is not difficult to see that the Covenant of Works concept was already broadly known at the time of the writing of The Heidelberg Catechism and the Canons of Dort, but unanimity that it be regarded a confessional truth was lacking at this early stage.

One of the chief defenders of Arminianism at the Synod of Dort was Episcopius, a theologian and leader of the Remonstrants. After the Synod "silenced" his views, he argued against the Covenant of Works until his death in 1643, and others in the Remonstrant party continued pressing the attack after his passing. Episcopius insisted that in God's relations with Adam, "there were commands, but only commands with warnings; there was no stipulation or promise without which there can be no covenant properly so-called" (*Institutiones Theologicae* in *Works of Episcopius*, 23).[37] Wesley White explains that "the result of the Remonstrant attack on the covenant of works was a widespread defense of this doctrine by the Reformed theologians in the 17th century," especially by such theologians as Johannes Cloppenburg and Johannes Coccejus. This resulted in the Adamic covenant becoming increasingly popular in the early seventeenth century, but at first without broad agreement that it was a *covenant of works*. Prior to the Westminster Assembly (1643 to 1649) Samuel Bolton described four different popular views for understanding the divine covenants:[38]

1. "Those who recognized a covenant of nature, a covenant of grace,

and a covenant mixed with nature and grace."

2. "Those who recognized a *foedus natura* (covenant of nature) made with man before the Fall, a *foedus promissi* (covenant of promise) made with Adam after the Fall, and a *foedus operi*, a covenant of works made with the Jews at Sinai."

3. "Those who recognized a *foedus natura* made with man before the Fall, a *foedus gratiae* (a covenant of grace made with us in Christ), and a *foedus subserviens* (subservient covenant) made with the Jews at Sinai."

4. "Those who never did recognize but two covenants, one of works before the Fall and one of grace after, "Yet…this covenant of grace was dispensed to the Jews in such a legal manner that it seems to be nothing else but the repetition of the covenant of works."

All of these perspectives acknowledged a covenant between God and Adam, but only one, the last, assigned to it the title, the *Covenant of Works*. Argument and debate ran its course and by the time the Westminster Assembly was called together, the *Covenant of Works* concept first understood in the Netherlands had become widely accepted, not only among Presbyterian churches of Great Britain and Reformed churches of the European Continent, but in some other branches of Protestantism as well. White comments on the broad consent that continued in the Netherlands, "When we examine the major streams of Reformed theology in the Netherlands in the 17th century, we see that all three major streams affirmed and defended the covenant of works. According to J. van den Berg, there were three major streams of thought in Reformed theology in the 17th century (Broeyer and van der Wall, *Een richtingenstrijd*, 16-17). They were the Cocceian, following Johannes Cocceius at Franeker and then Leiden; the Voetian, following the Utrecht professor Gisbertus Voetius; and the traditional stream, best represented by Samuel Maresius at Groningen. The last two eventually merged together … Whatever other difference there may have been, they all defended the covenant of works."[39]

In Great Britain, it remained for the Westminster Assembly to determine whether this relatively recent understanding of Scripture was to be regarded as Confessional, i.e., as truth beyond doubt, to be believed and confessed by all.

The Westminster assembly has been lauded as among the most significant in the history of the church, not only because of the number of notable participants recognized for their wisdom and erudition, but because of the exceptional creed they furnished to the world. That document, the Westminster Confession of Faith, (WKF, 1646), devotes an entire chapter to "God's Covenant with Man," and another to "The Law of God." It is in these chapters that the Covenant of Works at last found its rightful place among other orthodox Christian doctrines, "rightful" because it is as much a doctrine of Scripture as any other, even though it was placed in the sacred Word as a mystery to be discovered by diligent disciples of Scripture.

In Chapter Seven, the Confession provides only a few details, suggesting that the *fact* of the Covenant of Works is certainly confessional. But the obscurity of this covenant in Scripture demands little more from man's faith than the recognition that it mainly consisted of law that required "perfect and personal obedience."[40] The obscurity in Scripture may be intentional because the Covenant of Works can no longer be man's way of salvation and life: (Article 2) *"The first covenant made with man was a covenant of works, (Gal. 3:12) wherein life was promised to Adam; and in him to his posterity, (Rom. 10:5, Rom. 5:12–20) upon condition of perfect and personal obedience. (Gen. 2:17, Gal. 3:10)."* Article 3 adds only that *"Man, by his fall, having made himself incapable of life by that covenant, the Lord was pleased to make a second..."*[41]

With the exception of Gal. 3:10, where the historical account of this covenant was first recorded, the supporting verse references for WCF Article 2 are not from the Old Testament, nor from the words of the Lord in the gospels, *but are drawn exclusively from the epistles of Paul*, as if to say that it is from this single inspired teacher that the entire Assembly was convinced of the legitimacy and basic substance of this covenant. Therefore, it is necessary that we look into these words of Paul (from these supporting texts: Gal. 3:12; Rom. 10:5, Rom. 5:12–20; Gen. 2:17, Gal. 3:10) if we will comprehend the assembly's understanding of the *covenant of works*.[42]

Paul seems to imply that it is possible to establish righteousness by works in Galatians 3:12, "...the law is not of faith, but *the man who does them shall live by them."* The apostle expresses the same idea in his letter to the Romans, "For Moses writes about the righteousness which is of the law, *"The man who does those things shall live by them."* But in Gal. 3:10-11, he destroys all hope of achieving self-righteousness, "For as many as are of the works of the law are under the curse; for it is written, *"Cursed is everyone who does not continue in all things which are written in the book of the law, to do them."* But that no one is justified by the law in the sight of God *is* evident, for *"the just shall live by faith."* (NKJV)

These statements describe the obligation to perfectly obey the Law, the condemnation of those who disobey, and the promise of life to those who faithfully do the works of the Law. The same obligation and promise was implied in God's covenant with Adam, in Gen. 2:17, "… but of the tree of the knowledge of good and evil you shall not eat, for in the day that you eat of it you shall surely die."

The fact that the Westminster Assembly used these particular verses to substantiate the *Covenant of Works* is a reflection of how they viewed the Law of Moses. WCF, Chapter Nineteen, states that "the Law of God," *is* the covenant of works, (Article 1) "God gave to Adam a law, as a *covenant of works*, by which He bound him and all his posterity, to personal, entire, exact, and perpetual obedience, promised life upon the fulfilling, and threatened death upon the breach of it, and endued him with power and ability to keep it. (Gen. 1:26–27, Gen. 2:17, Rom. 2:14–15, Rom. 10:5, Rom. 5:12, 19, Gal. 3:10,12, Eccl. 7:29, Job 28:28)" The second article of WCF Chapter Nineteen explains the place of this same Law in the Sinai covenant: "This law, after his fall, continued to be a perfect rule of righteousness; and, as such, was delivered by God upon Mount Sinai, in ten commandments, and written in two tables: (James 1:25, James 2:8,10–12, Rom. 13:8–9, Deut. 5:32, Deut. 10:4, Exod. 34:1) the first four commandments containing our duty towards God; and the other six, our duty to man. (Matt. 22:37–40)"[43]

If the covenant of Law was first made with Adam, and was later revealed again in an expanded form at Sinai, it is easy to see why. The Covenant of Works is so vaguely detailed in Genesis and so long ago, that it was necessary to revive its essential points in order that it might be more readily taught that justification, when based on works of the law, demands perfect obedience. It was Paul's writings, from such statements as this: the "law is not of faith" "but of works", which convinced scholars that the first covenant, which was a covenant of the law, was indeed a *Covenant of Works*.

Chapter Eight Notes

1. L. Berkhof, *Systematic Theology* (Grand Rapids: Eerdmans, 1938), 211.

2. Examples of this can be found in the writings of Origen, "Homily 8 in Leviticus 12," "Homily in Luke 14," "Homily 9 in Joshua;" and in Augustine, "Anti-Pelagian Works, A Treatise on Forgiveness of Sins and Infant Baptism," Book 1, "Chapter 33 - Christ Is the Savior and Redeemer Even of Infants."

3. Ibid

4. Mark W. Karlberg, "Reformed Interpretation of the Mosaic Covenant," *Westminster Theological Journal 43*, no. 1 (Fall 1980): 8, Logos e-book.

5. Herman Bavinck, "Gereformeerde Dogmatiek, Vol. 2:528-529," quoted in *Creator, Redeemer Consummator: A Festschrift for Meredith G. Kline*, trans. Richard Gaffin, eds. Griffith and Muether (City: Reformed Academic Press, 2000).

6. Translation mine, from *NA26th Ed. Greek New Testament*.

7. *Analytical Lexicon of the Greek New Testament*.

8. Richard Hooker, "A Sermon by Richard Hooker with Introductory comments by James Kiefer." http://elvis.rowan.edu/~kilroy/christia/library/hooker-learned.htm (accessed June 16, 2011).

9. *Second Helvetic Confession*.

10. Bullinger, *Decades*,2:169.

11. Ibid, 211

12. Ibid, 350-351.

13. Ibid, 304-305.

14. Ibid, 368-399.

15. Ibid, 397-398.

16. Ibid

17. Mark Karlberg, "Covenant Theology and the Westminster Tradition." *Westminster Theological Journal 54*, no. 1 (Spring 1992), 141, Logos e-book.

18. R. Scott Clark, "A Brief History of Covenant Theology." (R.S. Clark, 2001). http://clark.wscal.edu/briefhistorycovtheol.php (accessed

June 16, 2011).

19. Donald K. McKim and David F. Wright, *Encyclopedia of the Reformed Faith*, 1st ed. (Louisville:Westminster/John Knox Press, 1992), 136.

20. *The Heidelberg Catechism*, Lord's Day 23, QA 60.

21. Postlapsarian means "after the fall," that is, the fall of Adam.

22. Lyle D. Bierma, "The Covenant Theology of Caspar Olevian," quoted in Mark W. Karlberg *Westminster Theological Journal 54*, no. 1 (Spring 1992): 145, Logos e-book. Bierma writes this of Olevianus' covenant theology, "Because God is immutably righteous and true, He accepts us into the covenant of grace only in such a way that the integrity of the covenant of nature is preserved. He does not deem us just or award us eternal life unless we conform perfectly to the standards of righteousness required in the foedus naturale or, failing that, unless someone else satisfies the stipulations of the law in our stead. Hence the covenant of grace complements the covenant of nature" (p. 87; cf. also p. 183). Karlberg says that "Weir is not persuaded that Bierma interprets this element in Olevianus' theology accurately. At this point he finds "inherent difficulties in Bierma's methodology" ("Foedus Naturale: The Origins of Federal Theology in Sixteenth Century Reformation Thought" [Ph.D. dissertation, University of St. Andrews, 1984] 165-66). Both Lillback and Weir share a similar understanding of the relationship between law and gospel, from which viewpoint Lillback asserts that "the covenant of creation [in Olevianus' thinking] is not radically opposed to the covenant of grace in the Christian's life. The covenant of creation which was the beginning of man's duty to live before God in His law is still the very 'demand' of the 'new covenant of grace'" ("The Binding of God," 458). Lillback derives the same teaching from his reading of Calvin. But Lillback's interpretation amounts to a misreading of Olevianus and Calvin, one which appears to obscure the biblical antithesis between law and gospel."

23. Ronald M. Johnson, "Covenant Hermeneutics," *Conservative Theological Journal 3* (2002), p. 321-322.

24. Zacharias Ursinus, "Zacharias Ursinus' Large and Small Catechisms, Harmonized with the Heidelberg Catechism." Translated by Fred H. Klooster and John Medendorp. http://links.christreformed.org/doctrinevision/ursinus_project.pdf (accessed June 9, 2011).

25. Ibid., 22.

26. Italics in this paragraph are my own—STP.

27. Zacharias Ursinus, *The Commentary of Zacharias Ursinus on the Heidelberg Catechism* (Cincinnati : Elm Street Print., 1888), 609-610.

28. John Williamson Nevin, *Introduction to The Commentary of Zacharias Ursinus on the Heidelberg Catechism*, trans. G. W. Williard, (Cincinnati: Elm Street Print., 1888), xix.

29. *Historic Creeds and Confessions* (Oak Harbor: Logos Research Systems, Inc., 1997), Article 12, Logos e-book.

30. *McClintock-Strong Cyclopedia.*

31. James Arminius, *The Works of James Arminius*, trans. by James Nichols (Albany, OR: Ages Software, 1997), 2:77, Ages e-book.. It is worth noting that John Wesley, history's foremost promoter of Arminius' teaching, at first agreed with his mentor, that Adam's posterity shares in the corruption of their first father, but not in his guilt. Later, perhaps through his frequent correspondence with his friend, George Whitefield, Wesley eventually retracted this position and affirmed his agreement that both aspects of original sin—ie. guilt and corruption—belonged to Adam's seed.

32. Wesley White, "The Dutch Reformed Doctrine of the Covenant of Works," under the *Johannes Weslianus blog*, entry posted February 6, 2008, http://www.weswhite.net/2008/02/dutch-reformed-doctrine-of-covenant-of/ (Accessed June 10, 2011).

33. *The Canons of Dort*, "First Head of Doctrine: Divine Election and Reprobation," Article 1.

34. Ibid, "The Third and Fourth Heads of Doctrine: The Corruption of Man, His Conversion to God, and the Manner Thereof," Article 1.

35. Ibid, "Third and Fourth Heads of Doctrine: Rejection of Errors, Paragraph 1."

36. But while this passage of Scripture presents Adam's single sin as the direct cause of the condemnation of all his descendants, it is not clear if the assembly understood by this the immediate imputation of Adam's guilt, for their purpose had been to explain the spread of Adam's corruption to the entire human race.

37. White, "Dutch Reformed," blog.

38. T. David Gordon, "Critique of Theonomy: A Taxonomy." *Westminster Theological Journal 56*, no.1 (Spring 1994): 34, Logos e-book.

39. White, "Dutch Reformed."

40. As Ursinus had observed nearly a century earlier.

41. Ibid, 2.

42. Romans 5:12 has been discussed in a previous section.

43. *The Westminster Confession of Faith* (Oak Harbor, WA: Logos Research Systems, Inc., 1996), 19: 2.

Nine
Why These Features in Sinai?

Observations on the Covenant of Works and the Sinai Covenant

In the previous chapter, it was observed that many in Reformed theology have concluded that the Sinai Covenant really is the Covenant of Grace. In addition it contains *a presentation of the Covenant of Works*[1] as a teaching device to lead the sinner first to the hopelessness of works and afterward to the confidence of grace. This was the understanding of Paul even if he never used the terminology of "Covenant of Works". Therefore, it was only natural for the Reformers to discover this in Paul as their understanding of covenant theology grew through the study of Scripture. In the late 16th century, Robert Rollock wrote of this, "For so the covenant of works, and the rule of the law of works, must be set before every one which is without Christ, seeking righteousness by the law, and the works of the law, to this end, if it may be, that by the sense of sin, and the feeling of misery, he may be prepared to embrace the covenant of grace in Christ."[2]

Paul's letters help us to see the most obvious reasons that God would deliver the Law to Moses with this double structure:[3] first, to reveal the essential points of the Covenant of Works, bringing what is obscure in the shadows of the distant past into the daylight of the present, and second, to make clear beyond all doubt that the Lord Jesus Christ, as the last Adam, fulfilled the first covenant's demands and is in fact the only person in human history who ever would or could obey God perfectly.

This chapter browses some additional considerations, both from Paul and others, to show why its still the best medicine to view the covenants in this way. Five centuries of theologians have recognized links between the Garden covenant and Mt. Sinai pact. The element of law is not the only connection. Many of the parallels between the covenants are easy to identify:

Demand and Promise. The Covenants, Adamic and Sinaitic, both include the elements of demand (of obedience) and the promise of life for those who do obey. Malcom Watts, in a lecture on the Covenant of Works, pointed out it that is precisely such details that constitute a covenant: "If you have a mere precept without anything else, than what you have is a commandment. If you have a promise, and nothing else, than what you have is a promise. But if you have a covenant, you have those two things incorporated in one; you have a certain command which forms the condition of the covenant, and you have a promise which is made upon fulfillment of that command; this is what makes it a covenant, it is an agreement, or a conditional promise."[4] In Eden, the promise was represented by the tree of life. The demand of sinless obedience was in the tree of the knowledge of good and evil. Paul frequently points out the same promise and demand in the Law of Moses. Discussing the Law in Romans chapter two, the apostle describes the reward for "those who by persistence in doing good seek glory, honor and immortality," affirming that, "He will give eternal life" (v. 7), while contending in the same breath that "All who sin under the Law will be judged by the Law" (v. 12), concluding that "there is none righteous, no, not one" (3:10), and that "Jews and Greeks alike are all under sin" (3:9)

Unilateral. They are both unilateral in design and imposition. It is true that Israel willingly agreed to the terms of the covenant in Exodus 24, yet it was not a covenant of their own making, but God sovereignly established a covenant with them. Later, when the covenant was reconfirmed in Moab, or another covenant was added to the first, there is no mention of the people giving assent; the Lord simply made known to them that He was establishing or confirming His covenant among them. Similarly, Moses says nothing of Adam agreeing to be party to the Covenant of Works; rather, upon becoming conscious he found himself already faced with its demands. In similar fashion, the Lord established his covenant with Noah, Abraham, and David, without asking these men for their consent, or agreement. Therefore, the absence of any mention of consent on Adam's part is irrelevant.[5]

Legal. A covenant consists of legal terms for a relationship with God. The Adamic and Sinaitic pacts were covenants of law, consisting of legal requirements and severe penal sanctions for law-breaking, namely death. This is easily seen in Adam, for that first covenant is kept free from extraneous clutter in order that the simple law, and its terrible penalty, might not be so easily misconstrued. Paul makes certain we do not fail to notice the legality in the covenant of Sinai, warning the Galatians, "All who rely on observing the Law are under a curse, for it is written: "Cursed is everyone who does not continue to do everything written in the Book of the Law" (Gal. 3:10). Since the covenant of Sinai has been aptly titled, the Law of Moses, or simply, the Law, further comment seems superfluous.

Life and Death. The two trees, representing life and death, blessing and cursing, were placed before Adam's eyes in the very center of the garden. The eternal life promised by this covenant, the life that comes from God Himself, was symbolized by the tree of life, in the center of the garden.[6] The tree stood for both the life and the means of attaining to this life. Whenever Adam partook of this sacramental fruit it was as if God was saying through the tree, "Take, eat, this is my life, offered to you."[7] Similar to other sacraments, such as the Lord's Table, this tree symbolized the life of Christ, the life that God shares with those who listen to His Word and are faithful to Him. The apostle John explains that the Word (Christ) was "in the beginning" with God; all things were created by Him, and at that time, in the beginning "in Him was life, and the life was the light of men." (John 1:1-4). Another tree stood beside the tree of life. Early Reformed theologians taught that this tree symbolized the terrible lesson that Adam would learn if he should disobey God and eat from it. God placed this tree beside the tree of life, with the foreknowledge that Adam would be tested there, well within sight of the promise of life. At that second tree, Adam would learn the difference between good and evil the hard way, through the bitterness of the curse, the misery of condemnation and the pain of death. So God called it the tree of the knowledge of good and evil, for its lesson would be learned only if Adam refused to learn the easier lesson that would be gained by eating only at the tree of life, that he must heed God's Word if he would live. In disobeying God and eating from the forbidden tree, Adam would finally learn through the curse what he had refused to understand through the blessing and promise of the tree of life, namely the difference between good and evil. Fallen mankind would inherit this knowledge eventually as the Law of Moses, the moral law that distinguishes between good and evil. In similar fashion in the Law, God set before the Israelites "life and death, blessing and cursing." Moses declares, "I call heaven and earth as witnesses today against you, that I have set before you life and death, blessing and cursing; therefore choose life, that both you and your descendants may live; that you may love the Lord your God, that you may obey His voice, and that you may cling to Him, for He is your life and the length of your days; and that you may dwell in the land which the Lord swore to your fathers, to Abraham, Isaac, and Jacob, to give them." (Deuteronomy 30:19–20, NKJV) God warned that Adam's disobedience would be punished with death, ie., loss of life, that penal sanction so well known in Paul, "the wages of sin is death." As this warning was represented by one of the trees, the other tree stood for the promise of life, or eternal life, as the reward for obedience. The way of life in Eden, represented by the Tree of Life, was to listen to God's Word and obey it from the heart in genuine love for God the Creator. The Sinai covenant held forth the same promise, viz, that those who listen to the Word and obey would live, "Therefore you shall keep the commandment, the statutes, and the judgments which I command you today, to observe them. "Then it shall come to pass, because you listen to these judgments, and keep and do them, that the LORD your God will keep with you the covenant and the mercy which He swore to your fathers. And He will love you and bless you and multiply you; He will also bless the fruit of your womb and the fruit of your land, your grain and your new wine and your oil, the increase of your cattle and the offspring of your flock, in the land of which He swore to your fathers to give you. " (Deuteronomy 7:11–13, NKJV) Again, "And he said unto them, Set your hearts unto all the words which I testify among you this day, which ye shall command your children to observe to do, all the words of this law. For it is not a vain thing for you; because it is your life..." (Deuteronomy 32:46-47a).

Responsibilities. The covenant God established with Adam contained such promises as friendship with God, the right to rule over the created world, the needs of man to be met by God, and children to be rewarded to him. These things were represented to man in the Word of God, as responsibilities for man's good and pleasure, to be done for the glory of God: "Let us make man in our image...and let them rule" (Gen. 1:26); "be fruitful and multiply" (Gen. 1:28); "God blessed the seventh day and sanctified it" (Gen. 2:3); "the Lord God took the man and put him in the garden of Eden to tend and keep it" (Gen. 2:15) . Adam was supposed to populate the world with godly children, children in God's image,[8] and rule the creatures as an image of God, all for the glory of the invisible God.[9] These were characteristics of the Covenant of Works, as Morton H. Smith explains,

> "As we have already suggested, the covenant relationship was more inclusive than the particular probation of Genesis 2:17. Adam as first created was to be the office–bearer for God. He was to be God's prophet, priest and king. In these offices he was to carry out the will of God. In order to make him a self–conscious covenant–keeper, God placed him under probation with regard to the tree of knowledge of good and evil. Perfect obedience was the condition of the test. It was a specific condition of specific obedience to a positive command of God. It was an obedience that would demonstrate the completeness of man's obedience to the will of God under the two–fold circumstance of probation and temptation."[10]

Adam was assigned these responsibilities as God's office-bearer. But we err if we regard these positive responsibilities—ruling, multiplying, and laboring in the garden—as the central feature of the covenant. They were the activities in which man was to be blessed as long as he continued in covenant faithfulness, which was essentially to love God with all His heart. To "rule" the earth is a privilege,[11] the "fruit of the womb is His reward," and "nothing is better for a man than that he should eat and drink, and that his soul should enjoy good in his labor." Solomon saw that the command to work was actually a blessing "from the hand of God."[12] These blessings, or gifts from God, were not to be merely for a moment, or a day, but for eternity. The covenant set eternal life before the man in the tree of life. God's covenant promised this life to Adam and to his descendants, and granted authority to rule over the world-kingdom forever with God, if Adam would truly love God and prove faithful to Him. These were those areas of life through which Adam was to honor God by displaying His image, and enjoy God's rich favor and blessings: ruling the earth and its creatures, laboring in the field to produce a harvest, bearing children who are images of God, and resting from his labor every seventh day. In the Sinai covenant, the blessings promised in Deut. 28:1-14, as the reward for the obedient, are expanded details of the broad categories that were first appointed to Adam: "the fruit of your body, the produce of your ground..." (Deut. 28:4).

When Adam broke the covenant and fell into sin these very blessings

151

became the curses of the covenant: the animal kingdom ruled by man was cursed and the world was subjected to futility, women bore the fruit of the womb in pain and sorrow, and the very ground was cursed in which man was to "enjoy good in his labor." The curses were directed against the very responsibilities in which man was to glorify God and receive blessing from Him. The covenant of Sinai likewise pronounces a curse in all of these same areas where there is deliberate disobedience of the Law (Deut. 28:15-68).

Consequences. The far-reaching consequences accompanying Adam's rebellion were extremely serious: both man and the world were placed under the curse: man was subjected to death and the world to futility, childbirth was cursed with pain, paradise was lost, the ground was cursed from producing its harvest, and the entire animal kingdom was cursed. Such penalties have no place in a mere pact of friendship. God warned in Deuteronomy 28, and elsewhere, that the covenant kingdom of Israel would face similar consequences should they rebel against Yahweh, the Lord of their nation: "The fruit of your womb will be cursed" (v. 18); "The Lord will send on you curses, confusion and rebuke in everything you put your hand to" (v. 20); "The sky over your head will be bronze, the ground beneath you iron" (v. 23); "Your sons and daughters will be given to another nation..." (v. 32).

Failed intention. Adam's covenant was *intended* to preserve life by warning of the penalty for rebellion. But the twisted tongue of Satan used the same covenant words to bring forth children cursed with death and spiritual slavery. In a similar vein, Paul says, "I found that the very commandment that was *intended* to bring life actually brought death" (Rom. 7:10). He knew that "the Law is holy and righteous and good," and that God's *intention* in giving it was to keep man from sin and its consequences. The commandment meant to preserve man from God's justice is the very instrument wielded by Satan to bring judgment, condemnation, and death from God. Therefore, Paul declares that "All who rely on the Law are under a curse..." (Gal. 3:10), that it is "the ministry of condemnation" (2 Cor. 3:9), and "the Law of sin and death" (Rom. 8:2), "because the Law brings wrath" (Rom. 4:15).

Paul's handling of the Law. It was clear to many Reformed theologians that the Law of Moses contains all the elements of the gospel of grace, especially in the ceremonial ordinances. Yet, Paul often describes the Law as condemning its adherents and leaving them with no hope. This is especially glaring when we see that Paul himself teaches that one of the main functions of the Law is to drive sinners to the grace of God. In the Old Testament, this grace was made available only through the atoning sacrifices. "Without the shedding of blood, there is no forgiveness of sin." (Hebrews 9:22) The meaning of these sacrifices would eventually be fulfilled by Christ alone, but God promised forgiveness in the Law of Sinai before Christ came (cf. Leviticus 4-6). Paul shows on one hand that grace was available to believers under the Law of Moses (Romans 4:4-9). On the other hand, he describes the same Law of Moses as if it is an impossible covenant of works, completely lacking grace. In the former instances, Paul seems to describe the Law as it truly is, the Covenant of Grace. But in the latter sense, he appears to highlight the elements of the covenant of works that are put on display within the Law of Moses.

Symbolism. The Covenant of Works was arranged in a garden sanctuary where God dwelt among and in His creation. The tree of life was the central feature, standing as the promise that God, or Christ, was sharing His own life with Adam. When Adam rebelled, he was driven out of the sanctuary of Eden and Yahweh set in place two cherubim and a flaming sword to guard the way back to the tree of life. In the Law of Moses, particularly in the ceremonial code, the Tabernacle was so arranged as to be reminiscent of the garden temple. Palm trees and fruits were carved into all the panels and columns. They were also displayed in the pattern of the veil that barred entrance into the Holy of Holies. In effect, the cherubim were still there, woven into the fabric of the veil, and standing wing to wing within the Most Holy sanctuary. The two cherubim adorned the mercy seat, their wings outstretched over the Divine Presence that would meet with Moses in the sanctuary. They were as sentinels forever at their post, still guarding the way back to the Tree of Life, illustrating that the life lost in the abandoned Garden was to be discovered only in learning the mystery of that mercy seat. Before the veil, the flaming sword still turned every way with wrathful vengeance, declaring, "The soul that sins shall die!" The flames of justice burned in the coals of the altar, and the sword was the bloody knife of sacrifice. Every person who would pass through that veil to the life-giving Spirit enthroned there, would be struck down before passing the altar, condemned by the Law that turned every way, searched out by the Living Word whose eyes were flames of fire, and the testimony that "there is none righteous, no not one." It was there Israel, seeking pardon and life, was commanded to bring her sacrifices. There that she must confess her sins on the head of the innocent substitute; there that she would plunge the sword, herself, into the lamb. A thousand times daily, ten thousand times, the ritual was repeated, but never did the flames or the sword find a resting place. The blood of every sacrifice was sprinkled all around the altar, and seven times before the veil, but still the sword was raised to kill relentlessly. It waited for only One Lamb, that One foretold in the garden, born of the woman, whose blood would be shed to cover over forever the sin of any of Adam's lost children who come searching for the way there.

The Restricted Food. To test Adam, God set in place a law that merely restricted him from enjoying one of the foods of the garden, declaring, "but of the tree of the knowledge of good and evil you shall not eat, for in the day that you eat of it you shall surely die." (Genesis 2:17, NKJV) When the Law came, thousands of years later, the Lord again restricted his people from eating certain foods. Obeying the food restrictions of Moses was as much a "work of the Law" as abstaining from adultery or helping an enemy's fallen donkey back on his feet. Yet, these restrictions were not moral absolutes but temporary ceremonial ordinances to separate Jews from Gentiles. When the new covenant was established, God made clear to Peter, "What God has cleansed, you must not call common" (Acts 10:15, NKJV). Just as these restrictions passed away with the new covenant, the law forbidding the fruit of a certain tree vanished after Adam's fall, when the Lord later reintroduced the covenant to a new type of Adam named Noah. Because these restrictions carry no essential moral quality in themselves, our apostle writes that regulations such as "Do not touch, do not taste, do not handle,"… "have an appearance of wisdom in self-imposed religion, false humility, and neglect of the body, *but are of no value* against the indulgence of the flesh." (Colossians 2:21, 23; NKJV)

The Test of Adam The sovereignty of God determined from eternity that Adam's love for God, and loyalty to Him, and complete submission to Him, would be tested by making a single food forbidden to him, and that the agent of testing would be the serpent of old. In this test, Adam would either stand faithfully and then go on to produce children for God, or he would fall and his children would be fallen with him. It is not difficult to see that a similar test was also faced by the Last Adam, when He came into the world to fulfill the condition of the Covenant of Works, perfect obedience to God. The covenant was really a legal imposition, demanding full obedience forever, but testing that obedience in a temporary probation. A.A. Hodge writes, "A probation is a trial. The word is variously used to express the state, or the time, or the act of trial." And there must be a time

154

limit to the period of probation, because "it is self–evident that either the infliction of the penalty or the granting of the reward would, ipso facto, close the probation forever, and the reward could not accrue until the period of probation was completed."[13]

The testing of Adam, who was the perfect representative of all humankind who came from him, was the probation of mankind. When man failed the test the covenant was broken. The depravity that corrupted the soul of all men made impossible any further thought of probation or of a conditional covenant. Adam was banished from the tree of life because he subjected himself to sin and death and could no longer live forever. The tree of the knowledge of good and evil was taken away because the sinful nature, by its very existence in man, violates the commandment not to eat of that tree.

It was a legal covenant. When Adam broke it, by listening to the Word of Satan rather than the Word of God, he brought upon himself and all his descendants: sin, corruption, separation from God, bondage to Satan, death, and condemnation. Adam rebelled deliberately against God, and God deliberately sentenced humankind to death.

The Nature of the Test: Fidelity of Love for God   Implied in the demand of the Covenant of Works, but unexpressed, is the requirement that man perfectly love his creator and subject himself sincerely forever to the sovereignty of God. It was actually Adam's love for God that was on trial. The test of his love, through law, was a simple legal prohibition against eating from the tree of the knowledge of good and evil. Paul shows that this is another parallel between Adam's covenant and Sinai, when he writes, "love is the fulfillment of the Law" (Romans 13:10). Paul, of course, learned this from his Master, who taught, "You shall love the Lord your God with all your heart, with all your soul, and with all your mind.' This is the first and great commandment. And the second is like it: 'You shall love your neighbor as yourself.' On these two commandments hang all the Law and the Prophets." (Matthew 22:37–40, NKJV)

This is one of the strongest reasons that it is correct to say that the covenant is a legal arrangement. God's covenant with Adam established a relationship between parties so vastly unequal, that it would seem incredibly ludicrous to consider the possibility of such a covenant. This is the very reason that there was indeed a covenant between God and Adam, unilaterally imposed by the superior party. The words of a covenant determine the form of legal relationship that shall be established: what obligations must be fulfilled, wholehearted love for God, what benefits shall be available upon fulfillment, God will share His own indestructible life with Adam, symbolized by the Tree of Life, and what penalty imposed for rejecting the Word of the covenant, death. Adam had rejected God's word, "From the tree of the knowledge of good and evil you shall not eat." This was tantamount to rejecting God's rule and lordship, in short, it was to reject God Himself.

The Accomplished Reward It has long been debated whether Adam would have gained life only for himself, or also for his children, by resisting Satan, passing the test of the tree, and holding firmly to his love for God with all his heart. Covenant theology, with its principle of the federal headship of the first and last Adam, argues that Adam represented all his children who were contained within him and that his fall was the fall of all. Jesus Christ also represented his children who were in Him, for the Father chose them "in Him" before the creation of the world. Therefore, he was their representative throughout his entire life, and not merely as their sin-bearer. When He was tested as the first Adam was, He had already resisted sin His entire life. This was the ultimate final test on behalf of His children, that in victory His righteousness might be shared by all who had a share in Him. Already declared righteous by the Father's "with whom I am well-pleased," He was now ready to fulfill His role as the Last Adam, the man through whom God will have His own children, made in his image. Driven by the Holy Spirit into the wilderness, the very first test of the Diabolical One was by sovereign design. The first Adam was not made hungry for forty days and nights. But as food was so important to the test of the first man, it must be for the Last. Satan's aim in urging Him to command stones to become bread showed shrewd discernment, for that cunning lizard understood after watching the Christ throughout His life that He was the perfectly obedient servant of God, an Adam who never does anything except what the Father commands. How unlike Him was the selfwill of His predecessor, Adam! Satan thought to use Christ's hunger to drive Him to act independently of God, and so disobey the will of God. But starving for bread, the Last Adam would not eat unless God Himself gave the Word, and responded instead with a Word God had given, not only to Him but to all, "Man shall not live by bread alone, but by every Word that proceeds from the mouth of God!" Where Adam failed, and passed down to all of his seed his unrighteousness, the Last Adam came off victoriously, "having been tested in all points even as we, yet without sin," displaying a righteousness approved both by the Law throughout His whole

156

life, by His Father at His baptism, and by the Covenant of Works at the dragon's test. Now at last the stage was set for Paul to write these words, "now the righteousness of God apart from the Law is revealed, being witnessed by the Law and the prophets, even the righteousness of God, through faith in Jesus Christ, to all and on all who believe" (Romans 3:21-22).

Federal Headship of Adam and Christ   It was because Adam was made in His image that God established a covenant with Adam and his descendants after him. The Lord designated Adam federal head of all mankind since he was created a perfect and sinless man, equipped in every way to represent the human race before God. Nevertheless, Adam did fall. Immediately after the fall God revealed to Adam the promise of the Redeemer (Gen. 3:15). The "seed of the woman," a person born from the fallen race would come into the world as the representative of all the elect to restore people to God through a "covenant of grace."   Then God demonstrated a sign of the Redeemer to Adam by slaying animals and covering Adam and Eve with their skins (Gen. 3:21). The Redeemer would sacrifice His own life as a perfectly righteous human to cover over their sins and to bring forth the children of God that Adam, in his fall, had failed to produce. Every time any Jew brought an animal to the temple, laid his hands on its head, and confessed his sins over it, he showed that Christ, the true Lamb, must be his representative if he will be saved. Representing every repentant seeker of God's mercy, Christ is the federal head of them all.

This is the reason that Romans 5:14 states that Adam was "a type of Him who was later to come." Just as Adam's one act of rebellion brought condemnation to all who were born of Adam, the Redeemer's one sacrifice would provide redemption to all who are born again through Him, to all who trust in Him for salvation.   The apostle Paul explains, in Romans 5:18, "Consequently, just as the result of one trespass was condemnation for all men, so also the result of one act of righteousness was justification that brings life for all men."

The Redeemer, our Lord Jesus Christ, saves us as our representative. Representing all believers before God's judgment throne, He takes our sins upon Himself, bears the full measure of God's wrath for those sins at the cross, and rises again from the dead as our righteousness before God. Therefore, Adam,when he was tested, represented every person who would be born of Him because he was a type of Christ. This is the reason that Eve also had to come from Adam; there had to be one head of humanity, one man

157

who represents all.

It should now be clear that the demand of Adam's obedience is the essential point of the Covenant of Works. As the representative of all mankind, his one sin was the sin of the human race; his guilt the guilt of all.

In the same way, Christ is the representative of all who were chosen in Him, all who would be born of His Spirit. He had to obey perfectly, for their sake, the commands and laws of the Father. The demand of Christ's perfect obedience throughout His entire life but especially in His death at the cross is one of the essential points of the Covenant of Grace. Without the perfect active and passive obedience of Christ, there can be no Covenant of Grace, no substitutionary atonement, no salvation, and no hope for sinners fallen in Adam.

The free gift of life given through Christ's one act of righteousness is the promise of the eternal plan of God; it is the tree of life of the new covenant. God required His Son to take upon Himself human form and to bear the full penalty of the sins of all those God had chosen to give to His Son. As the reward for His perfect obedience the Father promised to give to the elect the righteousness of Christ, justification, adoption as sons, and a share in the inheritance of Christ Himself. (Isa. 49:4; Heb. 12:2; Isa. 53:10-11)

Mankind, having been plunged into spiritual darkness and bondage by the fall of Adam, was separated from God and soon forgot the true God. Therefore, God began to speak through chosen prophets, revealing that He alone is the Creator of heaven and earth. He commanded His words to be preserved in a book. God's revelation of Himself is the main message of the Bible. It is of first importance. Second to this, the Bible reveals how the human race fell away from God, and teaches the only way to be restored to life and to God's loving favor. Salvation would be only through the death of the Redeemer. There would be only one Savior for all people everywhere. He would give His life for the sins of lost people from every tribe, language and nation.

To help sinners see the futility of their fallen condition, God provided an expanded presentation of the Covenant of Works, within the covenant of Sinai. This gives every person the opportunity to see that no one can establish righteousness by works of the Law. All who try fail. Because of the weakness of the flesh, every descendant of Adam fails to obey God. No sinner can live without sinning. By reading about the Covenant of Works in Genesis, sinners may comprehend the cause of man's ruin. When the Law of Moses then presses sinners with the demand of the Covenant of Works, sinful people learn the utter hopelessness of establishing perfect righteousness by works of the Law. The Law of Moses curses every person who does not continue in all things written in it, in perfect obedience. In this way it is a schoolmaster to lead the helpless to Christ, so that those who have no hope in themselves may be justified by faith in Christ the Redeemer.[14]

There are some who will not begin to consider the possibility of the Covenant of Works simply because *this title* is not found in Scripture. But the fact that the Adamic administration was not specifically labeled as a "covenant," or a Covenant of Works, does not necessarily imply that it wasn't. O. Palmer Robertson "has demonstrated the legitimacy of calling it a covenant. First of all, some scriptural precedent exists for the omission of the term 'covenant' in discussing a relationship which unquestionably is covenantal. Nowhere in the original account of the establishment of God's promise to David does the term 'covenant' appear (2 Sam. 7; 1 Chron. 17). Yet this relationship clearly is covenantal. God's commitments to David were covenantal in nature despite the absence of any formal application of the term 'covenant' in the original context of the establishment of the relationship. Subsequent Scripture specifically speaks of God's 'covenant' with David (cf. 2 Sam. 23:5; Ps. 89:3)."[15]

Robert L. Reymond writes that "the word "covenant" does not occur in Genesis 2," but argues that "there are four reasons for regarding the arrangement between God and Adam as a covenant as the Westminster Confession of Faith teaches (VII/i, ii):

> a. The word תיְרִב, *berît*, does not have to be actually used at the time a covenant is made in order for a covenant to be present, as is made clear from 2 Samuel 7, where, although the word is not employed, according to Psalm 89:19–37 God *covenantally* promised David that his dynastic house would rule over Israel.

> b. Covenant elements (parties, stipulation, promise, and threat) are present.

> c. Hosea 6:7, "But they, like Adam, transgressed covenant," states by implication that Adam's sin was a "transgression of covenant." Some commentators suggest that the phrase "like Adam" should be translated "like men," but this is to intrude an inanity into the text, for how else could Hosea's contemporaries transgress than "like

men"? Other commentators have wanted to emend the "like Adam" (כְּאָדָם, *keˌāḏām*) phrase to "in Adam" (בְּאָדָם, *beˌāḏām*), and then they speak of some transgression which occurred in the town by that name mentioned in Joshua 3:16. But the Scriptures are silent regarding such an event. It seems best to retain the most obvious sense of the phrase.

d. The New Testament parallels between Adam and Christ (Rom. 5:12–19; 1 Cor. 15:22, 45–49) imply that just as Christ was the federal (*foedus:* "covenant") representative of the New Covenant (Luke 22:20; Heb. 9:15), so also Adam acted as a federal representative of a covenant arrangement."[16]

Observations like those listed in this chapter have prompted every generation of Reformed theologians to explore afresh every possible dimension of the relationship between these two covenants. Most have finally concluded that the Law of Moses introduces, and amplifies, the main points of the Covenant of Works but only within the greater context of the Covenant of Grace. At the same time, there have always been voices of protest standing on the wayside. John Gill, the great Baptist commentator, was determined to prove infant baptism wrong. He thought he could strike a final blow by strangely arguing that not only the Sinai covenant, but Abraham's covenant also, was *nothing but* a Covenant of Works, "Now that this covenant was not the pure covenant of grace, in distinction from the covenant of works, but rather a covenant of works, will soon be proved; and if so, then the main ground of infant baptism is taken away, and its principal arguments in support of it overturned..."[17] Such comments are based on deductive handling of Scripture, rather than inductive, and seem ludicrous to cautious students of the divine covenants. Merrill Unger, in the Dispensational camp, due to the absolute distinction between these covenants in that theological system, also believed the Sinai covenant was a Covenant of Works, "It was a conditional covenant of works, a ministry of 'condemnation' and 'death' (2 Cor 3:7–9), designed to lead the transgressor (convicted thereby as a sinner) to Christ.[18]

But in Reformed theology, where the divine covenants have been under the microscope for hundreds of years, the parallel presentation of the two covenants within the Law of Moses has long been emphasized. In theological writings, these two covenants are often represented simply as "law and grace". Mark W. Karlberg, in a 1980 article on "Reformed Interpretation of the Mosaic Covenant," emphasizes "recognition of the dual principles of law and grace operative in the Mosaic Covenant administration. The Mosaic Covenant is to be viewed in *some sense* as a covenant of works. This has been the conviction of the vast majority of Reformed theologians in the early history of federalism (up to 1648)."[19] To press this point, Karlberg ably surveys the works of Zwingli, Bullinger, Calvin, Ursinus, Olevianus, Tyndale, Robert Rollock, James Ussher, William Perkins, William Ames, Tobias Crisp, David Dickson, Samuel Bolton, Edward Fisher, John Ball, and finally concludes with the Westminster Assembly and their creeds.

The Westminster Assembly agreed that the Covenant of Works was represented in Sinai, but it absolutely refused to view Sinai as an actual and literal reintroduction of that broken covenant. The first and last Adams are the only two men who could attempt to fulfill the Covenant of Works, because that covenant demands that its members must be uncorrupt in both heart and deed.

John Murray, in the twentieth century, held a different opinion, "The view that in the mosaic covenant there was a repetition of the so-called Covenant of Works, current among covenant theologians, is a grave misconception and involves an erroneous construction of the Mosaic Covenant, as well as fails to assess the uniqueness of the Adamic administration. The Mosaic Covenant was distinctly redemptive in character and was continuous with and extensive of the Abrahamic Covenants (p. 44)."[20] Murray not only failed to see the Covenant of Works as a didactic element in Sinai, he was in favor of putting aside the very concept of a Covenant of Works in Eden as well. But viewing the Sinai covenant as purely the Covenant of Grace, containing no elements of the Covenant of Works, leaves one wondering why countless thousands perished under that law, condemned and put to death by its very precepts?

There have been many others throughout history who agree that the Law of Moses must be the Covenant of Grace, yet see that it contains a clear presentation of the Covenant of Works. For example, Malcolm Watts comments that "a covenant of works was made because there was in some ways a re-exhibition of this covenant at Mt. Sinai. In that, obedience was required in Sinai as the condition of life, Deut.18:5; 'if a man keep my statutes he shall live in them.' There was some restatement of the covenant of works at Mt. Sinai in that commandment and promise … But what is important is that this exhibit is called a covenant; He called unto you His covenant at Sinai, even the Ten Commandments; again in Deut.5:2. If the restatement is expressly called a covenant, then the original draft in Genesis

2 must have been a covenant, too. But the covenant at Sinai was not a covenant of works, although there was another revelation of the covenant of works. There is indeed its repetition, but if you take the whole of the arrangement at Sinai with its Mediator and sacrifices, it is clear that Sinai is a covenant of grace."[21]

If the Adamic covenant is not revealed in the Law of Moses, then it becomes difficult to explain why characteristics that so strikingly reflect the Covenant of Works are present in any covenant after the fall of man. It must be pointed out that it was not the Sinai covenant alone that contained elements of God's covenant with Adam. Noah's covenant, which contained such gracious gestures on God's part that some have referred to it as the covenant of common grace, also includes the reintroduction of certain elements of the covenant God first established with Adam, such as the "creation mandate" to rule, subdue, and care for the earth; and the command to multiply and fill the earth; and the commandment to eat the plants and fruits of the earth. The fact that these responsibilities are presented to Noah in a covenant surely indicates that the first time that God gave them to Adam was also in the context of a covenant. Yet, it is clear that Noah's covenant is not the original Covenant of Works, but is of grace, for God swore the words of the covenant to Noah over the shed blood of a type of Christ, a substitutionary sacrifice.

Thoughts on Practical Application

If the majority of Reformed theologians were on the right track and this thesis is true, that the Law contained such a republication of the Covenant of Works, how should it be used in our preaching? George Whitefield, the prince of preachers at that time in history when the covenant of works had already become prominent, employed it to lead sinners to fully realize their condemnation, so that he might then proclaim to them the gospel of peace through Christ's atoning sacrifice, "First, then, before you can speak peace to your hearts, you must be made to see, made to feel, made to weep over, made to bewail, your actual transgressions against the law of God. According to the covenant of works, 'The soul that sinneth it shall die;' cursed is that man, be he what he may, that continueth not in all things that are written in the book of the law to do them."[22] The Law, by first condemning sinners with the threat of the Covenant of Works, was intended to drive them to the mercy of the God, also contained in the Law, who will at last "speak peace to your heart," but only where there is confession of sin and admission of guilt. This was emphasized by Calvin, who regarded it to be the first use of the Law:

> "First, by exhibiting the righteousness of God,, in other words, the righteousness which alone is acceptable to God,, it admonishes every one of his own unrighteousness, certiorates,[23] convicts, and finally condemns him. This is necessary, in order that man, who is blind and intoxicated with self-love, may be brought at once to know and to confess his weakness and impurity. For until his vanity is made perfectly manifest, he is puffed up with infatuated confidence in his own powers, and never can be brought to feel their feebleness so long as he measures them by a standard of his own choice. So soon, however, as he begins to compare them with the requirements of the Law, he has something to tame his presumption. How high soever his opinion of his own powers may be, he immediately feels that they pant under the heavy load, then totter and stumble, and finally fall and give way. He, then, who is schooled by the Law, lays aside the arrogance which formerly blinded him. In like manner must he be cured of pride, the other disease under which we have said that he labours. So long as he is permitted to appeal to his own judgment, he substitutes a hypocritical for a real righteousness, and, contented with this, sets up certain factitious observances in opposition to the grace of God. But after he is forced to weigh his conduct in the balance of the Law, renouncing all dependence on this fancied righteousness, he sees that he is at an infinite distance from holiness, and, on the other hand, that he teems with innumerable vices of which he formerly seemed free.... Thus the Law is a kind of mirror. As in a mirror we discover any stains upon our face, so in the Law we behold, first, our impotence; then, in consequence of it, our iniquity; and, finally, the curse, as the consequence of both. He who has no power of following righteousness is necessarily plunged in the mire of iniquity, and this iniquity is immediately followed by the curse. Accordingly, the greater the transgression of which the Law convicts us, the severer the judgment to which we are exposed."[24]

Calvin credits Paul with promoting this understanding, and encourages his readers to learn from the apostle, introducing the section quoted above with this comment, "Let it therefore be held incontrovertible, that, in consequence of the feebleness of our nature, it is impossible for us, so long as we are in the flesh, to fulfil the law. This will also be proved

163

elsewhere from the writings of Paul (Rom. 8:3)."[25]

Though Calvin comes short of mentioning the Covenant of Works, his description of the use of the law is synonymous with later Reformed theology's exposition of a republication of the Covenant of Works within the gracious covenant of Sinai. It is clear that he saw the same contrasting characteristics in the Law of Moses as later theologians, for he emphasizes in many places in his works that Sinai was the Covenant of Grace. We cannot expect to find a complete presentation of the Covenant of Works in his writing because he lived before this understanding blossomed in Reformed theology.

There may be some who ask, "How can the *Covenant of Works* and the *Covenant of Grace* coexist within the covenant of Sinai? Are they not opposites?"

Yes, they have certainly been presented as a dichotomy[26] by sound Reformed theologians throughout the past centuries. For example, Octavius Winslow writes, "The old covenant of works made with Adam, the federal head of his race, the terms of which were, "Do and live; sin and die," was broken by our first parents, and by its violation compromised the present and eternal happiness of their posterity. But the new covenant of Grace entered into by the Sacred Three on behalf of elect sinners, on whom grace and glory were eternally and forever settled in Christ Jesus, their covenant Head, Surety, and Mediator, is absolute and new, filled with all spiritual blessings, signed and sealed by the blood of the New Covenant, accepted and ratified, on the part of God, by His raising up Christ from the dead. "I will," says God, "make an everlasting covenant with you, even the sure mercies of David." "This is my blood of the new covenant," says Christ."[27]

This antithesis, in which the gospel, the Covenant of Grace, is juxtaposed against the Law, the Covenant of Works, is often set before us by the apostle. But this is usually done in contexts where he compares the covenant that Christ has established through His blood with the covenant introduced through Moses. This is not proof that there was no means of grace in Sinai. Rather, it should be clear that when Paul makes such a comparison, he points his readers to the presentation of the Covenant of Works within the Law of Moses. If it is the entire Law of Moses which Paul refers to when he says such things as "the Law brings wrath," or, "the letter kills," then why does the apostle avoid acknowledging the "means of grace" which constituted a very large part of the Sinai covenant and thus soften or balance his words? Paul is intentionally overlooking the elements of grace and the promises of forgiveness offered in the Torah (cf. Leviticus 4-6), so that the reader may discern something of the shadowy form of the Covenant of Works, as it is contained in the greater covenant of Sinai.

When Moses sketches these two covenants within one covenant, it cannot be assumed that the Sinai road follows precisely the same route as the Covenant of Works. Sinai leads to the broken covenant of Eden along a pathway lined with panoromic scenes of Edenic blessings that could have been: fruitful fields, an abundant womb, a blessed breadbasket, peace and protection from enemies, and the right to inherit and rule the earth. Here the tree of life is seen with its manifold fruits and foliage, the hope of life eternal in an earthly paradise in which nothing shall hurt or destroy. Walking this road with its bright earthly promises very soon becomes painstakingly difficult with every step forward impeded by dark thunderclouds of justice. Every demand of God's righteous Law strikes lightning bolts at our feet, halting further progress. Faced with the righteous demands of heaven and our abject failure, we are dismayed to find hopelessly blocked all efforts to enter that paradise by our own works, to gain the tree of life by our own righteousness. The way is obstructed with roadblocks, red flags, flashing warning lights, heavenly guardians and threats of impending doom. And it is only at this point, when we come to the end of all hope in ourselves, that we see in the Sinai Covenant there is another pathway, a narrow path stained deep with the sprinkled blood of a million sacrifices, leading through the altar directly before the face of the imposing veil, a way not afflicted with gloomy thoughts of terror, but illuminated with these words of comfort, "Thus shall the priest make atonement for him before the Lord, and he will be forgiven for any of these things he did that made him guilty" (Leviticus 6:7). It is only in recognizing this as the main principle of Law of Moses pointing to the divine King of Israel who will offer Himself as the Lamb who takes away the sin of the world, that we begin to see that the path was lined all along with signs pointing in this direction, and a trail of blood marked every step of the way.

These two paths are marked with such striking differences that there is a stark contrast in Paul's writings between the works of the Law and justification by grace through faith. He declares in the same breath that *"Therefore by the deeds of the law no flesh will be justified in His sight, for by the law is the knowledge of sin. But now the righteousness of God apart from the law is revealed, being witnessed by the Law and the Prophets,"* (Romans 3:20–21, NKJV) This dichotomy has led to the wrong confusion,

165

common in modern evangelicalism (as seen in Merrill Unger's comment, above), that the old covenant truly was a system of works righteousness.

Seeing that both principles are at work in the covenant of Sinai and learning to strike a balance between the proper place and use of both is one of the most important challenges of the Bible teacher.

Chapter Nine Notes

1. While finalizing this chapter, I came across a blog dated July 16, 2008, where Randy Scott Clark comments on this: "One of the interesting and useful features of the older (classic) covenant theology of the 17th century was the doctrine of "re-publication." It was widely held among 17th-century Reformed theologians that, in certain ways, the giving of the Law at Sinai was a "re-publication" of the Law given in the garden to Adam as part of the covenant of works (John Owen, Herman Witsius, Leonard van Rijssen, Johannes Marckius, Peter Van Mastricht and Thomas Boston taught it). They took the promulgation of the law at Sinai as evidence of the covenant of works in the garden with Adam. They thought this way because they had a doctrine of natural or creational law, i.e., there is a moral law that was given in the garden that is reflected in the law given at Sinai.

This re-publication of the Law was not a new "Dispensation" of salvation or way of being justified. Rather, the Mosaic national covenant with Israel was regarded by the Reformed as operating on multiple levels at the same time. As Paul says in Gal 3, the covenant of grace, the Abrahamic covenant is the administration of God's saving grace. It was and remains a covenant of grace. Paul's argument is that nothing about the Mosaic national covenant changes God's promises made to and through Abraham. Hence Paul says that Abraham (Rom 3-4) is the father of all believers, circumcised and uncircumcised (i.e., Jew and Gentile) before Moses, during the Old Covenant, and since.

Thus, before, during, and after the Mosaic national covenant, all the elect were saved and justified by grace alone (sola gratia), through faith alone (sola fide), in Christ alone (solo Christo)."

"...See Herman Witsius, *The Economy of the Covenants Between God and Man*, trans. William Crookshank, 2 vols. (1803; Phillipsburg: Presbyterian and Reformed Publishing, 1990), 1,336–337; Leonard van Rijssen, *Compendium Theologiae* (Amsterdam: 1695.), 89. John Owen, *An Exposition of the Epistle to the Hebrews*, ed. W. H. Goold, 7 vols., *The Works of John Owen* (Edinburgh: Banner of Truth Trust, 1991), 6.85. Johannes Marckius, *Compendium Theologiae Christianae* (Amsterdam, 1749), 345–346; Peter Van Mastricht, *Theoretico-Practica Theologia*, 3 vols (Utrecht: 1699), 3.12.23." Available at http://heidelblog.wordpress.com/2008/07/16/re-publication-of-the-covenant-of-works-1/ (accessed May 2011)

2. Rollock, *Select Works*, 1:36.

3. By the phrase, "double structure," I mean that both covenants, grace and works, are presented at Sinai. But the Covenant of Works is presented to show the necessity of the Covenant of Grace, and to provide the means of receiving grace through types and shadows of Christ centuries before He would come as the "Lamb of God who takes away the sin of the world."

4. Malcolm Watts, "Reformed Covenant Theology," Lecture, Puritan Reformed Theological Seminary, Grand Rapids, MI, April 14, 2008.

5. It has been argued by some that a covenant requires mutual consent and agreement, and since there is no evidence of this with Adam, thethey believe there was no covenant.

6. Genesis 2:9.

7. Meredith Kline, *Kingdom Prologue*, 96.

8. Malachi 2:15.

9. 1 Cor. 10:31. Every work and activity was to be for God's glory, just as man was "the image and glory of God." (1 Cor. 11:7) Therefore, to sin is to "fall short of the glory of God." (Rom. 3:23)

10. Smith, *Theology*, 1: 281.

11. Rev. 20:4, 6.

12. Ecclesiastes 2:24.

13. A.A. Hodge, *Outlines of Bible Topics*, Chap. 17: Covenant of Works, 9. What is a "Probation"? and when and where did the human race have its probation under the Covenant of Works?

14. Galatians 3:24.

15. Smith, *Systematic Theology*, 1: 280.

16. Robert L. Reymond, *A New Systematic Theology of the Christian Faith* (Nashville: T. Nelson, 1998), 430.

17. John Gill. *A Complete Body of Doctrinal and Practical Divinity.* (Paris, Arkansas: The Baptist Standard Bearer, 1999), 1799, Ages e-book.

18. Merrill F. Unger, *The New Unger's Bible Handbook* (Chicago: Moody Press, 1984), 595.

19. Mark W. Karlberg, "Reformed Interpretation of the Mosaic Covenant." *Westminster Theological Journal 43*, no. 1(1980): 1-57.

20. John Murray, quoted in Mark W. Karlberg "Reformed Interpretation of the Mosaic Covenant," *Westminster Theological Journal 43*, no.1 (Fall 1980): 1-57.

21. Watts, Class notes.

22. George Whitefield, "The Method of Grace: Sermon 58." *Selected Sermons of George Whitefield* (Oak Harbor, WA: Logos Research Systems, 1999), Ages e-book.

23. Certiorate means "to inform; assure." *Century Dictionary.*

24. Calvin, *Institutes*, II, vii, 7.

25. Ibid, II, vii, 5.

26. A dichotomy is "two especially mutually exclusive or contradictory groups" or "something with seemingly contradictory qualities." *Merriam-Webster's Collegiate Dictionary.*

27. Octavius Winslow, *Our God*, 1870, in "The Octavius Winslow Archive," http://octaviuswinslow.org/e-books/ (accessed June 17, 2011), PDF e-book.

Ten

Obedience Came First

T he previous chapters described perfect obedience as the requirement of the Covenant of Works, perfect obedience without a single violation. The reason for this demand must now be explored. It is especially important to do this because this essential point is denied by some today. Others give it very little attention even in conservative scholarship. Mark Karlberg comments on this. In his recent review of a book of essays on the covenant of Moses, he emphasizes "the crucial role of meritorious human obedience in the successful fulfillment of the original covenant of works,"[1] as a vital point some do not acknowledge. The bedrock of federal theology is that perfect obedience was required of Adam. This has been the consensus in covenant theology for hundreds of years, even with each new generation reexamining the Biblical data anew. A survey of theologians of the past 500 years would demonstrate this; the handful cited below is merely a representative sample.

In the 17th century, Edward Fisher believed the title, "covenant of works," fit perfectly. (Fisher is author of the famous *Marrow of Modern Divinity*, published in 1644). He wrote, "I conceive that the matter of it cannot properly be called the covenant of works, except the form be put upon it; that is to say, except the Lord require, and man undertake to yield perfect obedience thereunto, upon condition of eternal life and death..." Charles Hodge (1797-1878), the great Princeton theologian of the nineteenth century says, "...it is called the "covenant of works," because perfect obedience was its condition, and to distinguish it from the covenant of grace, which rests our salvation on a different basis altogether."[2] Arthur Pink (1186-1952),

169

popular author of the twentieth century wrote, "…under the covenant of works no provision was made for failure: the obedience required must be perfect and perpetual (Gal. 3:10)."[3] Contemporary author, R.C. Sproul concurs, "The original covenant between God and humankind was a covenant of works. In this covenant, God required perfect and total obedience to His rule."[4]

There are good reasons for this requirement. God's infinite glory and sovereignty demand wholehearted worship and obedience from all His creatures. This becomes easier to see when we observe the love that each member of the Trinity has for the others. The Son of God did not come into the world to seek His own glory, but the glory of the One who sent Him. He lived every day on earth in absolute surrender to the will of the Father, driven not by fear, but by unquenchable flames of love. Therefore, to this very day, wherever Christ leads a soul into fellowship with God, His foremost purpose and desire is that the heart of every redeemed one should, following His steps, be consumed with burning zeal for the glory of His Father, and walk in obedience.

The apostle Paul has expressed this in beautiful words. And the Son, "taking upon Himself the form of a servant, being found in appearance as a man, He humbled Himself and *became obedient to death, even death on a cross*. Therefore, God exalted Him to the highest place and gave Him the Name that is above every Name, that at the Name of Jesus every knee should bow, in heaven and on earth and under the earth, and every tongue confess that Jesus Christ is Lord, to the glory of God the Father." In another letter to the churches, the apostle describes this scene of glory with different words, "…He raised Him from the dead and seated Him at His right hand in the heavenly realms, far above all rule and authority, power and dominion, and every title that can be given, not only in the present age but also in the one to come. And God placed all things under His feet and appointed Him to be head over all things for the church…" (Ephesians 1:20-22) In his letter to the Corinthians, Paul sheds yet further light, "For he 'has put everything under his feet.' Now when it says that "everything" has been put under Him, it is clear that this does not include God Himself, who put everything under Christ."

God has given not only the world and the ends of the earth to the Last Adam, but has "placed under his feet" the entire universe. Yet, God will not subject Himself. Today, He still requires subjection and obedience from the Son of God. If this is forever required of Christ, the Last Adam, surely such obedience must have been required from the first "son of God",[5] the first Adam.

Furthermore, mankind are lowly creatures made by His own hand that God has exalted, stamping His own image on their souls and raising them to heights of glory. No human can ever be equal to the eternal Son of God. For Him, alone, it is not robbery to be called God's equal. He is co-equal with the Father and the Holy Spirit, co-Eternal, co-Infinite, co-Almighty. He is the shining forth of God's glory, the powerful Word of His mouth, the exact representation of His nature.

Nevertheless, in unashamed Love, Christ submits Himself to the will of the Father, being obedient to His will in every word He speaks, every step He takes, doing all things to please Him, not only during his life on earth, but forever and ever.

If then, the eternal submission of the Son of God is the model, in His most pure-hearted devotion to the Father, can anyone think that humans made in God's image should render anything less than perfect obedience? Paul sets this model before his readers when he outlines the following order, "Now I want you to realize that the head of every man is Christ, and the head of the woman is man, and the head of Christ is God." (1 Cor. 11:3) This is an important economy, dismissed by modernism, but vital to God's design.

What does it mean that the head of Christ is God? If it refers to the Trinity, it indicates that within the Godhead, there is not only headship on the part of the Father, but willing submission and obedience from the Son. It has already been seen that obedience is the most distinct characteristic of the Lord Jesus Christ.

It is likely this also refers to Jesus Christ as an incarnated human being; then it must have something to do with Christ's role as the Last Adam where He is seen standing at the head of a new humanity, yet required to be a Servant in complete submission to God. This is the Christ, sharing our humanity, actually seen in the world. His willing submission to the Father's headship is most beautifully displayed in every word He spoke, every deed, and every miracle. As this Last Adam entered the world in the role of Yahweh's forever faithful and obedient Servant, so the first Adam must have been called to the same duty, since the first Adam was also "head of every man." Or to say this another way, if perfect and absolute obedience is forever displayed by the Last Adam, this must have been God's requirement for the first Adam, howbeit through only a single commandment. If such

171

obedience was required from our first father, Adam, it is also required of Adam's children. Robert Haldane (1764-1842) wrote, "All men are by nature placed under the law, as the covenant of works made with the first man, who, as the Apostle had been teaching in the fifth chapter, was the federal or covenant-head of all his posterity."[6] To carry this into the new covenant, if our head, Jesus Christ, must submit wholeheartedly to the will of God, how can we be called to anything less? We are members of His body, to conform to His will. Walking in the footsteps of Jesus is more than trusting in Him for salvation. It is to follow His leading as He submits with all His heart, all His strength, and all His mind, to the Father's will.

The order in 1 Corinthians 11:3 describes not only headship, but willing submission, "Now I want you to realize that the head of every man is Christ, and the head of the woman is man, and the head of Christ is God." (1 Cor. 11:3) Christ showed what this headship means to Him throughout His life on earth. He obeyed the will of the Father in everything He did. In Ephesians 5:24, this pattern of Christ's subjection, "in everything," is brought to the wife as her example to follow, "Now as the church submits to Christ, so also wives should submit to their husbands *in everything*." There is an implied qualifier here, seen in the life of Christ. He submitted in everything to the Father's will, because the will of God in all things is perfect and just and right. But this is not true of the will of fallen sons of Adam. There will be many things a wife cannot be subject to. In 1 Peter 3, the apostle encourages wives to "be submissive to your husbands so that, if any of them do not believe the word, they may be won over without words by the behavior of their wives." Yet, he concludes by saying that godly women are daughters of Sarah "if you do what is right and do not give way to fear" (1 Peter 3:6) So a woman shows submission to her husband who is her head, but over him is another head to whom she has sworn wholehearted obedience, God the Father. She must always be careful to "do what is right" in His sight, even when her husband would lead her otherwise, "and not give way to fear," at the same time showing the desire to be subject to her husband, through "a gentle and quiet spirit." There are Biblical illustrations which bring this lesson to life. In Joshua 7 there is the story of Achan, who disobeyed God's ban on the goods of Jericho, coveted clothing and treasure, and hid them in his tent. When God revealed the crime to Joshua and the people, the entire family suffered the penalty of death with him. Yet God says elsewhere, "the son shall not die for the sin of the father, nor shall the father die for the sin of the son." (Ezekiel 18:4, 20) Therefore, there must have also been guilt in the wife, sons and daughters, for all paid with their lives. This is a shocking incident, but it is in the Scripture to teach us a very important lesson. A wife is to "submit to her husband in everything," that is, if her husband also submits to God in things he leads her to do. But if her husband leads her to commit sin, she must refuse. For she has an obligation higher than her husband "to do what is right" in the sight of God. If Achan's wife had resisted when her husband buried the treasure in her tent, she could have saved herself and her children. Her submission, following her husband *in everything,* was rebellion against God, and cost a dear price.

So here is the pattern. "God is the head of Christ." Christ clearly submits to the perfect will of the Father in everything, as an example for us to follow, even while serving as the Prophet, Priest and King of the new covenant, exalted to the highest throne in glory to this present day. Christ, as Last Adam, demonstrates the obedience that should have been shown by the first Adam. The wife is clearly commanded to follow Christ's example, for "the husband is head of the wife" (Eph. 5:23), "man is the head of woman" (1 Cor. 11:3). Therefore, Paul writes, *"Now as the church submits to Christ, so also wives should submit in everything to their husbands."* (Ephesians 5:24, ESV)

But where is the commandment that the husband "should submit in everything"? Paul writes, "Christ is the head of every man." (1 Cor. 11:3) If the wife must submit "in everything" to her head, the husband, the same principle must apply in the husband's submission to Christ. Just as Christ wholeheartedly follows the will and word of the Father, so the husband is to obey the word of Christ in all things, and lead his family to do the same.

When husbands and wives submit to God in this way, there is a dual picture of Christ before the eyes of the children. The husband, laying down His life for His wife, becomes an illustration of the love of Christ for His bride, the church. Any child who sees his father putting the needs of his wife before himself, will be deeply impacted by this selflessness and learn more than any vocal lesson. The same is true for the pattern of Christ shown by the wife. As she submits to her head *just as Christ submits to the Father in everything*, the children learn submission by the example of their mother who follows the leading of the father with a "gentle and quiet" spirit, that is, a submissive heart (1 Peter 3:4). Children learn far more quickly by example than command. Seeing submission in their parents in their tender formative years, they will imitate submission to authority and to God. When they see their father obeying God's Word when the whole world scorns him or pulls in another direction, and the mother willingly and quietly submitting to her husband as He follows the Word of God, they will understand who the true Head of their home really is, God Himself.

With Adam in the Covenant of Works, there was more than the principle of submission to God. Covenant theology has always held that Adam's obedience, required in the Covenant of Works, was a test for a certain period of time, *a probationary period.*

Since Adam was "a type of Him who was later to come," we look to Christ for the parallel that may shed light on Adam's own test. It is precisely where it should be found, immediately after Christ was anointed by the Holy Spirit at the River Jordan. He had lived "under the Law" of Moses as an ordinary Jew for thirty years, the age when a Levi would enter priestly service. When baptized with water by John, the heavens were opened and God Himself bore witness to the righteousness of Christ. Christ revealed that this was the purpose of his baptism, *"to fulfill all righteousness."* After years of waiting for this moment, John finally found himself face to face with the Lord. He had prepared all his life to be His forerunner. To prepare the way for Christ to appear, John called all Israel to repent of their sins, ceremonially cleansing them with the water of baptism to make ready a people for the coming of the Lord. Through the Holy Spirit, John knew the man standing before Him was the Messiah, just as he had once leaped for joy in his mother's womb when the mother of Jesus entered the room.

John was overwhelmed by the moment. He knew he is not worthy even to tie this man's sandal; he had said it many times. He pleaded with Jesus, "I need to be baptized by you, and do you come to me?" (Matthew 3:14). But Christ's answer shows why He, too, as other Jews, must present Himself to John for cleansing, "Let it be so now; it is proper for us to do this *to fulfill all righteousness"* (Matthew 3:15). Christ had lived thirty years to maturity without sin. He was ready to begin his ministry as the spotless sinbearing lamb. Only one command of the Father still awaited obedience for His righteousness to be confirmed by God; He had to present Himself to John with all Israel, and be baptized like everyone else, as a man who had lived under the Law. God had made John ready for this moment long ago; John revealed what the Holy Spirit taught him, "...he who sent me to baptize with water said to me, 'He on whom you see the Spirit descend and remain, this is he who baptizes with the Holy Spirit.'" (John 1:33; ESV) A few moments later, the heavens were opened, John witnessed the Spirit descending in the form of a dove, and the voice of the Father thundered from the heavens, "You are my beloved Son; with you I am well pleased" (Mark 1:11; ESV). John, catching his breath, began testifying to all who were present, "And I have seen and have borne witness that this is the Son of God" (John 1:34; ESV)

The righteousness of the Last Adam was fulfilled and confirmed. When the first Adam was created from dust, he had to be tested in the Covenant of Works already mature, perhaps as a man of thirty years would appear, before he could begin producing children for God. Now, the second sinless man has come into the world and attained to the age of manhood without once sinning. The time had come. Before He could fulfill His role as the Last Adam, from whom all of God's children would be spiritually born, there remained only the test. Mark writes, "At once the Spirit drove Him out into the desert, and he was in the desert forty days, being tempted by Satan" (Mark 1:12).

The covenant God established with Noah began with forty days of poured out wrath.

When the Sinai covenant was inaugurated, Moses told the people God's words, wrote the words into the Book of the Covenant, gathered the people again, and read all the words to them from the Book. After that, came the period of testing. Moses was taken away, with God on the mountain for forty days. Will the people follow the Word of God, the Book of the Covenant, as they have sworn? The words of Hosea 6:7 testify to their failure, not only at Horeb, but also in the wilderness and in the land of promise, "Like Adam, they have broken the covenant, they were unfaithful to me there."

When the new covenant was established it was different. The prophet, priest and king of the heavenly covenant was anointed by the Spirit from heaven. Before He should begin His ministry as the Great Prophet of the new covenant, He must overcome Satan where the first Adam had so miserably failed. The end of the forty days saw the Last Adam still standing faithfully on the Word of God, and Satan slinking away, licking the first wounds of the bruising of his head. Now Christ could begin to preach, "The time is fulfilled; the kingdom of heaven is at hand. Repent, and believe the good news!"

Since there was a probationary period of Christ's testing, we may assume the same for the test of Adam, though there is no revelation in Scripture to confirm how long this probation might have lasted. In any case,

Adam's wholehearted subjection to God and to His Word, was to prove itself before he would begin producing children bearing a flawless image of God. The test would not go on forever. Adam would stand by his one act of obedience and merit eternal life, life that would be confirmed to him and to his descendants; or his one act of disobedience would bring judgment, condemnation and death to all who were in him. They would be born as righteous children of a righteous father, or corrupt children of a fallen sinful father. Paul has already shown in Romans 5:12ff, that the latter was the miserable outcome.

The question of *merit* still remains.

The word, *merit*, has been in Reformed creeds for centuries. In the Westminster Confession of Faith, it refers to the righteousness Christ established by perfectly obeying the Law of Moses and the commandments God gave to Him personally, "This perseverance of the saints depends not upon their own free will, but upon the immutability of the decree of election, flowing from the free and unchangeable love of God the Father; (2 Tim. 2:18–19, Jer. 31:3) *upon the efficacy of the merit and intercession of Jesus Christ,* (Heb. 10:10, 14, Heb. 13:20–21, Heb. 9:12–15, Rom. 8:33–39, John 17:11, 24, Luke 22:32, Heb. 7:25) …"[7]

"The efficacy of the merit and intercession of Christ" is explained in the Westminster Larger Catechism, by answering the question, "How does Christ make intercession?" as follows: "by his appearing in our nature continually before the Father in heaven, (Heb. 9:12 ,24) in the merit of his obedience and sacrifice on earth, (Heb. 1:3) declaring his will to have it applied to all believers; (John 3:16, John 17:9,20,24) answering all accusations against them, (Rom. 8:33–34) and procuring for them quiet of conscience, notwithstanding daily failings, (Rom. 5:1–2, 1 John 2:1–2) access with boldness to the throne of grace, (Heb. 4:16) and acceptance of their persons (Eph. 1:6) and services. (1 Pet. 2:5)"[8]

Merit is mentioned in the second phrase, "the merit of his obedience and sacrifice on earth." The *New Dictionary of Theology* says that "Merit is that which in a good action qualifies the doer for reward."[9]

Some say that Christ could not establish righteousness under the Law, that is, he could not merit righteousness, since He is already perfectly righteous from eternity. True, Christ does have incorruptible righteousness, but the "righteousness that is according to the Law" is the assessment of a person on the basis of obeying or disobeying God's commands. The Law says that those who keep all of God's commands are righteous, those who do not are unrighteous. The Law promises that the righteous inherit life on their own merits. The unrighteous are condemned by the Law and are under the curse of the Law. For them, the only hope of rescue from curse and condemnation is through the grace that comes by the One Man who paid for their sins at the cross. Yet, they still need to have righteousness to ascend into heaven, live forever, become God's own children, rule over the nations and inherit the earth and the heavens. Since those who are forgiven do not have this perfect righteousness, they need to obtain it from God. It must be a human righteousness, confirmed by the Law. It must be a perfect righteousness approved by God's Law. There is only one man who has such righteousness. "...All have sinned and fall short of the glory of God" but one man, Jesus Christ. He is the only human rewarded with all things promised to those who obey God. Every other person in human history is condemned under the Law by His own sin. God describes only Christ as "My righteous One." There is no other human righteousness. Those redeemed from condemnation live only by the grace that comes through the One Man, Jesus Christ.

This is the reason that union with Christ is the only way to live forever in glory with God. Union with Christ is to be grafted into Him, to be a member of His spiritual body, to be baptized by the Holy Spirit into Christ, to be chosen *in Him* from the foundation of the world. All who are "in Christ" are members of Him and possess His merits, that is, the perfect righteousness the Law requires. Those in Christ also own His eternal life, His glorification and His inheritance of all things from the Father.

Merit has fallen on bad times. Many are raising questions today about the legitimacy of this word, *merit*, as it stands in the Westminster Confession of Faith, and other early Reformed creeds. The old adage, too many cooks spoil the broth, is a wise word for these times. Into the soup kettle every doubt is cast. They are mostly very common questions, circulated again and again. Did Adam need to merit anything? Could he merit anything? Wasn't he already a perfect image of God? What could he earn? Furthermore, wasn't God condescending in amazing grace simply in making a covenant with Adam? Isn't absolute obedience to God always mandatory anyway? The idea that Adam could do anything to merit life with God has become a raw soupbone that some disdain the thought of chewing. When the very concept of merit has become a brew of bitter herbs and rancid odor, into the mix is stirred questions on whether Christ Himself merited

177

anything all.

Calvin writes, "When Paul declared that all prophecy ought to be according to the analogy of faith (Rom. 12:6), he laid down the surest rule for determining the meaning of Scripture. Let our doctrine be tested by this rule and our victory is secure."[10]

Robert Dunzweiler explains what Calvin means by the phrase, "analogy of faith":

> "The "analogy of faith," to which we are to "bring every interpretation of Scripture," refers to the ultimate rule or standard of interpretation, the final test of all doctrine; namely, the teaching of Scripture as a whole. Analogy suggests comparison; thus we are to compare a proposed interpretation of a specific portion of Scripture with the interpretation which Scripture as a whole; either explicitly or generally, gives to itself. Analogy suggests proportion or measure; thus we are to ascertain the intention and importance of a single text of Scripture in proportion to its place and distribution in the whole body of revealed truth. Analogy also suggests relationship; thus we are to study the particular doctrines of Scriptures in relation to the system of doctrine revealed therein."[11]

The idea is that "the teaching of Scripture as a whole" is the test to determine if are our interpretations are on the right track. Calvin insists that the Reformers learned this "analogy of Scripture" *from Paul himself.*

Let us take the "analogy of Scripture" to the question of merit. Almost all Bible interpreters agree that the whole of Scripture teaches that all of us are sinners, and that a sinner cannot possibly merit righteousness with God on the basis of the works of the Law. For every one of us, salvation is by grace alone through faith alone, and righteousness is a gift from God, through faith. This is so universally understood that most churches will not keep a preacher if he can't see this point in Scripture. This is the reason the *New Dictionary of Theology* says,

> In a *superficial sense* the theological idea of merit arises from the many passages of Scripture which promise reward for obedience and punishment (or demerit) for disobedience (e.g. Dt. 5:28–33; Mt. 5:3–12). Paul affirms that God 'will give to each person according to what he has done' (Rom. 2:6). The apostle goes on to teach, however, that the rebellion of man precludes the possibility of relating to God on the basis of merit. Reliance on the principle of reward is fatal, for 'the wages of sin is death';

eternal life comes from 'the gift of God … in Christ Jesus our Lord' (Rom. 6:23).[12]

This statement explains Paul's position: *"The apostle goes on to teach, however, that the rebellion of man precludes the possibility of relating to God on the basis of merit. Reliance on the principle of reward is fatal…"* This is with respect to sinners. Paul certainly does teach this. But can we say that the "theological idea of merit" has only a *"superficial sense,"* because such merit is impossible for us to attain to? Doesn't God mean what He says in Scripture, that the obedient will be rewarded, the righteous will inherit life? This is impossible for sinners, but these words were written for the One Man who *could* fulfill them, "born under the Law, that He might redeem those who were under the Law". With respect to that one righteous man, there is a question to answer from Scripture "as a whole," from the *analogy of Scripture.* Does the Scripture promise repeatedly that eternal life will be the reward for obedience, such as for perfect obedience?

Let the evidence speak for itself. The Lord commands that by the mouth of two or three witnesses every fact is to be confirmed. The Master Teacher, Truth Himself, calls the witnesses to the stand with His familiar, "What do you read? What do the Scriptures say?"

Moses steps forward first. The voice of the great prophet speaks boldly, "This day I call heaven and earth to witness against you that I have set before you life and death, blessings and curses. Now choose life, so that you and your children may live, and that you may love the Lord your God, listen to His voice, and hold fast to him. For the Lord is your life…" (Deuteronomy 30:19-20a)

Paul takes the witness stand. First, he defends the testimony of Moses. "Moses describes in this way the righteousness that is by the law: "The man who does these things will live by them." Then Paul declares his own revelation from God, "To those who by persistence in doing good seek glory, honor and immortality, He will give eternal life."

Paul steps down, and Christ Himself takes the stand. He is cross-examined by a rich, young ruler, "Good teacher, what good thing must I do to get eternal life." The Lord answers, "If you want to enter life, keep the commandments" (Matthew 19:17).

At this point, court spectators begin murmuring. How can this be? It goes against everything Paul teaches about justification! It is best that Paul himself answer then. It is most certainly true, as Paul has written, that

179

"by the works of the Law no flesh will be justified in His sight, for through the Law comes the knowledge of sin." It is true that all who are born with a sinful nature, are under the curse and under the Law of sin and death. Paul himself has written, "The Law speaks to those who are under the Law, that every mouth may be closed, and the whole world become accountable to God."

Yet, this does not hold true for Christ. He was born under the Law, and yet without sin.

No other person in human history obeyed Moses perfectly and explicitly under the Law. Only Christ obeyed Moses. He "loved Yahweh" and "listened to His voice" without sin. He "held fast to Him" just as Moses said, without any transgression to be condemned by the Law. This was the obedience demanded of the first Adam. He entered the covenant without sin, and the tree of life held the promise of life before Him. Placing the two trees in the center of Paradise, it was as if God said, "Behold, I place before you life and death, blessing and cursing; now choose life, so that you and your children may live, Adam, and that you may love the Lord your God, listen to His voice, and hold fast to him. For the Lord is your tree of life..."

What of the second witness? Christ obeyed Paul's testimony perfectly. By His "persistence in doing good" Christ did "seek glory, honor and immortality," and He knew that God "will give eternal life" to Him. His righteous obedience, throughout His life, confirmed that He is righteous and worthy of eternal life, and death could not keep Him in the ground. It is the Last Adam's perfect righteousness and eternal life that all who are "in Him" have now been made partakers of.

On the other hand, the first Adam failed to obey and was driven from the tree of life. Being declared unrighteous by disobeying the Law, he and all who are "in him" are subject to death.

The third witness, Christ Himself, said, "If you want to enter life, keep the commandments." His whole life was an example of this. Christ did "keep the commandments" and looked to God for His reward of life. That reward raised Him from the dead, and all the elect with Him.

The first Adam disobeyed the command, and lost the tree of life. All his seed are dead in trespasses and sins with him. Paul confirms both the demerit and the merit, the penalty and the reward, "In Adam, all die; in Christ, all shall be made alive."

In the *analogy of faith*, what is accomplished by the Last Adam

180

through perfect obedience in His covenant with the Father, should have been true of the first Adam when his obedience was tested in the Covenant of Works. It is the merits of Christ, in both active and passive obedience, that the Law pronounces righteous. The Law rewards or punishes those under the Law, in direct relation to their submission to or rejection of the Law of God. The righteousness that covenant law recognizes and promises to reward is the merits of Christ established by faithful obedience to God under the covenant of redemption, the covenant of works, the covenant of Sinai and the new covenant today. Many do not recognize the idea of merit valid in Christ's case because the inherent righteousness of Christ is thought to preclude any necessity for the *rule of Law* to declare righteousness based on merits. But this is not so difficult. If we are condemned by our demerits under the Law, the *rule of Law* has only fulfilled the curses written in the Law. Condemnation based on demerits should help us understand righteousness based on merits, even if there is no possibility of a world of sinners meriting anything from God.

Chapter Ten Notes

1. Mark Karlberg. *Journal of the Evangelical Theological Society 52*, no. 2 (Lynchburg: Evangelical Theological Society, 2009), 411, Logos e-book.

2. Hodge, *Confession*, 122.

3. A.W. Pink, *An Exposition of the Sermon on the Mount* (Escondido, CA: Ephesians Four Group, 2002), 354, Logos e-book.

4. R.C. Sproul, "24. Covenant of Works." *Essential Truths of the Christian Faith* (Wheaton, Ill.: Tyndale House, 1996), Logos e-book.

5. Luke 3:37b.

6. Robert Haldane, *An Exposition of Romans* (Simpsonville, SC: Christian Classics Foundation, 1996), 287, Logos e-book.

7. *Westminster Confession of Faith*, XVII, 2.

8. *Westminster Larger Catechism*, Q55.

9. S.B. Ferguson and J.I. Packer, *New Dictionary of Theology* (Downers Grove, IL: InterVarsity Press, 2000), 422, Logos e-book.

10 . Calvin, "Prefatory Address to the King of France," *Institutes*.

11. Robert J. Dunzweiler, "Footnote D127," in Calvin, John. *Institutes of the Christian Religion.* (Bellingham, WA: Logos Research Systems, Inc., 1997). Robert Dunzweiler's footnotes were added to the 1997 Logos digital version of Calvin's Institutes.

12. Ferguson, *New Dictionary*, 422.

Eleven
The "Eternal Purpose" of God

In Isaiah 54:1, the prophet exhorts Sarah, the wife of Abraham, "Sing, O barren one, who did not bear; break forth into singing and cry aloud, you who have not been in labor! For the children of the desolate one will be more than the children of her who is married," says the Lord. " (Isaiah 54:1, ESV) Sarah is an illustration of the kingdom of heaven and its capitol city, Jerusalem. The heavenly Jerusalem had few children for centuries, while the worldly Jerusalem had many children born as slaves to Babylonians, Persians, Greeks and Romans. In Galatians 4:21-31, Hagar represents earthly Jerusalem and the Sinai Covenant. This covenant of earthly things was the slave woman who raised a son to Abraham as if she was the wife "who is married," but God was waiting to bless Sarah, the free woman, who represented the covenant of heaven.

Standing just before Isaiah 54, Chapter 53 foretells the death of Christ, the sacrifice of the new covenant, in remarkable detail. Immediately after these graphic details of Christ's sufferings, Isaiah declares in chapter 54, that *"the children of the desolate one will be more..."* and commands her in the next verse to *"Enlarge the place of your tent, and let the curtains of your habitations be stretched out; do not hold back; lengthen your cords and strengthen your stakes. For you will spread abroad to the right and to the left, and your offspring will possess the nations and will people the desolate cities. "* (Isaiah 54:2–3, ESV)

Isaiah 54:9 compares the promise of Noah's covenant to the promises of Christ's covenant, *"This is like the days of Noah to me: as I swore that the waters of Noah should no more go over the earth, so I have sworn that I will not be angry with you, and will not rebuke you. For the mountains may depart and the hills be removed, but my steadfast love shall not depart from you, and my covenant of peace shall not be removed," says the Lord, who has compassion on you."* (Isaiah 54:9-10; ESV)

In these words, Yahweh declares that the covenant of Christ is like the covenant of Noah. God made promises to Noah without adding any conditions, "I swore that the waters of Noah should no more cover the earth." These promises will most certainly be fulfilled. In Isaiah 54:9-10, He now swears to those redeemed by Christ in the "covenant of peace" that His "steadfast love shall not depart" from them. As with Noah, there are no conditions here, either. Rather, God declares an oath, "I have sworn that I will not be angry with you and will not rebuke you."

This is remarkable.

Surely, now whenever God sees the rainbow in the clouds and remembers his everlasting covenant with Noah, He also recalls this promise in Isaiah 54, His everlasting covenant made through Jesus Christ with all who are "in Him."

As a sign of the covenant, the rainbow is a fitting symbol arching over the heads of God's new covenant people. It begins on one end with God's eternal promises made to His Son from eternity and it ends with the coming of His Son into the world fulfilling all that the Father commanded, receiving promised blessings that are bestowed unconditionally upon all who belong to Jesus. There can be no conditions remaining since all the conditions were fulfilled by Christ Himself.

Sugerloaf Mountain, in the state of Maine, is the biggest ski resort in the eastern US. The mountain is covered with ski trails with lifts to bring skiers quickly back up to the top of the mountain. Skiers ride up the slopes in cable cars or bench seats hanging from a suspended moving cable. On one side of each lift, seats going up the mountain are full of passengers. A few feet away the same cable carries empty seats back down to pick up more people. In December, 2010, there was a freak accident at Sugerloaf mountain. Because of high winds the seats were flung up and down, one cable slipped from a trolley on a high pole and five skiers fell 30 feet to the ground below. Thankfully, no one was critically injured.

The covenants of God and His promises in the prophetic Scriptures are like that cable starting at the bottom, the origin in eternity, and ending in the victory of Christ for believers, securing heaven and eternal life. When passengers board at the bottom of the mountain their goal is to reach the top. The cable starts somewhere behind them as do the promises the Father made to His Son from eternity. The cable ends at the top in the full revelation of Jesus Christ dying for the sins of the world on Mt. Moriah, the perfect sacrifice to carry us to heaven. The cable going up is all the revelations and promises: of the Christ who will come into the world, the kingdom of heaven, and the everlasting covenant. From its eternal origin, the covenant of redemption leads us through all the course of history pointing only to Christ and bringing the elect to Him. When we reach the top and we are in Christ, the cable can be clearly seen leading back down through history making a straight line to only one starting point, the covenant established between the Trinity for redemption before time began.

Any slip from this track results in a disastrous fall away from God, like the five skiers who plummeted to the ground.

Even though *all the covenants* are traced back to promises God made to His Son in eternity, many even of theologians still don't get the point, that they were *covenant promises*. There was a covenant established between the Father and the Son for the redemption of God's elect in the world. That is why Adam, in the Covenant of Works, is "a type of Him who is later to come." Of course, for those Bible teachers who deny that Adam was in covenant with God, the fog at the base of the mountain obscures their vision of the covenant of redemption, also. But God has placed the signs where we can see them. There are allusions in every major covenant to the covenant between the Father and the Son, so that we can distinguish it in the murky depth that lies so far behind. If not, what does Paul mean when he says that the promises of Abraham's covenant "were spoken to Abraham and to his seed…a single seed, that is Christ" (Gal. 3:16). When were the promises spoken to Christ? God established the covenant with Abraham, a type of Christ, as a shadow of the covenant he had established with His Son from eternity. An understanding of how the promises to Christ were actually fulfilled makes it easy to understand the Father's meaning when He spoke words similar to these, from eternity:

My Son, leave your Father's house, and your Father's country, and go to the land I will show you, to the mountains of Moriah, where I make you a sacrifice for all peoples. There, I will make from you a great nation, the very kingdom of heaven, I will bless you and make your name very great in all the earth, so that you will be a blessing to all who trust in You.

185

Forevermore, I will bless those who bless you, and him who dishonors you I will curse, and in you, My Son, all the families of the earth shall be blessed. (Genesis 12:1-3); my own paraphrase of ESV).

Paul understood the Father's meaning perfectly (see Galatians 3:16) and left his own signs on the mountainside, "And the Scripture, foreseeing that God would justify the Gentiles by faith, preached the gospel beforehand to Abraham, saying, "In you shall all the nations be blessed."'" (Galatians 3:8; ESV)

Believers are supposed to figure out this mystery by watching the covenant cable that goes back down the mountain to its eternal origin. To say this another way, we are supposed to follow all the covenant clues scattered throughout Biblical history back to the eternal plan, and the covenant He established with His Son from eternity for our redemption. God is not going to state this plainly. It is one of the mysteries of the kingdom of heaven.

The apostle saw it clearly enough. Standing at the top, in the full revelation of Christ's appearance in the world, Paul's sharp spiritual insight could pierce down into the fog of the valley below and understand the mysterious origin which he calls, "the mystery of Christ, which was not made known to the sons of men in other generations as it has now been revealed to his holy apostles and prophets by the Spirit" (Eph. 3:4-5; ESV). So Paul left many markers and signs to help us see where the cable came from, without fully uncovering every detail.

The Lord Jesus revealed that certain mysteries about Himself are to remain mysteries. In Matthew 13, His disciples want to know why Jesus teaches the public with parables. He replied, "To you it has been given to know the secrets of the kingdom of heaven, but to them it has not been given." (Matthew 13:11; ESV)   So Jesus revealed truths in a hidden manner. Everything was not going to be plainly stated.

Just like Jesus, Paul describes mysteries in such a way that there is still a mystery, even after Paul's revelations, the truth is still in a form that is hiding something.

In Ephesians 1:4, he says of believers that "he chose us in him before the foundation of the world, that we should be holy and blameless before him. In love he predestined us for adoption as sons through Jesus Christ, according to the purpose of his will," (Ephesians 1:4-5; ESV)

What was this mysterious transaction between the Father and the

186

Son, when certain persons were "chosen in Him" from eternity? Paul doesn't tell us. He merely thrusts the signpost into the ground that directs us to look beyond Adam to eternal origins for God's secret purpose and eternal plan that He is fulfilling in the earth by sending Christ.

Shall we assume that there was no *consultation* between the members of the Trinity? But then why does God reveal a consultation when creating man, "Let us make man in our image, and let them rule..." "Behold the man has become as one of us, knowing good and evil."

No *agreement* between the Trinity? Maybe not. There was no agreement between Adam and God; the covenant was simply a sovereign imposition of the will of God. *Impose* is a better word for the administration of a covenant than *agree*. The English word, *impose*, means "to establish or apply by authority." God did not ask Noah to agree to His terms or promises; again, it was a sovereign imposition. There was no agreement with Abraham, no mutual drafting of terms, Abraham didn't sign on the dotted line, God did, when He commanded animals to be brought as a type of Christ and the second member of the Trinity passed between the pieces. He signed with blood. That's why O. Palmer Robertson wrote that a covenant is "a bond in blood, sovereignly administered."[1] It is a sign of Christ's blood, not Abraham's. It is a "signing" in blood, and the name is Jesus Christ.

What was actually imposed on the patriarch? It was a covenant of righteousness by grace through faith. The Covenant of Grace is an imposed gift, received by faith.

If the covenants were impositions, was there no *imposition* of the Father's will on Christ? Who can deny the evidence glaring at the reader so often when Christ speaks in Scripture? "I must do the will of the one who sent Me, and finish His work..." "The Father who sent Me has commanded me what to say, and how to say it..." "I will not speak much more with you for the ruler of this world is coming for me, and he has nothing in me, but the world must learn that I love the Father, and what the Father has commanded, even so I do." "Father, if possible, let this cup pass from Me. Nevertheless, not my will, but thine be done."

These statements and many more like them show that there is an *imposed* purpose for Christ's coming into the world. He was fulfilling commandments given to Him before time began.

There is an interesting passage in Hebrew 10:5, "Consequently, when Christ came into the world, he said, "Sacrifices and offerings you have not desired, but a body have you prepared for me..." (Hebrews 10:5; ESV) The prophet states that Christ said this "when He came into the world," yet the words were written one thousand years earlier. It seems obvious that when David wrote these words at that early date, they were already known by God from before the beginning of time when He first gave His eternal plan to His Son. He is said to have declared this by becoming a human born of Mary, because His physical, truly-human, flesh and blood body is the fulfillment of Psalm 40. If creation itself is a speaking of God, a Word telling the glory of God (Psalm 19), then the incarnation is the shout of God into the darkness of our world. With Psalm 40, His incarnation was a speaking into our humanity of that word prophesied ages before in the secret counsels of the Trinity.

Furthermore, in the Old Testament, Psalm 40 does not even state these words, "a body you have prepared for me," but rather has these words, "my ears you have dug for me" (Lit. Hebrew translation), or "you have given me an open ear." (ESV) This phrase is understood to refer to the custom, in Deut. 15:15-17, of boring a slave's ear with a pointed tool. When a Hebrew slave did not desire freedom in the year of jubilee, but loved his master and would serve him willingly, the master was to bore through his ear with a sharp tool against the door, thus making the man his slave for life.

The *Jamieson, Fausset, and Brown Commentary* explains this, "Christ's assuming a human *body,* in obedience to the Father's will, in order to die the death of a slave (Heb 2:14), was virtually the same act of voluntary submission to service as that of a slave suffering his ear to be bored by his master. His *willing obedience to the Father's will* is what is dwelt on as giving especial virtue to His sacrifice (Heb 10:7, 9, 10). The *preparing,* or *fitting of a body* for Him, is not with a view to His mere incarnation, but to His expiatory *sacrifice* (Heb 10:10), as the *contrast* to "sacrifice and offering" require."[2] This suggests that Christ "gave His ear" to the Father from eternity, or, to state plainly, He submitted Himself in wholehearted love to obey God perfectly in human form, live a sinless life, and die as the sin offering of His people.

The charge to live a sinless life is revealed in Zechariah 3. The Angel of the Lord shows the prophet a vision of Joshua, the High Priest. He's a picture of the true Y'Shua, the High Priest Redeemer who will one day bear the sins of God's people, and come through the fire of judgment with a clean robe of righteousness in the end. The angel of the Lord is Christ Himself. As He shows the vision to Zechariah, He reveals words the Father spoke to Him from eternity, in v. 7, "If you will walk in my ways and keep my charge, then you shall rule my house and have charge of my courts, and I will give you the right of access among those who are standing here." (Zechariah 3:7; ESV) The "right of access" is an allusion to His own right to enter behind the veil into the true Holy of Holies in heaven itself. In Zechariah 6, in another vision of Christ, the Holy Spirit shows that Christ will be perfectly obedient under the Law on earth, when He predicts that "He shall sit and rule on his throne. And there shall be a priest on His throne, and the counsel of peace shall be between them both." To rule in God's "house" and have "charge" of His "courts" depended on the perfect obedience of Christ described in Zech. 3:7. (Zech. 6:13; ESV).

Psalm 110 describes the words the Father promised to His Son from eternity. Because He knew He would most certainly obey perfectly, "The LORD said to my Lord, 'Sit at my right hand, until I make your enemies a footstool for your feet." David does not state that the call to ascend to the heavenly throne will be spoken in the future, but is revealed as past tense even in David's time. It was from eternity that God spoke the words of v. 4, "The Lord has sworn and will not change His mind, you are a priest forever after the order of Melchizedek." It was a priesthood that existed as a sworn promise from eternity, awaiting only the fulfillment of the obedience required in the covenant.

There are many more passages could be referenced, all pointing at certain transactions between the Trinity before the creation of the universe, such as numerous statements by Christ Himself, declaring that His own were given to Him by the Father long before He went to the cross to die for their sins (John 6:37, 39; 10:14-16, 25-30; 17:2, 6, 9, 24).

But consider what has been presented so far. That there was election of certain persons, to be regarded by God forever as "in Christ" before the foundation of the world. Revelation 17:8 declares that their names have been "written in the book of life from the creation of the world." (NIV) There was a commandment that Christ must come into the world for the elect to serve the Father's will, His eternal purpose, before time began. There was, from eternity, the plan that God would prepare a human body for His Son, and that He must, as a human, "walk in all God's ways and keep His charge," and the command that Christ must surrender Himself to die at the hands of the ruler of the world, Satan. In Rev. 13:8, Christ is "the Lamb slain from the creation of the world." God reveals here, at the end of the written Scripture, what was established in the covenant of redemption from the creation of the world. Throughout human history, God has always regarded His Son as the "Lamb slain," and has granted forgiveness to sinners only on this basis.

In the covenant, he was not to remain a "Lamb slain," He could not be kept by death, held in the grave. Rising from the dead to be the High Priest of His people, He would ascend bodily into heaven to serve forever as human King and High Priest in heaven, the Mediator of the new covenant who intercedes for the people He redeems.

Theologians who trace the clues of this covenant in Scripture call it the pre-creation *covenant of redemption* to distinguish it from the Covenant of Grace that God establishes with His people in human history. But it could also be regarded as Christ's personal *Covenant of Works*.

It is a *covenant of redemption* because it demanded Christ's death as payment in full for the sins of the elect, to provide redemption, forgiveness of sins, peace and eternal life for all who are in Christ. George Whitefield, (1714–1770), the greatest evangelist during the Great Awakening in the early American colonies, preached in one of his sermons, "Would to God this point of doctrine was considered more, and people were more studious of the covenant of redemption between the Father and the Son! We should not then have so much disputing against the doctrine of election, or hear it condemned (even by good men) as a doctrine of devils. For my own part, I cannot see how true humbleness of mind can be attained without a knowledge of it…"[3]

It is a *Covenant of Works* because it required that Christ obey God perfectly throughout His entire life as a human born under the Law, then in the final act of obedience, offer Himself to die willingly for the sins of all the elect at the hands of his human and demonic persecutors. With his last gasps of breath, He cried out, "It is finished," to declare that He had fulfilled perfectly all the obedience, all the requirements of this "covenant of works".

In Isaiah 42:6, God declared to His Son from eternity, "I, the LORD, have called you in righteousness, I will take hold of your hand. I will keep you, and will make you to be a covenant for the people and a light for the Gentiles" (Isa. 42:6; ESV).

Because Christ fulfilled the requirements of the Covenant of Works (demonstrating this by His perfect righteousness under the Law of Moses), He gives righteousness and eternal life to all who are in Him. And having fulfilled the covenant of redemption (by obeying God's command to pay for the sins of the elect with His own blood), He provides forgiveness of sins to all who are in Him. Therefore, God now gives the benefits of Christ's death, His broken body and shed blood, the remembrance of His death, and his righteousness as a free gift to those in Him as a *Covenant of Grace*. On the basis of the finished work of Christ in the covenant of redemption, we are saved by grace through faith in the Covenant of Grace, saved by faith in His righteousness, His death, His shed blood, His resurrection, all summarized as "faith in Christ." This grace was secured forever for the elect when Christ represented them in the covenant of redemption. The grace is appropriated by the elect whenever a person learns the gospel and believes in Christ as his or her personal Lord and Savior.

This mysterious eternal plan of God is mentioned in various passages of Scripture, but especially in the writings of the apostle Paul. He hints at it in Ephesians 1:11, "In him we have obtained an inheritance, having been *predestined according to the purpose* of him who works all things according to the counsel of his will..." (Ephesians 1:11; ESV)

Paul understood God's eternal purpose as beginning with election. So when he writes about God's purpose, He almost always mentions election or predestination, as in 2 Timothy 1:9, ""who saved us and called us to a holy calling, not because of our works but because of his own purpose and grace, which he gave us in Christ Jesus before the ages began..." (2 Timothy 1:9; ESV)

In Romans 9:11, he states this most plainly, "though they were not yet born and had done nothing either good or bad, in order that *God's purpose of election* might continue, not because of works but because of him who calls, " (Romans 9:11; ESV)

This entire chapter on election flows from Paul's powerful statement about God's eternal purpose in Romans 8:28-30, "And we know that for those who love God all things work together for good, for those who are *called according to his purpose. For those whom he foreknew he also predestined* to be conformed to the image of his Son, in order that he might be the firstborn among many brothers. And those whom he predestined he also called, and those whom he called he also justified, and those whom he justified he also glorified." (Romans 8:28-30; ESV)

In this passage the apostle reveals why, ultimately, everything works together for good in the life of a true believer. There may be suffering, loss, or hardship in this life for those whom God has foreknown, but every person who is foreknown has also been predestined, called, justified and glorified. These are all past tense terms to indicate that it was determined from eternity, from the time that God the Father established the covenant of redemption with His Son. There are no exceptions. No person that God has predestined will fail to be called, justified or glorified. These words have been a great comfort to those who have faced terrible ordeals as Christians, at the hands of Satan and his children, in this present evil age. On the other hand, some have suffered greatly, simply for accepting Scriptural statements about predestination with childlike faith.

One such person was an Augustinian disciple named Gottschalk of Orbais. Around 400 AD, Augustine articulated the doctrine of predestination, seeing in the Scriptures the election of some to salvation and eternal life, and the just condemnation of those not elected. Named "doctor of the church" by later centuries, his views were nonetheless abandoned by many in favor of the semi-pelagianism advanced by Gregory the Great, so that in later centuries those who embraced Augustinian teaching were sometimes persecuted. Gottschalk of Orbais endured enormous cruelties simply for believing the doctrine of double predestination. Adolf Harnack describes how Gottschalk's understanding began to take root and blossom in his life and teaching:

> "With the devotion, at first of resignation, and afterwards of fanaticism, he committed himself to the hands of God who does all things according to his good pleasure, and does nothing without having determined it irrevocably from the beginning. [Gottschalk believed that] predestination is the content of the Gospel, is the object of faith. It is the truth, that twofold predestination to life and death, according to which eternal life is decreed for the good, and death for the sinner, in which, therefore, some are appointed to life, and the rest to death. Nothing is to be set aside that the Church elsewhere teaches, or that it does; but it is a revolt from the Gospel to obscure in the hearts of men the certainty of this eternal unchangeable dispensation of divine grace, for justice and punishment are also good. Until his death Gottschalk defended inflexibly this faith of his, in the living and original language of the convinced advocate."[4]

Falsely charged with teaching a doctrine of predestination to sin, he was condemned as a "heretic, deposed from the priesthood," and "shut up in the prison of a convent." Philip Schaff writes, "According to the report of eye-witnessses, he was scourged "most atrociously" and "nearly to death," until half dead he threw his book, which contained the proofs of his doctrine from the Scriptures and the fathers, into the fire."[5]

After some time in prison allowed him to think carefully, he decided to compose two confessions of faith "in which he strongly re-asserted his doctrine of a double predestination."[6] Determined never to deny God's Word again, He offered, "in reliance on the grace of God, to undergo the fiery ordeal before the king, the bishops and monks, to step successively into four cauldrons of boiling water, oil, fat and pitch, and then to walk through a blazing pile; but nobody could be found to accept the challenge."[7]

There are some in church history who have denied certain statements in God's Word for less noble reasons. Referring to the doctrines of election and predestination as "the horrible decree," they imagine that Calvin, and other Reformers, viewed God as being sadistic and moody, delighting to create some people to enjoy the bliss of heaven, while finding sadistic pleasure in predestining others to become sinners who suffer forever in hell for the sinful nature God Himself made of them. But that strawman was never the God of Reformed theology. Rather, Calvin understood that God is holy and just, and that He hates all sin. Sin is very serious to Him, much more than it is to us. Inherently sinful, we have by nature such a liberal view of sin and disobedience, that we need the conviction of the Holy Spirit, convicting the world of sin and righteousness and judgment, before we begin to sense that we ourselves are in serious and imminent danger of facing that Day of Judgment. Denny Burke explains why, with sin, there are different degrees of seriousness:

> "Sin will always appear as a trifle to those whose view of God is small. If you were to discover a little boy pulling the legs off of a grasshopper, you would think it strange and perhaps a little bizarre. If the same little boy were pulling the legs off of a frog, that would be a bit more disturbing. If it were a bird, you would probably scold him and inform his parents. If it were a puppy, that would be too shocking to tolerate. You would intervene. If it were a little baby, it would be so reprehensible and tragic that you would risk you own life to protect the baby. What's the difference in each of these scenarios? The sin is the same (pulling the limbs off). The only difference is the one sinned against (from a grasshopper to a baby). The more noble and valuable the creature, the more heinous and reprehensible the sin. And so it is with God.

193

If God were a grasshopper, then to sin against Him wouldn't be such a big deal and eternal punishment wouldn't be necessary. But God isn't a grasshopper, He's the most precious, valuable, beautiful being in the universe. His glory and worth are infinite and eternal. Thus to sin against an infinitely glorious being is an infinitely heinous offense that is worthy of an infinitely heinous punishment.

We don't take sin seriously because we don't take God seriously. We have so imbibed of the banality of our God-belittling spirit of the age that our sins hardly trouble us at all. Our sin seems small because we regard God as small. And thus the penalty of hell, eternal conscious suffering under the wrath of God, always seems like an overreaction on God's part. If we knew God better, we wouldn't think like that."[8]

This is a very important point, but we may need to take a step farther than Burke. It is necessary to consider not only who we sin against, but also who is offended by the sin. It is a great and terrible crime to sin against Jesus Christ. Nevertheless, he says He could forgive such sin and blasphemy against Himself, but whoever blasphemes the Holy Spirit, He will not forgive, neither in this age, nor in the age to come. What does this mean? The members of the Trinity are humble, but their love for each other is such that they simply cannot tolerate wicked acts committed against the other persons. Christ's love for the Holy Spirit is incredibly high and holy, and His wrath will be kindled forever against those who abuse Him with careless words or hateful mockery. We should assume that the Father's love for the Son, and the Son's love for the Father is of the same degree of seriousness.

Some have tried to explain that the key to understanding these ideas is the word, "foreknow." Thomas R. Shreiner comments, "One's understanding of Paul's soteriology is significantly affected by one's understanding of the verb προγινώσκειν (proginōskein, to foreknow), for predestination unto salvation is limited to those who were foreknown."[9] Shreiner's discussion of proginōskein sheds light on this consideration of election and the covenant of redemption, and should be read carefully to understand the point he is making. He says:

"Some have argued that the verb προέγνω (proegnō, he foreknew) here should be defined only in terms of God's foreknowledge. That is, God predestined to salvation those whom he saw in advance would choose to be part of his redeemed community. This fits with Acts 26:5 and 2 Pet. 3:17, where the verb προγινώσκειν clearly means "to know beforehand." According to this understanding

194

predestination is not ultimately based on God's decision to save some. Instead, God has predestined to save those whom he foresaw would choose him. Such an interpretation is attractive in that it forestalls the impression that God arbitrarily saves some and not others. It is quite unlikely, however, that it accurately represents the meaning of προγινώσκειν when the reference is to God's foreknowledge.

"The background of the term should be located in the OT, where for God "to know" (עָדַי, *yāda*‹) refers to his covenantal love in which he sets his affection on those whom he has chosen (cf. Gen. 18:19; Exod. 33:17; 1 Sam. 2:12; Ps. 18:43; Prov. 9:10; Jer. 1:5; Hos. 13:5; Amos 3:2).

"The parallel terms "consecrate" and "appoint" in Jer. 1:5 are noteworthy, for the text is not merely saying that God "foresaw" that Jeremiah would serve as a prophet. The point is that God had lovingly chosen him to be a prophet before he was born. Similarly, in Amos 3:2 God's knowledge of Israel in contrast to that of the rest of the nations can scarcely be cognitional, for Yahweh had full knowledge of all nations of the earth. The intention of the text is to say that Yahweh had set his covenantal love only upon Israel. Romans 11:2 yields the same conclusion, "God has not rejected his people whom he foreknew." The verb προέγνω here functions as the antonym to ἀπώσατο (*apōsato*, he rejected). In other words, the verse is saying that God has not rejected his people upon whom he set his covenantal love (cf. also Acts 2:23; 1 Pet. 1:2, 20). Similarly, in Rom. 8:29 the point is that God has predestined those upon whom he has set his covenantal affection."[10]

Shreiner guides the reader to the Old Testament to look for shades of meaning because the Jews were by heart speakers of Hebrew/Aramaic. Their use of the common Greek of their day was tempered by the connotations of terms that were carried over into Greek when they translated their thoughts from Hebrew into a dialect that, for many of them, may have been little more than a business language. Exegetes are mistaken when they seek the meanings of NT Greek terms exclusively from secular Greek usage. They had been converting Hebrew ideas into Greek terms for 250 years before the New Testament was written. This affected the particularly Jewish understanding of those terms which were written in the gospels and the epistles to churches.

It should be pointed out that there is an artificial introduction with those who say that God foreknew those who would choose Him, and for this reason alone, He chose them. This idea is not expressed anywhere in the context. The object of "foreknew" is not something believed or done by people in future generations, but is simply the persons themselves, *"those* he foreknew."

R.C. Sproul explains more about the OT and Hebrew sense of the phrase, "He foreknew," showing that it must refer only to those whom God elected and predestined for justification and glorification:

> "Some have argued from Romans 8:29 that predestination is based on God's foreknowledge in the sense that God looked down the corridors of time and saw who would freely choose to believe, and then predestinated them. This position assumes that foreknowledge here only means "knows in advance." In the Bible, however, knowledge is often used in a sense of personal intimacy, as when Adam "knew" Eve and she conceived a son (Genesis 4:1). God's foreknowledge is linked to His foreloving. We see in Romans 8:30 that everyone who was "foreknown" was also "predestined, called, justified, and glorified." Does God glorify everyone? Does God justify everyone? No. Clearly then, in terms of what this passage is dealing with, God does not call everyone, does not predestine everyone, and does not foreknow everyone. In Romans 8:29–30, "foreknowledge" must have the sense of intimacy and personal calling, and can refer only to God's elect. God's predestination does not exist in a vacuum, and it is not simply for the purpose of saving us from sin. Verse 29 shows us the goal or purpose of salvation: that we might be conformed to the likeness of His Son. Ultimately, the reason God has saved you and me is for the honor and glory of His Son, "That He might be the firstborn." The goal in creation is that God would give as a gift to His Son many who are reborn into Christ's likeness."[11]

Jesus tells this story about the predestination of those God foreknew in Matthew chapter 13.

> "He put another parable before them, saying, "The kingdom of heaven may be compared to a man who sowed good seed in his field, but while his men were sleeping, his enemy came and sowed weeds among the wheat and went away. So when the plants came up and bore grain, then the weeds appeared also. And the servants of the

master of the house came and said to him, 'Master, did you not sow good seed in your field? How then does it have weeds?' He said to them, 'An enemy has done this.' So the servants said to him, 'Then do you want us to go and gather them?' But he said, 'No, lest in gathering the weeds you root up the wheat along with them. Let both grow together until the harvest, and at harvest time I will tell the reapers, Gather the weeds first and bind them in bundles to be burned, but gather the wheat into my barn.' " " (Matthew 13:24–30, ESV)

Later, when they were alone with the Lord in a house, the disciples come to Jesus, saying, "Explain to us the parable of the weeds of the field."

"He answered, "The one who sows the good seed is the Son of Man. The field is the world, and the good seed is the sons of the kingdom. The weeds are the sons of the evil one, and the enemy who sowed them is the devil. The harvest is the close of the age, and the reapers are angels. Just as the weeds are gathered and burned with fire, so will it be at the close of the age. The Son of Man will send his angels, and they will gather out of his kingdom all causes of sin and all law-breakers, and throw them into the fiery furnace. In that place there will be weeping and gnashing of teeth. Then the righteous will shine like the sun in the kingdom of their Father. He who has ears, let him hear. " (Matthew 13:36–43, ESV)

The details of this story describe predestination. The man *"sowed good seed"* in *"his field,"* indicating that the owner of the field is the Son of Man. Jesus further explains that the field is the whole world. The Son of Man is planting good seed in His field, that is, everywhere in the world.

During the night, during the age of spiritual darkness, this present evil age, his enemy, the devil, plants bad seed among the sprouting wheat plants.

The good seed are described as the sons of the kingdom. The Son of Man plants *only* good seed, and they sovereignly grow, under His care, to be sons of the kingdom of heaven. They are planted as sons of the kingdom, and harvested as sons of the kingdom. Jesus makes very clear, however, that the bad seed are the "sons of the evil one." These, the Son of Man has no part in "planting," but, "an enemy has done this!" They are children of their father, the devil, and it will be seen that they are his children in the bearing of fruit in their lives and character. Satan disguises them as sons of the kingdom, planting them in the church in order to corrupt or spoil the wheat as much as he can.

These plants, described as weeds or tares, are *darnel*. Darnel is a plant that looks almost exactly like wheat until the time comes to bear fruit, and there is no wheat to harvest. When there is no fruit these plants are finally seen to be false. This is a picture of those so-called Christians, planted among true believers, who appear to believe but are the seed of the serpent They are found anywhere that the church exists in the world. There is no fruit of holiness, godliness, or hungering and thirsting after righteousness. These do not struggle against sin's many colors, but are marked by a love for the devil's worldliness, the self-righteousness of the unrepentant religious Pharisee, and the self-indulgence of Sodom and Gomorrah.

The workers who tend the field for the landowner are angels. As the plants reach the age of tender maturity, it is already becoming obvious to them that many of the plants are not wheat, but weeds. The angels report this to the Son of Man, asking if they should "go and gather them" now. But he answers, *"Let both grow together until the harvest, and at harvest time I will tell the reapers, Gather the weeds first and bind them in bundles to be burned, but gather the wheat into my barn."*

The children of Satan are permitted to grow together with God's children in the church until the day of judgment. To remove them all sooner would harm the wheat plants, because of the close relationships growing up together. At the end of the age, the Son of Man will send forth his angels to remove the sons of the evil one and cast them into the fire, where there will be weeping and gnashing of teeth. Then, says Jesus, *"the righteous will shine like the sun in the kingdom of their Father."*

Now it can be understood that the sons of the kingdom are planted by preaching the gospel to people who appear to be the seed of the serpent because they are "dead in trespasses and sins" like everyone else. They become seedlings of the kingdom when they are raised to life with Christ. They are the blessed souls Paul is describing when he says, "Those whom God foreknew, He also predestined…and those whom He predestined, He also called, and those whom He called, He also justified." Both Romans 8 and Matthew 13 describe children of God brought forth by God's sovereign election and calling. But from their time of spiritual rebirth, having been born of Word and Spirit, they remain children of God throughout the rest of their lives.

There are others, however, in the church, and in Christian fellowship, who will never truly embrace the gospel. Perhaps they do not believe they are such sinners that they desperately need a Savior. Or maybe they secretly continue in their sinful ways while pretending to be repentant. Whatever the reason, they have failed to receive the truth that God is holy judge, that they are utterly sinful, that the day of judgment is coming, and that Jesus Christ is the only person in the history of the world who *can* save them. There are many who will take Jesus as Savior, but not as Lord, they will receive grace, but not if it calls for repentance. The Word of God did not find soil made ready and has borne no lasting fruit. There is no birth from the Word and Spirit and consequently no transformed life. A person with an unregenerate spirit responds to the Word like dead persons in a cemetery. Souls dead in sin may follow for opportunism, if the pay or foreign support or the comfort or the pleasure is appealing, but will not in heart come to Christ that they may have life. That's why Jesus says, "He who has ears to hear, let him hear." Sharp sickle in hand, ready to "burn up the chaff with unquenchable fire," Jesus confronts weeds of the evil one, the seed of the serpent who have ears but cannot hear, in John 8:44, "Why do you not understand My speech? Because you are not able to listen to My word." (John 8:43; NKJV)[12] They were Jews, God's covenant people, but they would not accept Jesus Christ, and even wanted to kill him. His words shocked all who regarded him a prophet, "You are of your father, the devil, and your will is to do your father's desires. He was a murderer from the beginning and has nothing to do with the truth…" The two-edged sword from out of His mouth had found its mark.

Jesus saw people in black and white. Either they are children of God, or children of the devil. "Anyone who is not with me is against me, and whoever does not gather with me scatters" (Luke 11:23). Sons of the kingdom, or the seed of the serpent. Wheat or weeds. There was no middle ground.

"Sir, did you not plant good seed in your field?"

The story of the Bible begins by presenting a man created perfect in all respects, the image and likeness of God in righteousness, holiness, and truth. Paradise was made for him, the earth is given into his hands, eternal life stands before him. Then an astonishing thing happens. Almost immediately, in only the third chapter, this perfect likeness of God, this sinless man, rebels against his Creator and throws in his lot with the Serpent.

The rebellion against the holy God, the highest majesty of the

199

universe, was costly; Adam and his descendants were cut off from God and fell into spiritual death, corruption, and slavery to sin and Satan.

And he said to them, "An enemy has done this!" (Matthew 13:28).

The rebels stood before God in troubled Eden. The LORD God said to the serpent, *"Because you have done this, you are cursed more than all cattle, and more than every beast of the field; on your belly you shall go, and you shall eat dust all the days of your life. And I will put enmity between you and the woman, and between your seed and her Seed; He shall bruise your head, and you shall bruise His heel."* (Genesis 3:14–15, NKJV)

In the first prophetic revelation in human history, God reveals that there will be the seed of the serpent, and there will be the Seed of the woman, and God Himself will stir up hostilities between them, *"I will put enmity between you and the woman, and between your seed and her Seed."*

Love is an attribute of God. It is sometimes said that a loving God must give equal opportunity to all people to be saved. This sounds very right and true. Some insist a loving God is an equal opportunity Savior, but why isn't a righteous God also an equal opportunity judge of all sinners? The meaning of Biblical love will not be expounded in this chapter. Love is a covenant promise and blessing in Scripture, so a later chapter explores Biblical love.

But consider, God has said that all have sinned, and fallen short of the glory of God. There is none righteous; no, not one. He has declared that the wages of sin is death, and that the soul that sins will die.

What if God as judge did not execute justice against sinners? What would people think if the highest criminal court decided to stop prosecuting criminals, insisting that there would no longer be any judgment of wrongdoers in our society? After all, the justices are all loving people. They love their families, their friends and their neighbors. So they insist it is inconsistent for a loving judge to condemn criminals, or send anyone to death row. How would the people respond if the high court declares it is wrong to punish the wicked, all criminal prosecution ceases, prisons are emptied, and all violaters simply told that the judges are not the least troubled by all the terrible things they have done, because it would go against their loving nature.

Will not the nation rise in protest? Will they not say the judges are mad?

It is necessary that the true judge of the earth fulfill every word He has said He will do, and execute righteous justice against all sin. Many times, in writing, He has stated that He will judge every sin on the last day. He would be a liar if He fails to keep His word.

Yet, most sinners insist that God cannot execute justice. They disapprove of His threats of the coming day of judgment, and insist that a loving God would not condemn them.

But let us return to this concept that salvation is about equal opportunity. Does God truly give such opportunity for everyone in the world in all generations and in every nation to learn the gospel of Christ? The Scripture says "It is appointed unto men once to die, and then comes the judgment" (Heb. 9:27). It is necessary, therefore, to learn the gospel and be saved within this one lifetime. Yet, millions of people pass from the cradle to the grave without learning the gospel.

In the universality of sin, believers know that "there is none righteous; no, not one." All deserve the penalty that Adam's rebellious children will receive on the Day of Judgment. The world rejects this foolish message that all people need to repent of their sins and trust in the Savior. Because all are dead in sin, corrupt and depraved, and in spiritual bondage to the will of the evil one, only God's direct intervention will convince sinners that they should not follow the devil and his ways to his final destiny.

This is the reason that God's eternal purpose is according to election. This is important to emphasize again, "And we know that for those who love God all things work together for good, for those who are called according to his purpose. For those whom he foreknew he also predestined to be conformed to the image of his Son, in order that he might be the firstborn among many brothers. And those whom he predestined he also called, and those whom he called he also justified, and those whom he justified he also glorified." (Romans 8:28-30; ESV)

There is a "call" that is "according to His purpose." It involves God "knowing" His elect before they exist, predestining them, calling them, justifying them, and glorifying them. Every person who was elected is predestined, called, justified, and glorified. Then what of those millions of lost sinners who went to the grave without a call?

Does God always give the same opportunity? He told Israel that He showed them signs and wonders that He had never done for any people (Deut. 4:32-40). Those signs and wonders did not offer any opportunity to

Pharoah. Paul reminds us of God's word to the Egyptian king, "For this very purpose I have raised you up, that I might show my power in you, and that my name might be proclaimed in all the earth. So then He has mercy on whomever He wills, and He hardens whomever He wills" (Rom. 9:17-18; cf. Exodus 9:16). Nor did God offer an opportunity to Pharoah's army when they followed Israel into the Red Sea. They were only obeying the orders of their king, but they all perished in the waters after Israel had passed through safely.

When the Amalekites attacked the stragglers in Israel, God was so angry that He commanded Moses to tell Joshua, "I will have war against the Amalekites unto all generations until they are completely destroyed." And he gave instructions that no Amalekite may ever enter the temple area. David was still executing the judgments of God on the Amalekites more than three centuries after Moses.

God was so terribly angry at the evil customs of the miserable Canaanites that He determined to exterminate them from the earth and give their lands as a gift to his covenant people. One city after another was completely destroyed at the command of Yahweh, without permitting a single soul to learn the ways of the true God.

Abraham's call may be the best example of God's purpose in election. Two thousand years before Christ came into the world, God chose the patriarch Abram and gave Him the covenant of justification by grace through faith. In Ephesians 2: 12, the apostle Paul makes very clear that all those who were not members of Abraham's covenant throughout those two millennia were "without Christ...without God, and without hope in the world." This shocking revelation must be accepted or the obvious meaning of the text must be explained away so the reader will feel more comfortable with it.

But why show this mercy to Abraham? He was also a sinner. Before God revealed Himself to Abraham and transformed his heart, he was as dead, as lost and miserable as any in this world. Abraham did not deserve God's love but His justice. He should have received the wages of sin, death. He came from a family of idolaters. Yet God says to all who are pursuing righteousness, to those who truly seek the Lord, "...look to the rock from which you were hewn, and to the quarry from which you were dug. Look to Abraham your father and to Sarah who bore you; for he was but one when I called him, that I might bless him and multiply him." (Isaiah 51:1-2; ESV) God "chose" him,[13] and revealed Himself to him, and "called" him.[14] He blessed Him with justification by grace through faith,[15] and gave him many promises he could never deserve. Truly, in Abraham's case, it did "not depend on him who wills or him who runs, but on God who shows mercy" (Romans 9:16; NKJV).[16] Paul quotes the Lord's words to Moses, but he's applying it to Jews who rejected Christ 1400 years later, showing that God's sovereignty is the same in old covenants as in the new covenant, "I will have mercy on whomever I will have mercy, and I will have compassion on whomever I will have compassion."[17]

If Abraham deserved life, and righteousness, and eternal glory, righteousness would not be gifted to him. But sinners do not deserve any of these things. Therefore, where God bestows His gifts, no one can claim they have a right to the same thing. All sinners have an equal right! Another illustration of criminal justice is helpful here. There may be many sentenced to life imprisonment or death. The Prime Minister, or the President, has the authority to pardon the crimes of any such one. If he does, the rest who are fully guilty of wrong cannot press claim to the same pardon. A criminal, or a sinner, has no right to a gracious gift of pardon. "I will show mercy on whomever I show mercy." Though these are the words of Almighty God Himself, countless expositors, ashamed of God and His words, have endlessly wrestled to explain that God can't possibly mean what He says. Unwilling to accept the God whose eternal purpose is in election, they present a God to the world who fits our taste much better. All of us who are Calvinists today were once like them. We, too, hated these words; they couldn't possibly be right. But this is refusal to believe what God has said about Himself, and when we finally came to terms with our own unwillingness to accept God as Scripture reveals Him, each one of us decided in our own hearts to simply accept what He says, even if our friends don't like the real Biblical picture of a God who is both just *and* merciful, loving *and* angry at sin, righteously condemning the sinner with his sin, *but* still determined to produce children for Himself out of our hopeless stock of fallen humanity. If left to ourselves, all of us would reject Him, all of us would turn away and follow him no more, all of us would spit in His face, beat Him with sticks, and crucify Him. The Synod of Dort described this work of God in this way:

> "For this was the sovereign counsel and most gracious will and purpose of God the Father that the quickening and saving efficacy of the most precious death of His Son should extend to all the elect, *for bestowing upon them alone the gift of justifying faith, thereby to*

bring them infallibly to salvation; that is, it was the will of God that Christ by the blood of the cross, whereby He confirmed the new covenant, should effectually redeem out of every people, tribe, nation, and language, all those, and those only, who were from eternity chosen to salvation and given to Him by the Father; **that He should confer upon them faith**, which, together with all the other saving gifts of the Holy Spirit, He purchased for them by His death; should purge them from all sin, both original and actual, whether committed before or after believing; and having faithfully preserved them even to the end, should at last bring them, free from every spot and blemish, to the enjoyment of glory in His own presence forever."[18]

As I think about this doctrine of election that has been the cause of so many storms of debate and divisions in churches, my thoughts turn to Paul and I can't help wondering what more he would explain about it. I imagine a great edifice rising up around me. "According to the grace of God given to me, like a skilled master builder I laid a foundation, and someone else is building upon it" (2 Cor. 3:10). *I'm amazed when I realize that, just like the Sinai Covenant temple was a picture of Christ, the new covenant temple bears His exact likeness, even more than that, He Himself is this great construction. The temple is the body of Christ, the true vine, and we are its branches.*

With the blueprints for the new covenant temple on my desk (the Holy Scriptures), I see it more clearly rising in all nations, among all peoples, "built on the foundation of the apostles and prophets, Christ Jesus, Himself, being the Cornerstone, *in whom* the whole structure, being joined together, grows into a holy temple in the Lord" (Eph. 2:20-21). The words of the apostle's pen draw my attention to the detail, to the individual stones being pushed and pulled into place to complete and decorate the temple walls. Paul's words explain, "…He chose us in Him before the foundation of the world, that we should be holy and blameless before Him...." (Eph. 1:4). *"Chosen, in Him." How much differently God thinks than us. Which came first, were they chosen because God regarded them as "in Him" from eternity? Or were they "in Him" because God chose them from eternity?*

Not far away, standing in the bright sunlight of the Word, there is a pile of such stones that Paul explains "once were far off" but now "have been brought near through the blood of Christ" (Eph. 2:13). Peter's word encourages them, "As you come to him, a living stone rejected by men but in the sight of God chosen and precious, you yourselves like living stones are being built up a spiritual house, to be a holy priesthood, to offer spiritual sacrifices acceptable to God through Jesus Christ" (1 Peter 2:4-5). *My thoughts are carried away to the vision of Zechariah 6, of the Branch, branching out from His place into all the earth, building the Temple of the new covenant among all Gentile nations. Every stone of the temple, like the Cornerstone, is "in the sight of God chosen and precious," grafted into the body of Christ, living stones because He lives to share His life with them, stones made Holy by the tabernacling of the Holy One within us, where the worship service never ends and the path of the righteous grows brighter and brighter until the full light of glory dawns in the Second Coming of Christ. Zechariah is told, "He shall build the temple, and He will bear the glory within it." But who could have known at the time that He would construct it out of His own body?*

Paul's scribbling pen points us to the foundation, where our eyes, focusing through the darker shadows cast down there, make out the shapes of many scrolls, neatly laid in rows leading directly to the Cornerstone. *Hmmm, almost like they are all pointing in one direction...* As if reading my mind, the apostle's words flow from His pen like streams of living light, "For no one can lay a foundation other than that which is laid, which is Jesus Christ." (1 Cor. 3:11).

Paul's teaching is designed for this, to draw us close, to gaze more intently at that foundation. After all, it is his entire life's work to lead crowds of people to gaze upon this Cornerstone, until finally, with face unveiled, they begin to see "the light of the knowledge of the glory of God in the face of Jesus Christ" (2 Cor. 4:6). Peering through the haze of our own ignorance, having our understanding darkened by long ages of Satan's war against the truth, the words inscribed on the foundation are difficult to see. Paul gives them to us, "God's firm foundation stands, bearing this seal: "The Lord knows those who are his..." 2 Timothy 2:19b.

I realize... that this is where it all begins. God started with this one truth, "The Lord knows those who are His." This is the foundation of everything, the beginning of all that He would accomplish in history. Now the letters that glowed dimly in the darkness stream brilliant light, illuminating Paul's own words inscribed on one of the ancient scrolls lying in the foundation. The meditation words of this chapter, "For those whom He foreknew, He also predestined to be conformed to the image of His Son, in order that He might be the firstborn among many brothers. And those whom

205

he predestined, he also called, and those whom he called he also justified, and those whom he justified he also glorified."

"This is the beginning, and glorified is the end," I muse, "Here is the alpha, and glory the omega. Doesn't the potter have a right over the clay?" (Romans 9:21). *But what about all the theologians who argue that a loving God should not have sovereign right over His own clay?*

"Who are you, O man, to answer back to God." writes Paul, "God's firm foundation stands having this seal..."

But doesn't that result in people of God who are just like the world? The only difference about them is that they were chosen, and others were not? Don't good deeds and righteousness have anything at all to do with our relationship with God?

"...having this seal, "The Lord knows those who are His," and "Let everyone who names the name of the Lord depart from iniquity."

You mean from eternity God started with not one, but two vital truths, sealing His foundation? There is another saying on the foundation of God's works. It is not only, "The Lord knows those who are His," but also, "Let everyone who names the name of the Lord depart from iniquity." This would mean that, though God elects, there must also always be repentance, with each and every elect person.

Paul's pen is really stabbing my heart now, as if to say, "Look at all that I've written about this:

"God is now calling all people everywhere to repent, because He has fixed a day on which He will judge the world in righteousness..." (Acts 17:30-31; ESV).

"For if you live according to the flesh you will die, but if by the Spirit you put to death the deeds of the body you will live..." (Romans 8:13; ESV).

"Cleanse out the old leaven...I am writing to you not to associate with anyone who bears the name of brother if he is guilty of sexual immorality or greed, or is an idolater, reviler, drunkard or swindler, not even to eat with such a one....Purge the evil person from among you" (1Cor. 5:7, 11, 13).

"Or do you not know that the unrighteous shall not inherit the kingdom of God? Do not be deceived: neither the sexual immoral, nor idolaters, nor adulterers, nor men who practice homesexuality,

206

nor thieves, nor the greedy, nor drunkards, nor revilers, nor swindlers will inherit the kingdom of God. And such were some of you, but you were washed…" (1 Cor. 6:9-11; ESV)

This is really Pauline; I see this in all his letters.

"This is the sign of genuineness in every letter of mine; it is the way I write." (2 Thess. 3:17)

I think you mean that you have a characteristic way of signing your letters with your own large print signature, because of your nearly blind eyes.

"It is the way I write," Paul explains, "Now in a great house there are not only vessels of gold and silver but also of wood and clay, some for honorable use, some for dishonorable. Therefore, if anyone cleanses himself from what is dishonorable, he will be a vessel for honorable use, set apart as holy, useful to the master of the house, ready for every good work." (2 Timothy 2:20-21; ESV)

Things are beginning to add up. I think I see it. These two belong together like salt and pepper. A person is elected from eternity to be saved from sin. When he or she finally learns the gospel and believes, there has to be the evidence of a genuine conversion. God really does grant repentance.[19]

The apostle writes, "For we know, brothers loved by God, that he has chosen you, because our gospel came to you not only in word, but also in power and in the Holy Spirit and with full conviction….and how you turned to God from idols to serve the living and true God, and to wait for his Son from heaven, whom he raised from the dead, Jesus who delivers us from the wrath to come." (1 Thessalonians 1:4-5, 9-10; ESV)

JC Ryle has a helpful comment on this, "…let us never forget that the great thing we have to do, is to repent and believe the Gospel. We have no right to take any comfort from God's *election*, unless we can show plain evidence of repentance and faith. We are not to stand still, troubling ourselves with anxious speculations whether we are elect or not, when God commands us plainly to repent and believe. (Acts xvii. 30. 1 John iii. 23.) Let us cease to do evil. Let us learn to do well. Let us break off from sin. Let us lay hold on Christ. Let us draw near to God in prayer. So doing, we shall soon know and feel whether we are God's elect. To use the words of an old divine, we must begin at the grammar school of repentance and faith before we go to the university of election. It was when Paul remembered the faith, and hope, and love of the Thessalonians, that he said, "I know your election of God…" (1 Thess. 1:4)[20]

The foundation of God is sealed with election on one hand and human responsibility on the other. Election is entirely God's department, hidden away from us in His secret counsel, but repentance, turning from all sin, confessing our guilt, and trusting in Christ to save us from sin, is what every person who has been elected must do. We are responsible to listen to the truth, and then follow it wholeheartedly in true love for God, in sincere fear of God. "Let everyone who names the name of the Lord depart from iniquity." *Well, then Whitefield could finally sleep in peace, and people would actually stop calling election a doctrine of devils.*

R.B. Kuiper's illustration of *election* and *responsibility* may be well known, but its worth repeating here,

> "I liken them to two ropes going through two holes in the ceiling and over a pulley above. If I wish to support myself by them, I must cling to them both. If I cling only to one and not the other, I go down.

> "I read the many teachings of the Bible regarding God's election, predestination, his chosen, and so on. I read also the many teachings regarding 'whosoever will may come' and urging people to exercise their responsibility as human beings. These seeming contradictions cannot be reconciled by the puny human mind. With childlike faith, I cling to both ropes, fully confident that in eternity I will see that both strands of truth are, after all, of one piece."[21]

God knows those who are his from eternity, long before repentance reveals they are children of God. If you think about it, that's where Peter starts his writing, "Peter, an apostle of Jesus Christ, to those who are elect…"

And that's where many of Paul's letters start: his epistle to the Romans is penned to those "who are called to belong to Jesus Christ"… and his first epistle to the Corinthians is addressed to those "called to be saints." *Those whom He predestined, He also called.* He launches his word to the Ephesians with the declaration that they are "chosen in Him before the foundation of the world;" and his first letter to the Thessalonians with, "we know, brothers loved by God, that he has chosen you." His second letter to Timothy begins with the "grace which he gave us in Christ Jesus before the ages began;" and to Titus, "Paul, a servant of God and an apostle of Jesus Christ, for the sake of the faith of God's elect…"

We must begin where God does, with the foundation, and Adam.

Chapter Eleven Notes

1. O. Palmer Robertson, *Christ of the Covenants*, 4.

2. Jamieson, R., A. R. Fausset, & D. Brown, *A Commentary, Critical and Explanatory, on the Old and New Testaments* (Oak Harbor, WA: Logos Research Systems, Inc., 2000), Hebrews 10:5, Logos e-book.

3. *Sermons of George Whitefield*, Sermon 36.

4. Adolf Harnack, *History of Dogma* (Grand Rapids, MI: Christian Classics Ethereal Library, year), 5:293, CCEL e-book.

5. Schaff, *History*, S. 121.

6. Ibid

7. Ibid

8. Denny Burke, under "Rob Bell Outs Himself," http://www.dennyburk.com/rob-bell-outs-himself/ (Accessed June 17, 2011). Denny Burke's internet response to Rob Bell's book (a book denying the Scriptural teaching on hell) may be already known to many who read this chapter, but the point he makes is so important and helpful I include it here.

9. Thomas R. Schreiner, *Romans* (Grand Rapids: Baker Books, 1998), 451–452.

10. Ibid, 452.

11. R.C. Sproul, *A Daily Guide for Living from the Book of Romans*. Vol. 1 of Before the Face of God (Grand Rapids: Baker Book House Company, 1992), pgs. 288-289

12. The NKJV translation is more accurate in this verse. The greek is "ὅτι οὐ δύνασθε ἀκούειν τὸν λόγον τὸν ἐμόν" (John 8:43; NA26), which is literally, "because you are not able to hear my word." The ESV renders it "It is because you cannot bear to hear my word." The translators have included their own interpretation of the meaning of the statement with the word, "bear." This is only one of a long list of possible connotations. But the context is what should guide us here. Jesus describes their true nature as children of the devil. It is because of their nature, not their

circumstances, that they are not able to hear. They are spiritually dead and in slavery to the evil one.

13. Nehemiah 9:7-8.

14. Isaiah 51:2; Joshua 24:2-3.

15. Genesis 15:6.

16. The NKJV closely follows the Greek text here. Most modern translations attempt to interpret the meaning instead of a literal rendering.

17 . Romans 9:15 (NKJV).

18. *Canons of Dort*, Second head, Article 8.

19. 2 Timothy 2:25; Acts 5:31 (ESV)

20. J.C. Ryle, *Matthew*, vol. 1 of *Expository Thoughts on the Gospels* (Grand Rapids: Baker Book House, 1977), 284-285.

21. John Morren, quoted in *10,000 Sermon Illustrations* (Biblical Studies Press, 2002), Logos e-book.

Twelve

The End is the Beginning

Standing at this juncture, at the completion of this brief study of the Covenant of Works, there is a strong feeling that this is not the end, but the beginning.

In the first part of the book, an attempt has been made to display the Covenant of Works within the overall context of covenant theology. This has been by necessity a history of the covenants, since the covenants themselves are God's terms for His relationship with His people within the context of real history, from generation to generation. Quotes in this section are primarily from Calvin to demonstrate that most elements of the Covenant of Works are found in his theology even if the terminology itself had not yet been used in his time. In Part Two, definitions and descriptions of the Covenant of Works flowed into a survey of the history of this foundational covenant, and its importance within Reformed theology. These two chapters may be helpful to address very loose assumptions that easily get tossed from one author to another, or to explain why the Covenant of Works had become so essential to many excellent theologians who worked together to frame the Westminster Standards in the 17th century. Chapter Eight examined a number of parallels between the Covenant of Works and the covenant of Moses to draw forth the republication, or display, of the Covenant of Works, out of the machinery of that important covenant God established with Israel. God's purpose was to take the Covenant of Works out of the darkness of its past and put it on display for all to see, to prepare for the coming of Christ who saves believers from the fall of Adam. This is not to say that the Sinai covenant is a covenant of works, but to demonstrate that the likeness of its details are used by God to highlight Adam's failed covenant and to drive sinners to the true function of the Sinai Covenant, the revelation of the Covenant of Grace in Christ. A smaller chapter, Ten, took up the theme of obedience, central to the Covenant of Works, to highlight the relationship between the concepts of obedience and works. To end this study, Chapter Eleven considered the importance of election. This is necessary because election "before the creation of the world" was a principle already functioning when God created the first man and established the Covenant of Works with him.

The sense of only beginning while standing here at the end is clear as midday sunlight. The Covenant of Works was broken by Adam. Darkness, doom, depravity and death flooded not only man's heart, but the entire world. The world was fallen. Paradise was lost. Death, not life, reigned over Adam's descendants. It was the worst of endings.

But God's eternal plan of redemption to restore people from all nations, His plan to give His own Son as a covenant, flooded darkened Eden with a new beginning even while the curtain was closing on that scene of deathly sorrow. God who commanded light to shine out of darkness on the first day of creation, now caused the hope of grace to shine where absolutely no light of grace had been promised and none should have been hoped. The woman would have a Son. He would crush the serpent's head. God directed these bright beams of the gospel upon Eden's rebels, showing them that God would provide only one way out of the curse. "A Son is born, a child is given to us, and His Name shall be the mighty God, the everlasting father, the prince of peace..."

The covenant of works is revealed in cryptic form in only three chapters in Genesis. One of those chapters describes how Adam broke the covenant. After this, several more chapters portray the world as fallen, cursed and condemned. But the rest of the Bible narrates the unfolding drama of the history of redemption in a cursed world where even the lives of those redeemed are punctuated by painful episodes of struggling with their own sinful natures.

The writing of many books, analyzing this drama from all possible angles, never ends. Seminary libraries stocked with tens of thousands of the excellent fruits of these labors bear this out. But many even of good books ignore the covenant structure of the inspired Scriptures, or minimize the importance of the Old Testament Scriptures which were carefully designed by God to prepare for the coming of Christ and the gospel for all the nations.

Therefore, the next two volumes of this series will address the Old Testament covenants God made with Abraham and Israel, before the final chapter considers the New Covenant and its New Testament completions.

Clearly, the story of God's covenant dealings with men does not end with this first covenant broken by Adam. It is plain to see that this is really where the Bible begins. It is also where God's covenant of grace takes hold of people languishing in Adam's dust and stains to mount up with wings like eagles and soar with Yahweh over the weakness of the flesh in the fallen world.

The next volume in this series, Camp of the Saints, follows the footsteps of the faith of Abram, a man who lay dead in dust with Adam. He was a lost sinner, steeped in the sin of idolatry and deceived by demons. But the Lord chose Abram in His grace, revealed Himself to him, and took him out of the horrible pit of his fallen nature and sinful life to make him a child of God and the father of all who believe.

In Asia, I have heard the story of Abram's call told as if his journey to another country is an example for all who desire to travel abroad and settle in a more developed country with better business opportunities. But Abram was really called to leave the world of sin and seek the kingdom of heaven. In this sense, his call is an example of the calling of all lost sinners. Abram was also called to make the first preparations for the Son that God would send into Satan's world-kingdom of spiritual darkness, to set free souls moaning in bondage. Abram was sent to the very land, and the very mountain, where the Christ would give His life for the sins of people from all nations. It is a marvelous story of new beginnings!

Broken Covenant, Fallen World and the next volume, *Camp of the Saints* are theology books. As such, they describe more of what true Christians should believe than what we should do and practice. This remains important because we are forgiven and justified and heirs of God's promises not by our works but by believing the truths of God's Word. Theology is the logical cohesive arrangement of the truths God has revealed in His Holy Scriptures. Good theology is purely logical, contemplative, and sometimes philosophical (like Bavinck) and not exegetical, but bases its conclusions upon the exegesis and translation work of other scholars. However, when God's doctrinal truths have been removed from the interesting story of the Bible's true history and arranged in a system of theology the result can be

213

boring and difficult stuff for all but pastors and seminary professors and their students. Therefore, *Broken Covenant, Fallen World* has aimed to be a theological work with at least some devotional or pastoral liveliness. Academic content has been minimized to make the study more accessible to readers-of-English-as-a-second-language, and to lay leaders and teachers serving the ordinary people of the Lord's church. At times this work has overstepped these boundaries, but it is hoped that those interested in the divine covenants have seen their way through.

In this last word, there is also a sense in which this study of the Covenant of Works is only beginning. Aiming for brevity, many concepts have been given brief mention so that more space may be devoted to difficult doctrines such as imputation and predestination. Books written against the Covenant of Works have not been responded to. The thirst of those looking for solid exegetical arguments supporting various aspects of the Covenant of Works has not at all been quenched. This has been by design. God permitting, a more academic volume on the Covenant of Works, following sometime after this series of four volumes, may pursue deeper trails through regions only scouted and sketched out on this brief journey.

This volume also mentions Covenantal Eschatology. Very little explanation is given because two volumes on this subject are planned to follow, God willing, on the heels of this series.

Lastly, having mentioned that this series is first concerned with the substance of faith, and with the structure, meaning and purpose of the covenants, it must also be acknowledged that the covenants are very practical, and that it is through His covenants that God gives His Law (what we are to do) to His people, and teaches us wisdom, and sets before us the patterns for relationships, church worship and polity, home life, and many other things. Look for these considerations in later volumes.

The apostle Paul once wisely wrote, "We do not proclaim ourselves, but Jesus as Lord, and ourselves as servants of Christ for your sake." It is the prayer of this author that the true God alone will be glorified in the eyes and hearts all who read *Broken Covenant, Fallen World*, even through such inadequate efforts of feeble-minded fallen men.

Soli Deo Gloria!

Bibliography

Arminius, James *The Works of James Arminius,*vol. 2, trans. by James Nichols. Albany, OR: Ages Software, 1997, Ages e-book..

Baugh, S.M. "Covenant Theology Illustrated: Romans 5 on the Federal Headship of Adam and Christ," *Modern Reformation* 9, no. 4 (2000): 16-23, http://www.modernreformation.org/default.php?page=articledisplay &var1=ArtRead&var2=496&var3=authorbio&var4=AutRes&var5= 247, 15 June, 2011.

Bavinck, Herman. *Gereformeerde Dogmatiek, Vol. 2:*528-529. Quoted in *Creator, Redeemer Consummator: A Festschrift for Meredith G. Kline,* eds. Griffith and Muether. Translated by Richard Gaffin. Reformed Academic Press, 2000, Logos e-book.

———, John Bolt, & John Vriend. *Sin and Salvation in Christ.* Vol. 3 of *Reformed Dogmatics.* Grand Rapids: Baker Academic, 2006, Logos e-book.

Berkhof, Louis. *Systematic Theology.* Grand Rapids: Eerdmans, 1938. Quoted in *Conservative Theological Journal Volume 1.* Tyndale Theological Seminary, 1997, Logos e-book.

Bierma, Lyle D. "Federal Theology in the Sixteenth Century: Two Traditions?" *Westminster Theological Journal 45.* Philadelphia: Westminster Theological Seminary, 1983, Logos e-book.

Brakel, Wilhelmus a. *The Christian's Reasonable Service.* Simpsonville, SC: Christian Classics Foundation, 1996, Logos e-book.

Bullinger, Heinrich. *The Decades of Henry Bullinger.* Ed. by Thomas Harding. Cambridge: Cambridge University Press, 1850.

Denny Burke, "Rob Bell Outs Himself," http://www.dennyburk.com/rob-bell-outs-himself/ (Accessed June 17, 2011).

Calvin, John. *Institutes of the Christian Religion.* Bellingham, WA: Logos Research Systems, 1997.

Carson, D.A., "The Emerging Church." *Modern Reformed Magazine 14,* no. 4 (2005), Online article:

http://www.modernreformation.org/default.php?page=articledisplay
&var1=ArtRead&var2=128&var3=issuedisplay&var4=IssRead&var
5=12, 06-15-2011.

Clark, R. Scott. "A Brief History of Covenant Theology." R.S. Clark, 2001.
Available at http://clark.wscal.edu/ briefhistorycovtheol.php.
Accessed 10 June, 2011.

Dick, John. *Lectures on Theology.* New York: Robert Carter and
Brothers,1851.

Dunzweiler, Robert J. "Robert Dunzweiler's Footnotes," in John Calvin,
Institutes of the Christian Religion. Bellingham, WA: Logos
Research Systems, Inc., 1997, Logos e-book.

Edwards, Jonathan. *The Works of Jonathan Edwards* - Vol. 5. Albany, OR:
Ages Software, 1997.

Ehlert, Arnold D. "A Bibliography of Dispensationalism." *Bibliotheca Sacra
102,* no. 405 (1945): 83-92, Logos e-book.

Ferguson, S. B., & Packer, J. *New Dictionary of Theology.* Downers Grove,
IL: InterVarsity Press, 2000, Logos e-book.

Gill, John. A Complete Body of Practical and Doctrinal Divinity. Paris,
Arkansas: The Baptist Standard Bearer, 1999, Ages e-book.

Gordon, T. David. "Critique of Theonomy: A Taxonomy." *Westminster
Theological Journal 56,* no. 1 (Spring 1994): 21-43, Logos e-book.

Grudem, Wayne A. *Systematic Theology: An Introduction to Biblical
Doctrine.* Leicester, England: Inter-Varsity Press, 1994, Logos e-
book.

Haldane, Robert. *Exposition of the Epistle to the Romans.* Simpsonville,
SC: Christian Classics Foundation, 1996, Logos e-book.

Harnack, Adolf. *History of Dogma* . Williams and Norgate, 1897, Christian
Classics Ethereal Library e-book.

Hodge, A.A. *Outlines of Theology.* Escondido: The Ephesians Four Group,
1998, Logos e-book.

———, Hodge, C., & Hodge, A. *The Confession of Faith : With Questions
for Theological Students and Bible Classes.* Simpsonville SC:

Christian Classics Foundation, 1996, Logos e-book.

Hooker, Richard. "A Sermon by Richard Hooker with Introductory comments by James Kiefer." http://elvis.rowan.edu/~kilroy/christia/library/hooker-learned.htm (accessed June 16, 2011).

Jamieson, R., A. R. Fausset and D. Brown. *A Commentary, Critical and Explanatory, on the Old and New Testaments.* Oak Harbor, WA: Logos Research Systems, Inc., 1997, Logos e-book.

Johnson, Ronald M. "Covenant Hermeneutics." *Conservative Theological Journal Volume 3* (1999): 315-328, Logos e-book.

Karlberg, Mark W. "Covenant Theology and the Westminster Tradition." *Westminster Theological Journal 54*, no. 1 (Spring 1992): 133-152, Logos e-book.

———. "The Search For An Evangelical Consensus On Paul And The Law." *Journal of the Evangelical Theological Society 40,* no. 4 (December 1997): 562-579, Logos e-book.

———. "Reformed Interpretation of the Mosaic Covenant." *Westminster Theological Journal. 43,* no. 1 (Fall 1980): 1-57, Logos e-book.

Kline, Meredith G. *Kingdom Prologue.* South Hamilton, MA: M. G. Kline, 1991.

Koehler, Ludwig, et al. *The Hebrew and Aramaic Lexicon of the Old Testament.* Leiden: E.J. Brill, 1999, Logos e-book.

Ladd, George Elden, *A Theology of the New Testament.* Rev. ed. Grand Rapids: Eerdman's, 1993.

Law, William. *The Works of the Reverend William Law.* Brockenhurst: G. Moreton, 1892.

Long, Gary D. "The Grace of God and Departures From It." *Reformation and Revival Ministries 3,* no. 1 (1994): 78-99, Logos e-book.

MacArthur, John. *The Truth War: Fighting for Certainty in an Age of Deception.* Thomas Nelson, 2007.

Machen, J. Gresham. *A Rapid Survey of the Literature and History of New Testament Times.* Oak Harbor, WA: Rose Tree Press, 2000, Logos e-

book.

Martin, Hugh. *The Atonement.* Edinburgh: James Gemmell, 1882.

Martin, R.P. *Dictionary of Paul and His Letters.* Downers Grove, Ill.: InterVarsity Press, 1993.

McKim, Donald K. and David F. Wright, *Encyclopedia of the Reformed Faith*, 1st ed. Louisville: Westminster/John Knox Press, 1992, Logos e-book.

————. *The Westminster Handbook to Reformed Theology.* Louisville: Westminster John Knox Press, 2002.

Murray, Andrew. *The Holiest of All: An Exposition of the Epistle to the Hebrews.* New York: Anson D.F. Randolph, 1894, DJView e-book.

Murray, John. *Studies in Theology.* Vol. 4 of *Collected Writings of John Murray.* Edinburgh: Banner of Truth, 1982.

Nevin, John Williamson. Introduction to *The Commentary of Zacharias Ursinus on the Heidelberg Catechis,* by Zacharias Ursinus. Translated by G. W. Williard. Cincinnati: Elm Street Printing, 1888.

Paine, Homer Lemuel. "Contemporary Amillennial Literature." *Bibliotheca Sacra.* Vol. 106. Dallas, TX: Dallas Theological Seminary, 1949, Logos e-book.

Pink, A. W. *An Exposition of the Sermon on the Mount.* Escondido: Ephesians Four Group, 2002, Logos e-book.

Reymond, R. L. *A New Systematic Theology of the Christian Faith.* Nashville: Thomas Nelson, 1998, Logos e-book.

Riddlebarger, Kim. *A Case for Amillennialism: Understanding the End Times.* Grand Rapids: Baker, 2003.

Robertson, O. Palmer. *Christ of the Covenants.* Grand Rapids: Baker, 1980.

Rollock, Robert. *Select Works of Robert Rollock.* Vol. 1. Edinburgh: Wodrow Society, 1849

Ryle, JC. "Matthew." Vol. 1 of *Expository Thoughts on the Gospels.* Grand Rapids: Baker Book House, 1977.

Schaff, Philip. *The Nicene and Post-Nicene Fathers, Second Series*. Vol. 5. Albany, OR: Ages Software, 1996, Ages e-book.

Schreiner, Thomas R. *Romans*. Grand Rapids: Baker Books, 1998.

———. *Systematic Theology*. 2 vols. Simpsonville, SC: Christian Classics Foundation, 1997.

Sproul, R.C. A Daily Guide for Living from the Book of Romans. Vol. 1 of Before the Face of God. Grand Rapids: Baker Book House Company, 1992, Logos e-book.

———. *Essential Truths of the Christian Faith*. Wheaton: Tyndale House, 1996, Logos e-book.

Unger, Merrill F. *The New Unger's Bible Handbook*. Chicago: Moody Press, 1984.

Ursinus, Zacharias. *"Zacharias Ursinus' Large and Small Catechisms, harmonized with the Heidelberg Catechism."* Translated by Fred H. Klooster and John Medendorp. Available at http://links.christreformed.org/doctrinevision/ursinus_project.pdf (accessed June 9, 2011).

Watson,Thomas. *A Body of Divinity*. Grand Rapids: Christian Classics Ethereal Library, 2002, PDF e-book.

Watts, Malcolm. "Reformed Covenant Theology." Lecture, Puritan Reformed Theological Seminary, Grand Rapids, MI, April 14, 2008.

Wells, David F., *The Courage to Be Protestant: Truth Lovers, Marketers and Emergents in the Postmodern World*. Grand Rapids: Wm. B. Eerdmans, 2008.

Wenham, Gordon. J. *Genesis 1-15*. Vol. 1 of *Word Biblical Commentary*. Dallas, TX: Word Books, 1987, Logos e-book.

White, R. Fowler and E. Calvin Beisner, "Why the Covenant of Works is a Necessary Doctrine: Revisiting the Objections to a Venerable Reformed Doctrine," in *By Faith Alone: Answering Challenges to the Doctrine of Justification,* edited by Gary L.W. Johnson and Guy Prentiss Waters. Wheaton, Illinois: Crossway Books, 2006: 147-170, Mobipocket e-book.

White, Wesley. "The Dutch Reformed Doctrine of the Covenant of Works,"

under the *Johannes Weslianus* blog, entry posted February 6, 2008,
http://www.weswhite.net/2008/02/dutch-reformed-doctrine-of-
covenant-of/ (Accessed June 10, 2011).

Whitefield, George. *George Whitefield's Sermons*. Oak Harbor, WA: Logos
Research Systems, 1999, Logos e-book.

Winslow, Octavius. *Our God* (1870), under "The Octavius Winslow
Archive," available at http://octaviuswinslow.org/2011/01/27/the-
names-of-christ-emmanuel-or-god-with-us-part-1-of-10/ (accessed
June 17, 2011), PDF e-book.

Woodbridge, Noel B. "Understanding the Emerging Church Movement: An
Overview of Its Strengths, Areas of Concern and Implications for
Today's Evangelicals." *Conspectus 4*, no. 1 (2007): 95-113, Logos e-
book.

Interested in More?

Have a question about anything you've read in this book? Post questions and comments to the author at http://narrowpathway.com/blogs/

Books by Steven T. Poelman are available at www.narrowpathway.com/books.html

Other books planned for the series, *Covenants of the Almighty*:

Volume Two: Camp of the Saints. (Release date: January 2012). God's Covenant with Abraham promised justification by grace through faith for believers from all nations. A study of the basics of the Covenant of Grace within the Abrahamic Covenant. Important lessons for all pilgrims who walk in the steps of Abraham's faith today.

Volume Three: The Lighthouse Kingdom (Spring 2012). God created the kingdom of Israel for His own glory, to reveal His righteousness to the nations, and to proclaim the future appearance of the Messiah who would bring salvation to all the earth and rule over all nations. Understand the old covenant through the illumination of the apostles, and sit at Moses' feet to ponder mysteries of the Messiah and the kingdom of heaven and gain insights valuable for citizens of heaven's kingdom.

Volume Four: Dawn of Heaven's Light (Summer 2012). The way into the kingdom of heaven is opened only through the death and resurrection of the King of heaven. He came from heaven to establish His kingdom in the hearts of believers from every language, tribe, people and nation. After conquering the grave, Christ returned to heaven to serve His kingdom forever as King and High Priest of the new covenant.

Volume Five: Heaven's Lamps in the Valley of Sorrows (Late 2012). The close relationship of the lines of covenant and eschatology throughout Biblical history until they come together and find their fulfillment in one man, Jesus Christ.

www.ingramcontent.com/pod-product-compliance
Lightning Source LLC
Chambersburg PA
CBHW051953090426
42741CB00008B/1372